"[Fallaci's] interviews remain studies in speaking truth to power… Fallaci was a piquant, stylish beauty, self-consciously photogenic in the Joan Didion way, a midcentury woman writer vigilant about her public image. Fallaci lived a genuinely romantic life, too, with stormy loves and war wounds. But De Stefano, who had access to living friends, family members, and colleagues as well as archives and letters, reveals another side to her life."
—*New York Times Book Review*

"A new biography gets Oriana Fallaci the way people who knew her couldn't… a fascinating and utterly sui generis life."
—*Los Angeles Times*

"[This] authoritative examination… offers bracing insight into a woman who defied convention… Fallaci's era is over but the stories remain as vivid as her adventure-filled life."
—*Boston Herald*

"Exceptional… this biography is a must read."
—*Literary Hub*

"Brisk, even-handed… I suspect that Oriana Fallaci would have enjoyed it."
—*Times Literary Supplement*

"In this meticulous, perceptive, and dramatic portrait, De Stefano reveals the full intensity and sensitivity of a trailblazing warrior writer."
—*Booklist* (starred review)

"The great Italian writer gets her due in this short but captivating biography...a superb introduction to the life of an irreplaceable figure."
— *Kirkus Reviews*

"De Stefano peels away the layers of mystery surrounding journalist Oriana Fallaci...an intimate investigation into a larger-than-life personality."
— *Publishers Weekly*

"In Cristina De Stefano's *Oriana Fallaci,* the stories about Italy's most controversial journalist have the power to stun as they race forward, one more astonishing than the next...De Stefano handles Fallaci's turbulent personal side with care...[and] has a terrific ear for Fallaci's most piquant quotes...the spirit of the book: headlong and direct, all the while maintaining an understanding of a reporter's commitment to asking hard questions."
— *Washington Independent Review of Books*

"The first major work to emerge in English since its subject's death...[*Oriana Fallaci*] offers the most readable and approachable overview of Fallaci's life."
— *Standpoint*

"De Stefano's work offers a deeply perceptive insight into the fascinating Italian journalist, delivered in a riveting and engaging narrative style that's evocative of Fallaci herself."
— *PopMatters*

"This is as powerful a life story as you will ever read."
— *Foreword*

ORIANA

the journalist, the agitator, the legend

FALLACI

CRISTINA DE STEFANO

translated from the Italian by Marina Harss

Other Press   *New York*

First softcover edition 2021
ISBN 978-1-63542-053-1

Copyright © 2013 Cristina De Stefano
Copyright © 2013 RCS Libri S.p.A., Milan
First published in Italian as *Oriana, una donna* by Rizzoli, Milan, in 2013.

English translation copyright © 2017 Other Press
Published by arrangement with the Agenzia Letteraria Roberto Santachiara

Oriana Fallaci's quotes are drawn from articles and interviews
published in *L'Europeo* and *Corriere della Sera*, her books,
quotes that have appeared in other books about her, and her private papers.

The publisher makes itself available to all those parties who hold rights
and who, despite repeated attempts, the publisher was unable to contact.

Excerpt from "Memory" by Natalia Ginzburg, from *It's Hard to Talk About Yourself*,
translated by Louise Quirke (Chicago: University of Chicago Press, 2003).
Copyright © 2003 by The University of Chicago Press.

Production Editor: Yvonne E. Cárdenas
Text Designer: Julie Fry
This book was set in Arno with Alternate Gothic.

1 3 5 7 9 10 8 6 4 2

Library of Congress Cataloging-in-Publication Data
Names: De Stefano, Cristina, 1967– author. | Harss, Marina translator.
Title: Oriana Fallaci : the journalist, the agitator the legend /
Cristina De Stefano ; translated by Marina Harss.
Description: New York : Other Press, 2017.
Identifiers: LCCN 2017002632 (print) | LCCN 2017003761 (ebook) |
ISBN 9781590517864 (hardcover : alk. paper) | ISBN 9781590517871 (e-book)
Subjects: LCSH: Fallaci, Oriana. | Women journalists — Italy — Biography.
Classification: LCC PN5246.F35 D4713 2017 (print) |
LCC PN5246.F35 (ebook) | DDC 070.92 [B] — dc23
LC record available at https://lccn.loc.gov/2017002632

CONTENTS

You won't have time to accomplish things, or even to understand them. This time we're given, this thing called life, is brief. So everything must happen in a great hurry.

The airplane flies high above an ocean immersed in darkness. Suddenly, the windows are bathed in light. "Look, Oriana, it's the aurora borealis," her nephew whispers. She remains silent. Dazed with weakness, she has dozed off. She sits in her reclined seat, draped in a fur coat. It's September 4, 2006, and Oriana is on her way back to Florence.

The tumor is in its terminal stage. No commercial flight from New York is willing to take her, so they have resorted to chartering a private plane. For several weeks, she has been surviving on sugar water; she weighs only sixty-six pounds. In truth, she never weighed much more than that: five foot one, ninety-two pounds. She often jokes, "When people meet me, they're surprised by how little there is of me. I just spread my arms and say, 'That's all there is!'"

This trip is her decision. She has lived in New York for almost five decades, but she wants things to end where they began. The cabin light is kept low to protect her failing eyes. Two doctors, both women, accompany her, in case of an emergency. But she barely moves during the whole trip; she sits, folded in on herself, immersed in memories. Florence advances slowly to meet her, bringing with it the past.

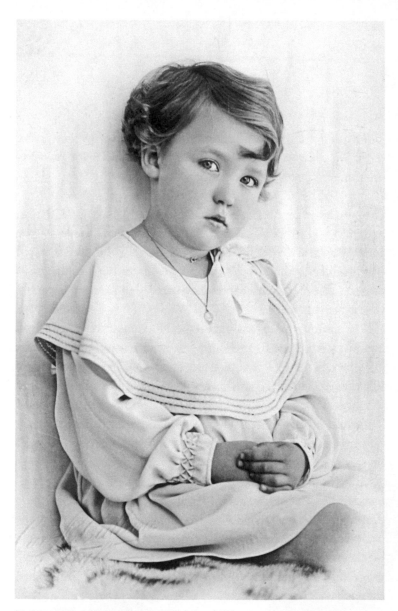

Studio portrait of Oriana at the age of three.

1. A FAMILY IN WHICH NOBODY SMILES

"I don't know anything about how my father and my mother met. The only clue to the mystery of my birth is a phrase my mother used to repeat: 'It all happened because of a hat full of cherries.'" Among all the family stories she heard as a child, this was the detail she loved the most: a bright red hat, worn like a beacon. Years later, placed on the head of someone other than her mother, it would supply the title to her posthumous novel, *Un cappello pieno dei ciliege* (A hat full of cherries). Anything else is speculation.

The meeting must have occurred somewhere in Florence on a late-summer afternoon in 1928, one of those hot days that drive people outdoors. Edoardo Fallaci, twenty-four, has just a few coins to his name. He works as a wood-carver and lives with his parents. He dreams of immigrating to Argentina to seek his fortune. He is not especially tall but has an attractively chiseled face and impertinent blue eyes. Tosca Cantini is twenty-two. After losing her mother when she was young, her anarchist sculptor father sent her off to work for two seamstresses. They have grown fond of her and raised her to be a well-mannered young lady. Eventually, they find her a job with a dowager who wants to take her to Paris as a companion. But on that day, Tosca decides to wear an eye-catching hat decorated with red fruit. It shows off her pretty face and high cheekbones. "What pretty cherries," the gallant Edoardo comments. Sometime later, on a ramble on Monte Morello, Oriana is conceived.

"My mother always said that when she first got pregnant, she didn't want me. She drank Epsom salts every night all the way through the fourth month of her pregnancy, to induce an abortion. But one night, just as she was about to put the glass to her lips, I moved in her belly, almost as if I were saying, 'I want to be born!' And then and there she poured the Epsom salts into a flower vase. 'And that's why you were born,' she used to say." Tosca had other dreams. She wanted to travel the world, to meet artists. She had friends in Florence's bohemian circles, particularly the painter Ottone Rosai, who courted her. "She used to say he was a 'handsome bear of a man,' quite the opposite of my father, who was small and lean."

When it becomes clear that there is no way around it, Edoardo introduces Tosca to his parents. His mother, Giacoma, known for her unpleasant character, is unwelcoming and takes every opportunity to be unkind. In contrast, his father, Antonio, takes a liking to the girl. This only makes matters worse. Tosca quickly becomes a kind of Cinderella in their home. "One of my first memories," says Oriana, "was of my mother crying as she did the laundry." The sight of this highly intelligent woman forced to serve the entire family marks her profoundly. Often in interviews she recalls that her mother was the first to encourage her ambitions. "It was my mother who used to say, in tears, 'Don't be like me! Don't become a slave to your husband and your children! Study! Go out into the world!' I didn't want to follow her footsteps, I wanted to vindicate her." In 1977, during the acceptance speech for an honorary degree

Oriana's father, Edoardo, wearing motorcycle gear.

Six-month-old Oriana in the arms of her mother, Tosca.

from Columbia College in Chicago, she declares, "I dedicate this honor to my mother, Tosca Fallaci, who was unable to go to college because she was a woman and because she was poor at a time when women and the poor could not get an education."

On June 29, 1929, the baby is baptized. Oriana is an unusual name for the time. Her parents, who are passionate readers, name her after Oriane, Proust's Duchesse de Guermantes. "'You weren't red and wrinkly like the other newborns,' my mother used to say. 'You were pale, smooth-skinned, and beautiful. And you never cried. Babies cry, but not you. You were always silent. You observed the world around you, and us, without a sound. By the eighth day I started to worry. I thought you had been born without vocal cords, so I took you to the doctor. He checked you and said, no, no, there's nothing wrong. Then he tickled your feet and you exploded in great peals of laughter.'"

Everyone lives together in the big house on Via del Piaggione: Edoardo's parents, grandparents, and unmarried sisters. As an adult, Oriana can remember every detail of the house, and over time, bit by bit, she takes it with her. A painted wardrobe goes to her apartment in New York; her parents' bed and a glass-fronted bookcase goes to her apartment in Florence; a side table from the parlor ends up in her country home. The house overlooks the whole city, with Brunelleschi's dome and Giotto's bell tower in the foreground, and farther off the rooftops and bridges of Florence. One room contains Grandfather's worktable, where he repairs the family's shoes. Oriana watches him for hours and enjoys carrying out small tasks. She avoids Grandma Giacoma, who is always in a bad mood and has a heavy hand. She considers Grandfather Antonio's room a kind of refuge: "He was a very affectionate man and always looked out for me. In a family where nobody smiled, he was always smiling."

After her, two more girls are born: Neera in 1932 and Paola in 1938. Later, in 1964, when they are adults, the family adopts an orphan, Elisabetta. There are no boys, but Edoardo treats Oriana like a son. "My father was upset that I wasn't a boy. So he took me hunting with him." He teaches her how to shoot and takes her everywhere with him. He waits with her at dawn in the shooting hut when flocks of thrushes descend on the fields. Years later Oriana will recall every detail — the pungent cold of the early morning, her eyes staring up at the sky, whispered voices. "If a bird comes from the left, it's mine. If it comes from the right, it's yours. And if they come in a flock, we both shoot, on the count of three." "Sì, Papà!"

Edoardo is a man of few words, demanding of himself and of others. He raises his eldest daughter like a soldier. One of Oriana's most vivid childhood memories is related to this toughness. She's fifteen; she and her father are walking down a street in Florence. A bomb siren rings out. They take refuge in a building. The thunder of aircraft becomes deafening. Oriana can't find the courage to embrace her father. She cowers in a corner, rolled up in a ball. As the bombs begin to fall, the floor and walls shudder, and she starts to cry. She is surprised by a slap; it takes her breath away. "Young ladies don't cry," her father hisses. Oriana often recounts this episode in order to illustrate why she tries never to cry in public. She will often have reason to cry, and she does — "Crying helps, it allows you vomit out your pain" — but almost never in the presence of others.

Another male relative who plays a central role in her life is Bruno Fallaci, her father's elder brother, whom everyone refers to as Settecervelli (seven brains). Bruno is the intellectual of the family. He belongs to a world apart, the world of writers. He is married to Gianna Manzini, a successful journalist. He edits the cultural page in the Florentine newspaper *La Nazione* and later becomes the editor of the magazine *Epoca*. He is Oriana's first, perhaps only, teacher, and she will make references to him her whole life: "When he enumerated the rules of journalism, he would say, 'First of all, don't bore the reader!'"

Tosca often cleans for them, and she brings her daughter along. Gianna Manzini sits on the couch, reading a book and smoking fragrant cigarettes through a long black cigarette holder. Every so often, without interrupting her reading, she extends a beautiful bejeweled hand toward a glass bowl of *gianduiotti* chocolates. "Don't dare ask for one!" Tosca warns Oriana before every visit. In one of her books, Oriana evokes the humiliation she felt watching her aunt unwrap each chocolate without even a glance in her direction, as if she didn't exist. Thirty years later, she can still taste the bitterness of this injustice. And yet she can't help but be struck by Gianna's beauty. She watches as her aunt prepares to go out, adjusting her fur hat and wrap. Gianna Manzini is tall and elegant, with a slender face and large eyes that she accentuates with great care.

No one in the family likes her. Oriana remembers her grandmother Giacoma slamming down a bouquet of flowers, a gift from her daughter-in-law, as she mutters, "Who needs flowers?! Why don't you sew the buttons on my son's shirts instead?!" One afternoon during a walk with Oriana and Grandfather Antonio, Gianna Manzini climbs up on the parapet of the Ponte Vecchio and cries out, "Look, I'll jump! I'll jump!" He taps his cane impatiently on the paving stones. "Go ahead, jump! Jump! But hurry, I need to take the girl home." Gianna Manzini leaves Bruno in 1933 and moves to Rome, disappearing from Oriana's childhood. However, she leaves behind one trace: her elegant handwriting, with its rounded vowels, which Oriana effortfully imitates, copying out letters for hours in her school notebooks. Thus, her signature — which will one day be famous and unmistakable — is born.

But most of her childhood memories are memories of poverty. There's not enough to eat, and her mother often feigns a lack of appetite so that her daughters will have more. When Oriana is sent out to buy food, she is ashamed of the tiny quantities she can afford. As the shop owners crane their necks to see her over the counter, she requests two ounces of cheese, two ounces of jam. "But we held our heads high," she later says. "You wouldn't have guessed we were poor. We were always well dressed and clean. Mamma was good at turning our clothes inside out and making a new dress out of an old one." Edoardo is a fine carpenter; he works passionately, filling the house with furniture he has made with his own hands. But he doesn't have much business sense and the family's finances are precarious. "Don't forget that your father is an artist," Tosca reminds her daughters.

From a very young age, Oriana is drawn to one particular object, a relic of another age. It is a carved trousseau chest with lions' feet and iron latches. Everyone calls it "Ildebranda's trunk," after an ancestor who, it is said, was burned at the stake as a heretic. Oriana stares at it for hours, making up stories about her. Whenever someone opens it, she eagerly digs through its contents. It contains the family keepsakes, all piled together: a spelling book and an abacus, a French medical textbook, a stringless lute, a clay pipe, a pincenez, a Catalan passport, a mended Italian flag, an ancient coin, the last letter written by a Napoleonic soldier before freezing to death in Russia. Each object inspires endless questions. When her grandparents are in the mood, she is able to elicit bits and pieces of information, rich with promise: Montserrat played the lute, even after she was confined to the madhouse...Caterina used to treat

the whole county with the help of Dr. Barbette's medical tome...
Giobatta came back from the war with his face disfigured by a
cannon shot.

The trunk is destroyed, along with the rest of the house, during
a bombing raid in 1944. Oriana will pine for it the rest of her days.
Later, she will ask her father to build an exact replica, which she
keeps in her apartment in New York. A few letters, written in Cur-
tatone and Montanara by an ancestor who volunteered in the First
War of Independence, will be saved because Oriana has copied
them out in a school workbook. Even at a young age, she knows
that every object tells a story, if you know how to listen.

When Edoardo Fallaci becomes ill with pleurisy in 1934, money
becomes even more scarce. The family moves to a basement on
the Piazza del Carmine. Oriana whiles away the hours watching
people's legs and feet as they pass by the family's barred window.
Her father is weak and spends most of his time in bed. His friends
try to convince him to apply for a Fascist Party card, which would
allow him a pension, but he refuses. "I can still see him lying there
in bed," Oriana says, "burning with fever, coughing, and saying,
'Never, never.'" Everyone in the family is opposed to the Fascists.
One day, old Antonio Fallaci is arrested. "Grandfather was seventy-
eight at the time, but he used to get into fights with the Fascists.
On that day he had yelled out, 'Mussolini stinks!' They took him to
the Fascist headquarters, shut him in a storage closet, and said he
would be put on trial. His wife went and apologized on his behalf,
and they wanted to take her too."

Resistance runs in the family. Oriana speaks admiringly of her
maternal grandfather, Augusto Cantini, who died penniless in a
beggars' hospital. An anarchist, as a young man he had deserted
in order to avoid going to a war that, to his eyes, was a quarrel among imperialist forces. "Other kids grew up brainwashed

by the cult of the First World War, but in my family people told stories about this grandfather, a deserter. My mother would say, proudly, 'My father was a deserter in the First World War.'" As a small child, Oriana listens with fascination as he sings old revolutionary songs: "As long as we behave like oxen / The landowners will decide / As long as the Anarchist Sun don't shine / We'll be the first to die."

Edoardo Fallaci becomes a card-carrying Socialist at seventeen; in 1923, he is injured in a fight with a group of Fascists. In 1929, he begins collaborating with the clandestine group Giustizia e Libertà and comes into contact with other antifascists in the city. Tosca agrees with his political stance, but she stays away from party meetings. "To my mother, politics were a male luxury. She was too busy keeping us alive, making sure we were fed and warm, and overseeing our studies to have time to explain why Mussolini was bad. He just was and that was that." Edoardo and Tosca are Oriana's first heroes; for the rest of life, she will ascribe great importance to the notion of heroism: "I was lucky enough to be brought up by courageous parents. Both physically and morally. My father was a hero of the Resistance and my mother was just as brave."

As a child, she is often left in the care of her aunt Lina for long periods. Lina is one of her father's sisters; she has no children but is married to a wealthy man. With her, Oriana discovers another world: vacations on the shore at Forte dei Marmi, a maid who calls her "miss," tea with cookies from the Robiglio bakery. In the spring, her aunt takes her to concerts at the Maggio Fiorentino and has a long black velvet dress made for her. Her uncle is quick with his fists; she doesn't like him. And he's a Fascist. "He had a truncheon in his room. I didn't understand what it was for until one day he took it with him to Incisa Valdarno; when he returned, it was stained in blood. "'Do you know whose blood this is?' he asked. 'The pharmacist's. We gave him a lesson. Sooner or later, we'll give all those *bigi** a lesson.' I locked myself in the bathroom and cried. He referred to my father, too, as a *bigio*, as in, 'that *bigio* who believes in democracy, who admires France and England!' My father never knew: he was convinced that underneath, he was a good man."

In 1938, Oriana's aunt takes her to watch Hitler and Mussolini parade down the streets of Florence in an open limousine covered in red lilies and black swastikas. Ever-darker clouds are gathering over Europe. The Second World War is about to erupt. Oriana's childhood is about to come to an end.

---

*Bigio (pl. *bigi*), derived from *grigio* (gray), was a term for people who were on the fence about the Fascists, neither with them nor against them.

As a courier for the Partisans at the age of fourteen. On her bicycle, Oriana rode through Nazi roadblocks carrying leaflets and weapons to the Resistance.

2. A LITTLE GIRL ACCUSTOMED TO FEAR, AND TO THE COLD

The date June 10, 1940, is deeply imprinted in her memory. Oriana is playing with her sisters on the terrace when her father comes home earlier than usual. Edoardo looks upset. He drops his jacket on the floor and slumps in a chair, yelling, "That madman has declared war!" Tosca is in the kitchen preparing dinner. The only thing that changes is that she slams the pots down with more force, muttering "scoundrels, cowards, murderers!" in a voice crackling with rage.

The war is the central event in Oriana's life: "I grew up in the war. As a little girl that's all I saw, all I heard about." The bombings, which were particularly brutal in Florence, are among her most burning memories. The rumble of planes that fills the air like the growls of a dangerous beast, sparks illuminating the sky, shelters filled with people who cry and pray as her mother tells her not to be afraid. "I didn't miss a single bombing. By some bitter twist of fate, I was always in the wrong place when the bombs began to fall. But I was never injured. Considering the danger, I had strange, even extraordinary luck." Oriana recalls seeing an old man, a neighbor, fall as they run toward the shelter. No one stops to help. She remembers a priest shot by the Fascists. She remembers months spent with her grandparents in the country, at Mercatale Val di

Pesa. "I was accustomed to hunger, fear, and to the cold," she would say many years later during a speech in Germany.

The months between September 1943 – after the fall of Mussolini – and August 1944 mark her life deeply, because it is then that she comes in contact with the Partisans. "Everything I am, my entire political worldview, dates from the Resistance. It marked me just as Pentecost left its mark upon the apostles." Her father is the leader of an antifascist revolt in the Galileo Workshops, where he works. Then he goes to ground to fight with the urban Resistance. As usual, he brings fourteen-year-old Oriana with him, despite Tosca's protestations. "Not even her hatred for fascism was strong enough to calm her fear that something might happen to me. 'Even the child!' she would groan." In order to shield her, Edoardo never tells Tosca when he has sent his daughter on a mission. The two of them are part of the citywide Giustizia e Libertà group, linked to the Socialist Partito d'Azione.

Oriana's nom de guerre is Emilia. It is chosen for her by Margherita Fasolo, her philosophy teacher, now too a member of the Partisans. Oriana is clever, resourceful; she is used mostly as a courier, to ferry notes, newspapers, sometimes weapons. If she has to carry a hand grenade, she hides it in a head of lettuce in the basket of her bicycle, after having carefully carved out its core. If she's carrying a message, she folds the slip of paper into a tiny ball and sticks it in one of her braids. Once, when she is carrying a bundle of clandestine newspapers, she falls off her bicycle and the precious cargo rolls out onto the pavement. She picks it up quickly, keeping an eye on her surroundings. No one notices. She's so tiny, and she looks young, even younger than she is, so she can slip by unobserved.

Among the members of Edoardo's band are people who will become important figures in Italian history: Enzo Enriques Agnoletti, Tristano Codignola, Carlo Furno, Maria Luigia Guaita, Nello Traquandi, Paolo Barile, Leo Valiani, Ugo La Malfa, Emilio Lussu.

Oriana observes them in tense situations. She remembers Carlo Levi hiding in an apartment across from Palazzo Pitti. One day her father sends her to deliver a pistol and some food. Levi opens the door just a crack, revealing a room full of books. He doesn't invite her in. He opens the package and makes a face. "It's a woman's gun, I don't want it," he says. "And is this all the food there is?" Oriana is not intimidated. She looks at him defiantly and says that her family goes hungry in order to feed people like him who are living in hiding.

One night in 1943, Edoardo Fallaci brings home two strangers dressed as railway employees. Their names are Nigel Eatwell and Gordon Buchanan, and they are British soldiers. They are escapees from the Laterina prisoner of war camp, near Arezzo. They had been traveling northward on a convoy, headed to Germany, when they threw themselves off the train in a tunnel near Florence. Nigel is middle-aged and more sure of himself. Gordon is much younger and seems scared. He looks like a child who has grown up too quickly and has the expression of someone who hasn't eaten in a long time. Oriana's mother gives them Oriana's room; she sleeps in the hall. At night, the clock rings out the hours, keeping her awake. She misses her room, the bed with the white lace bedspread and her schoolbooks neatly arranged on the shelves.

The soldiers stay for a month. They never go out and the shutters are kept closed in order to avoid prying eyes. Oriana spends a lot of time with them, asking questions in her limited English, fascinated by these two men who come from a land where there is freedom, the kind of place her father often speaks of. Later, in her novel *Penelope at War*, she will describe one of them as the adolescent heroine's first love, lost in the tragedy of war. She approaches him, enters the room to talk to him, sits next to him on the bed, listens to his stories for hours. He caresses her face and tells her that she is beautiful. Then, one day, disaster strikes. The other soldier discovers them in an embrace, on the bed, and becomes enraged. She flees. Behind her she can hear a bitter quarrel. Her mother covers her mouth: "What have you done?!"

When they receive the sign that it is safe to smuggle the two soldiers out of Florence, it is Oriana who, along with her father, travels with them to Acone, near Pontassieve, to pass them off to the local Partisans, who will take them across the front line. The road to Acone is long and dangerous—forty kilometers by bicycle with the looming threat of being caught by the Germans, who have promised to shoot anyone aiding a foreign soldier. As they approach a German crossing, one of the soldiers falls off his bike. "Uncle, get up!" Oriana exclaims, praying that the Germans won't notice. In the novel, she describes the moment she says goodbye to the younger soldier. The girl is too shy to embrace him. She says, simply, "If the war ends, come back." He answers, "The war will end, and I will come back." A tear descends slowly down his cheek. "Remember, Daddy?" she says. "You were there. When the tear reached his neck, he turned around and walked away. I watched him go, blond, thin, vulnerable. A boy almost my age. And just like that, my childhood, my fourteenth year, ended, and with it my ability to forgive."

They hear nothing for months. One day a friend of her father's gets news that one of the two made it to the other side but the other is dead. He doesn't know which. It is not until 1993 that Oriana will learn more, from a British historian. Nigel and Gordon hadn't immediately left enemy territory. They remained in Tuscany and joined a Partisan band of fifteen men. On May 4, 1944, Nigel was captured and shot by the Germans near Norcia. On June 14, Gordon was caught just as he was about to blow up a bridge being used by the Germans in their retreat. By some miracle, he survives. Three days later, the Partisans liberate the area. Oriana will try to locate him; she writes to England and Australia, without success. The only trace of them in the archives of their military unit, the Second Transvaal Scottish Regiment, is a mention of the medals awarded to Gordon and, posthumously, to Nigel.

Oriana keeps a letter sent by the soldiers after their departure from Acone. It's written in English, on a crumpled page, dated December 14, 1943.

Dear Oriana, as you know, we've gone. I'm writing because I know your father will return to Acone before Christmas. We will be unable to write to the priest with our news while we're in transit. But by the time your father sees the priest, he will have our news. And once the British army has reached Florence, I'll write to your family. Please thank your father again for everything he did for us. I'll never forget. Perhaps in a few years we'll be able to see each other again. I would like very much to return to Italy. We leave tomorrow, I hope it doesn't rain. The road will be difficult, I know, but not impossible, and I know that all of you are thinking of us and wishing us luck. I send you my embrace and my warm regards to your family, Nigel.

Below, in a different hand, just one line: "Gordon sends his love to his little wife."

"Important things happen at that age: you fall in love for the first time, and for the first time you experience doubt," Oriana will say later in an interview. It is not known how much of her novel is based on real events. But certain ideas formed during this period stay with her. The idea of courage, for example, which, for Oriana will always remain the supreme virtue in a man. As an adult, she will find it almost impossible to find a man worth falling in love with. "Whatever I did, whatever I saw, whatever I heard, I measured against that measuring stick, even love. I wasted the first years of my youth comparing the men I met against my heroes, and turned my back on them because they did not measure up. Few have been haunted by their memories or by a misunderstanding to the degree that I have."

In her novel she writes about another soldier housed by her family, a Russian, describing him in great detail. He is so fat that the buttons on his jacket often pop off. He wears thick glasses and looks profoundly unhappy as he gazes at a map of the Soviet Union, muttering "Mamma." Oriana detests him because he has taken Gordon's place and because he's alive, while they have no news of the young soldier. This character, too, is based on a real person. In her papers, she keeps a note he wrote in broken Italian: "Dear friends, today we leave homeland! We escape Germans! I hope defeat Germans after rebuild my country. Best wishes and salutations, your Vladimir."

In February 1944, Edoardo Fallaci is captured during a roundup after someone informs the police of his activities. He is taken when he is on his way to pick up materials from a clandestine hideaway. That evening, as the family waits, Tosca cries over the stove, comforting herself by repeating, over and over, "He must still be at work." The following day, news of the roundup spreads. "I'll never forget the day I read the headline in the paper: 'Terrorist Leader Arrested,'" Oriana will say in an interview many years later. Tosca goes to the villa where the Fascist militia holds its prisoners for interrogation. She manages to see the leader of the militia, Mario Carità, who tells her to dress in black because the next day her husband will be shot.

Oriana will often describe Tosca's reaction to that meeting. She considers it one of the most dramatic examples of her mother's courage. "I've always asked myself how I would have reacted in her place," she says, "and the answer has always been: Who knows? But I know how she reacted. She remained perfectly still for a moment.

As if struck by lightning. Then, slowly, she raised her right hand. She pointed her right index finger at Mario Carità, and in a steady voice, using the familiar pronoun *tu*, as if he were her servant, she said, 'Mario Carità, tomorrow at six I'll do as you say. I'll wear black. But if you were born of a woman, I warn you, she should do the same. Because your day will come, and soon.'" Tosca is pregnant at the time. She falls ill on the way home and soon after loses the baby.

Edoardo isn't shot. He is tortured for days and days, in hopes that he will give up the names of his collaborators, but he refuses to talk. He will never speak of those days. At Mario Carità's trial, however, several of his comrades describe their torture in detail. "They placed me half-naked on a bench, my feet and forearms chained, and blindfolded me," one of them says in his deposition. "Then they left me there for a few minutes. When they returned, something touched my belly; after a bit I felt a burning sensation there, hotter and hotter until it felt as if my skin would catch fire. The pain was terrible. I screamed and felt myself losing consciousness, and then fainted. Unable to take the pain, I managed to say that I would sign whatever they wanted me to sign. But they kept me there awhile longer. Finally, when they released me, I saw they had placed a glass on my stomach containing a strange insect, like a cockroach. The glass was airtight so the insect had tried to scratch its way out."

After the questioning, Edoardo Fallaci is transferred to the Murate prison. In May, he is released. According to Oriana, this is mostly her mother's doing. For days she searches for evidence of her husband's innocence. She doesn't find it, but she finds something more useful: a forgotten accusation of antifascist activity against one of the torturers. With this in hand she is able to black-mail him and obtain his assistance. When Tosca visits her husband in prison, she takes her children. "We would arrive with a bag full of food that would be taken by the guards. They pushed us into a lurid room that they called a visiting room, with a long table. Behind the table stood a dozen men. Among them there was a man with a swollen face covered in bruises, purple lips, and an eye sealed shut. No one went to him, so we sat there, waiting in silence for our father to arrive. A voice whispered, 'My babies, won't you even say hello?' It was my father's voice, and it came from the disfigured man we hadn't recognized. Then he said, 'Don't worry, everything will be all right. I didn't talk, they know nothing. Worst case, they'll send me to a German concentration camp.' When we left, I asked our mother, 'Why?' And she said, proudly, 'because your father is involved in politics. He fights to make this world a little bit more decent.'"

During that summer, the front line nears the city. Bombardments destroy entire neighborhoods. Oriana and her family take shelter on the outskirts of town, in a convent where other Partisans are hiding. One day a group of trucks carrying Nazi-Fascists surrounds the area. The doors are kicked open. Oriana has just enough time to destroy a list of names and addresses of people associated with the Partito d'Azione, which she has kept hidden in a squash. "As long as I live I'll remember the sound of those trucks and their voices howling Fascist songs, 'Our wives don't love us anymore, because we're the Brown shirts,' and then the echo of their boots down the hall as my father flees through the garden. The blows on our bedroom door, the door giving way, the way they burst into the room. And then the machine-gun fire, screams, crying." Her father escapes through the window, after instructing her to warn two Yugoslavian soldiers hiding in another wing. It is too late to flee, so instead they climb down a dry well in the courtyard and tell Oriana to close the cover. But it is too heavy for her. "I think the soldiers saw me, and this sealed their fate. My mother and I realized that the Germans had found them because they started laughing. I'll never forget how they laughed when they found the two Yugoslavians."

The final battle for Florence takes place in August. For days there is fighting in the streets. There's no electricity or water in the city; every inch of infrastructure has been destroyed by the German mines and mortar shells. Nor do they spare the bridges over the Arno. On the night of August 10–11, the final round of German parachutists retreats from the city. "They were covered in mud and shame, and dying of thirst. Beneath every window they cried out, '*Wasser, acqua, wasser!*' The windows stayed closed; they sprayed them with bullets, then kept walking."

On the morning of August 11, Oriana distributes red armbands with the words "Giustizia e Libertà" to the Partisans for the liberation parade. In her rush, she falls, dropping them on the street, and the exultant crowd picks them up and puts them on. "How young I was! I was a little girl. One of the bandleaders slapped me across the face. The precious armbands had gone to people who, in the best of cases, had done nothing to fight the Nazi-Fascists, and in the worst, had been Fascists themselves."

Now that the battle for the city has ended, she and her family can return home. The house has been partly destroyed by the bombs; there is an enormous crater in the garden, but nothing can dampen the joy of that moment. "I felt happy and light. I was wearing a white dress my mother had just made for me, and white socks, and I was careful where I put my feet because I didn't want to get mud on my white shoes. I felt a bewildering burst of joy and life, as if it were Easter. It was the end of the war."

Florence is reduced to a pile of rubble, but the streets are filled with people celebrating. Oriana goes to see the Americans who are parading through the city. One of them pulls her braids, another gives her chocolate, which she accepts shamefacedly, knowing that her mother will scold her. Tosca has a gentler nature than Edoardo, but she has always treated Oriana like an adult, teaching her that life is a constant battle, to be won through rugged determination. "One day my mother and I were walking across some rocks and she called out to me, 'Step lively, come on!' 'The rocks hurt my feet,' I answered her, 'carry me.' To which she responded, 'The world is full of rocks, as you'll soon find out.'"

One of the American soldiers becomes friendly with her father. They call him Ohio, because that's where he's from and because his real name is too difficult to pronounce. Often he comes over in the evening with a big loaf of white bread and stays for dinner, talking for hours about the war and eating what little food the Fallacis have managed to scrounge up for a meal. When he leaves, Tosca shakes her head as she tidies up the kitchen. "All the other Americans give away food, except for this one. In exchange for a bit of bread, he eats our food!" She becomes even angrier when her husband gives him his grandfather's pocket watch. Edoardo is very attached to the family relic, but when the soldier leaves, he gives him his own watch, saying solemnly, "Remember Ohio." Oriana's father feels obliged to do the same, saying, in turn, "Remember Florence." When Oriana travels to America for the first time, many years later, her mother will tell her, "If you can find that old bore, try to get Daddy's watch back; offer to pay for it."

After the liberation of Florence, Edoardo Fallaci joins the executive committee of the Partito d'Azione and is put in charge of union activities. He is one of the founders of the city's metalworkers' union and, for a time, the editor in chief of the union newspaper *La Libertà del Lavoro*. Everyone in the family cooperates in the city's reconstruction by volunteering for the Partito d'Azione: father, Uncle Bruno, many Fallacis and Cantinis. Their names are recorded in the archives of the Resistance in Florence. Oriana's name appears in a file labeled "High School Students." For a short period she also works as a secretary at L'Unione Donna in Italia, the union of Italian women, which is associated with the party.

She is discharged from the volunteer corps of the Italian Liberation Army with the rank of private. She is proud of having fought for her country's freedom. The discharge includes a payment of 15,670 lire [equivalent to about $23], she has no idea what to do with the money. After all, she says, she simply did her duty. In the end, she buys shoes for herself and her sisters. No one in the family has decent shoes, but "Mother and Father said they didn't want them." Later, she enrolls in the youth brigade of the Partito d'Azione, the only party she will ever be a member of. "It was a tiny party; everyone was a general. I think I was the only private." As the youngest member of the Resistance, she is asked to speak at a party meeting. She is wearing a red-and-white checked dress. "I remember the microphone and how I was introduced: 'People of Florence! A young girl will speak to you now! Young people, listen!' I don't remember anything after that because I must have been in a state of shock."

3. A HOUSE FULL OF BOOKS

For as long as Oriana can remember, she has been fascinated by the written word. Every page speaks to her, every line unleashes her imagination. "When I was a little girl, my mother would buy skeins of wool and roll the wool up in balls. She would start off these balls with a scrap of paper, sometimes a bit of newspaper, a receipt from the grocer. Each time she knit a sweater, I would be devoured by curiosity as I watched the ball of wool get smaller and smaller, wondering: What did she use this time? As soon as the ball was unwound, I would unfold the paper. Often, it was blank. And when it was, my disappointment was great. But if there was something written on it, I would give it to my mother for her to read, and listen, rapt, to the story. Even a shop receipt contained a story."

She grows up in a house of serious readers, where books are purchased on the installment plan. Unlike most of their friends, her parents have a passion for literature. "We were poor people with lots of books because my mother and father had a 'weakness for reading,' as they put it. The house was always full of books; books were sacred. They were a luxury, our only luxury, and they represented culture." As an adult, she will remember, with emotion, that the only object of value left to her by her father were two volumes of the Bible, illustrated by Gustave Doré.

The books are kept in a small sitting room that has been baptized the Book Room. In that room, the most sacred spot is a shelf with all of Edoardo's favorite books. And it is there, in that book-filled room, that Oriana sleeps as a child. Her bed is a tiny couch. On one shelf, a large book takes pride of place. Both the image on the cover — of a veiled woman — and the title, *The Thousand and One Nights*, are irresistible to her. These are her childhood fairy tales, and they will stay with her for the rest of her life. As an adult, she will never stop acquiring new volumes, often in expensive antique editions.

"The cabinet with the glass doors was my forbidden paradise because I wasn't allowed to open it." She is nine years old when she is given permission to touch one of those books for the first time. She has been sick for days, confined to her bed by a fever. She is bored and demands something new to read. Finally, her mother opens one of the glass doors and hands her Jack London's *Call of the Wild*. From the first lines, Oriana falls in love with the dog Buck and his struggle for freedom. "Turn off the light, will you?!" her mother urges. Years later she will describe the experience of reading that book: "Buck taught me about war, struggle, and living. And as such he guided my adolescence, that verdant season that would bear fruit in the woman I hope and strive to be: disobedient and intolerant of any imposition. Others had more imposing heroes. Mine was a dog."

If Buck is her first hero, Jack London is her first role model. Her mother spends hours telling her about his adventures, his travels around the United States, Alaska, across oceans. Uncle Bruno, on the other hand, is scandalized that she wastes her time reading an author who, in his opinion, wrote too prolifically and not always well. Oriana disagrees: "I liked his books. I liked them even when they were poorly written. I loved his imagination, his intelligence, and his ability to skip from one subject to another. I even loved his incoherence, the disorderliness that allowed him to write about anything, from hunting to politics, from science fiction to sociology." To her, Jack London is the embodiment of the journalist writer who combines curiosity and adventurousness. Uncle Bruno tells her stories about Virgilio Lilli, the *Corriere della Sera* correspondent who traveled around the world several times, and about Curzio Malaparte, who was present at every important event of his time. Oriana listens in rapt silence.

From the age of five or six, she begins to imagine becoming a writer, a word she always uses in its masculine form. It is something she senses within herself, set in stone. But her parents shake their heads. "A writer! Do you know how many books you would have to publish to make a living?" her mother argues, describing Jack London's life of privations, how he alternated between working and starving. Her uncle Bruno scolds her: "First you have to live, then you can write! What can you possibly write about if you haven't lived?" Then he tells her that Tolstoy had the luxury of writing because he was a prince and Dostoyevsky earned his keep in the gambling house. "They made me believe that writing was a pastime for the rich, for the old. I couldn't possibly do it because I was poor and young." Convinced that she has to wait until she is old enough and rich enough, she begins to think about becoming a journalist, something that everyone in the family seems to consider an honorable compromise.

She reads everything she can get her hands on. First the Greeks and the Romans and later, Anglo-Saxon writers: Americans, starting with Melville, and British, starting with Shakespeare. The latter will profoundly influence her writing. Among French writers, only Proust interests her. Despite being an autodidact, and chaotic in her readings, she soon develops a prodigious breadth of knowledge. She reads voraciously and writes even more. "I've discovered old notebooks filled with ridiculous stories and fantastical tales.

Were these encouraged by my mother?" she asks years later in an interview. "I suppose," she says, "that along with a genuine and spontaneous love of culture, rare for a woman born into a family of impoverished artists, her enthusiasm was born of a furious desire for vindication. Yes, I really believe that my mother interpreted culture as a form of personal and social victory."

As soon as her homework is done, Oriana writes in her notebooks while Tosca sews quietly in a chair nearby. She fills page after page, fascinated by the way words can create a world apart. In one of her school notebooks from that period she writes, in a rounded script, "It's strange how melancholy holidays make me feel, especially in the afternoons, and how sad the bells sound as they toll slowly in the distance. This moment is a perfect example: there is a light fog, it's cold, the light is whitish-gray, there's no sun, the rooster crows hoarsely, the pear tree is losing its leaves, and the bells are clanging away, making a wild, stirring noise. All this, for me, is the essence of Sundays in early winter... If I were a poet, or at least a man of letters, I could put together these impressions and create a work of art, but I am not, so I must limit myself to reflecting, feeling, describing."

Tosca, who never had the chance to finish her studies, pushes Oriana to study. "Beware of ignorance!" she warns. "Ignorant people are taken advantage of!" She demands that Oriana receive the highest grades at school. In elementary and secondary school she is a good student, always one of the best in her year. Her school essays are read out loud at home and often win prizes. She is very serious for her age, disciplined and introverted, determined to be the best. A neighbor remembers that she used to pedal furiously on her way to school on a bike several sizes too big for her. "My personality already was fully formed — my unpleasant personality," Oriana writes later. "They tell me that before I started school I was much more docile. At school I became hard and aggressive.

I was angry when I realized that I was smarter than my classmates even though they came from families with money, so their mothers didn't have to suffer to send them to school."

She attends the Gino Capponi middle school in Florence and gets good grades. In the fall of 1944, she begins high school at the Liceo Classico Galileo and passes a test that allows her to make up the year she lost while fighting with the Partisans. She is a brilliant but unruly student, quick to act out. "I was impossible. Poor teachers, I tormented them. I was very intelligent, so I was always first in my class, but I was insufferable. If a teacher said something wrong, I couldn't keep my mouth shut." She is very politicized. "Every time I raised my hand to complain or contradict something, my philosophy teacher would mutter, 'Let's hear what the ball-breaker has to say or else she'll complain that we're censoring her.'" With two friends, she founds a students' union and tries to organize a few strikes, but she soon realizes no one cares about her causes, or if they do, it's for the wrong reasons. She even manages to annoy the priest who teaches religion at school. "Whenever Don Bensi walked into class, I would walk out. Deaf to his exasperated comments — 'Go, go, there's no saving that soul of yours' — I would eat my midmorning snack in the hallway. There were no repercussions. Every day he would ask, 'How was your sandwich?' with a snicker."

She loses her faith at a young age, deciding after an intense bout of soul-searching that God does not exist. As will often happen later in life, her decision is brought on by an act of injustice. To prepare for her first Communion, her mother sends her to a convent for a short retreat. Before sending her off, she gives her some chocolate and a banana, an extraordinary luxury. The nuns tell her to leave everything on the altar, as a gift to Jesus. "A little while later I crept into the church to see whether Baby Jesus had eaten the banana and chocolate, but there was nothing left. Not even the banana peel or the chocolate wrapper. This made me suspicious. I left the church, went down a hallway, and there, on the balustrade, was a nun eating my banana." For the rest of her life she describes herself proudly as an atheist, saying that she never asked God for help, even at her lowest point.

She graduates with very good grades: nine (out of ten) in Italian, seven in Latin, eight in Greek, eight in history, eight in philosophy, seven in math, seven in physics, seven in natural sciences, and nine in art history. She takes her exams very seriously, drinking coffee all night long in order to stay awake to study. For her Italian exam, she chooses to write on "the concept of fatherland from the ancient Greek *polis* to our times." She writes a highly polemical essay, in which she asks the test writers why they have chosen the fatherland as a subject, since the concept of fatherland is constantly changing while the concept of liberty is eternal. The head of the exam panel tells her, "We argued over your essay. Some wanted to give you a zero, others wanted to give you a ten. So we gave you a ten minus." Then came the eternal question: "What do you want to do when you grow up?" "I want to be a writer," she answers, peering up at him.

4. THE KID AT THE PAPER

"My father spun around, surprised, and exclaimed, 'Medicine? You want to study medicine?' I said yes. 'I thought you wanted to write and travel like Jack London? Where does medicine fit in?' 'Cronin was a doctor,' I answered him." After high school, Oriana enrolls at the University of Florence. It is a moral obligation she feels toward her mother. There are long discussions about which faculty she should choose. Oriana knows she wants to write, but Uncle Bruno insists that it's not necessary to study literature to become a writer. Better to study medicine, a subject that reveals the mysteries of men.

Oriana attends her first-year courses — physics, chemistry, biology, histology, and anatomy — but doesn't make close friends. She is one of only a few women and a year younger than her classmates. Tiny, clothed in homemade dresses and cotton socks, she looks like somebody's younger sister who somehow slipped in unnoticed. She hates being teased and can't stand it when the older students look at her smugly. On days when the teasing is particularly intense, she comes home furious and has to be calmed down. "During a dissection, one of those assholes stuck a piece of brain in my bag, which I found later as I was digging for my cigarettes. I was upset, but my father laughed. 'Think of it as an initiation rite,' he said. 'Turn it around. Take it back and tell them that maybe one of them forgot his brain in your bag, since clearly he wasn't using it.'" She smokes, collecting tobacco from her fathers' cigarette stubs.

"How proud I was to be a medical student! I was thrilled by the limitless horizons opened up by the study of biology and physiology and pathology. I pushed myself relentlessly to learn the name of every bone — I had a particular hatred for the sphenoid bone — in my anatomy classes, and in the painful task of dissecting cadavers. I was horrified by those mounds of flesh, the smell, the sight of blood! I couldn't stand it. Now I smile to think of how much blood and stench and how many bodies and how much flesh I saw as a war correspondent." During autopsies, her mind wanders. With her imagination, she seeks to penetrate the mystery of the human soul. In the margins of a notebook, she scribbles in pencil, "The other day in the necropsy room, a doctor was dissecting a brain, the brain of what had been a man. That man had a name, lovers, children. Maybe he was an ambitious man who liked to go around well dressed and clean shaven." She will spend her life arguing with doctors and questioning their diagnoses, but she will never hide the admiration she feels for them. She considers them to be the most humanist of scientists, engaged in a constant battle with the scandal of death. "I've always believed that doctors were more suited to politics than other people. Doctors and pregnant women."

Her parents don't have enough money to pay for her studies. From the start, Oriana knows she will have to find work, and for her, work means journalism. It's what Uncle Bruno, one of her first teachers, does, and to her it is a symbol of the freedom of speech her family had fought for during the Fascist years. "One day I came across a newspaper that said things that were different from what I had heard at school. Among other things, it said that Hitler and Mussolini were murderers. I took the article to my father and asked, 'What is this?' And he answered, 'It's a newspaper that says the truth.' So I asked him, 'Why isn't it sold on newsstands?'

And he answered, 'because it tells the truth.' And I was so struck by that, so scandalized, that I yelled out — or so they tell me — 'One day I'll write for newspapers that tell the truth and that are sold on newsstands!'"

One late summer day she puts on her best dress and heads over to Via Ricasoli, where Florence's three newspapers are headquartered: *La Nazione, Il Nuovo Corriere*, and *Il Mattino dell'Italia Centrale*. She wants to write for *La Nazione*, the oldest newspaper in Florence, where her uncle Bruno has worked for years, but she goes to the wrong floor and ends up at *Il Mattino*, a new newspaper with Christian Democrat tendencies, founded just after the war. She is received by Gastone Panteri, a veteran news editor, who looks her up and down, taken aback by the determination of this young girl. When she tells him her name, he asks if she is related to Bruno Fallaci. "He's my uncle," she answers, lifting her chin in a gesture almost of defiance. He decides to give her a chance and hands her a piece of paper with the address of a dance hall on the Arno. He wants her to check it out and write something. "I was so embarrassed, I remember, at the idea of setting foot in a dance hall. But I went and wrote a feature; I reread it recently and it wasn't bad at all. But I wrote it by hand on piece of lined paper, the kind we used at school. Panteri said, 'What the hell is this? You don't know how to type?' He led me to a monstrosity — a typewriter. I hadn't the foggiest idea how it worked. It took me nine hours to type up my article, from ten in the morning until seven at night."

She soon becomes a regular columnist for *Il Mattino*. Every day she goes out to look for stories. Then in the evening she writes at the newspaper's offices. She goes home at three in the morning, hitching a ride on the truck that delivers the newspapers to the train station. At nine in the morning she's back at school. She's always tired, starts to lose weight, and is continually ill. At the start of her second year, she's still enrolled in medical school, but two months later she asks to be transferred to the journalism school. Then she leaves school altogether. "Forced to choose between medicine, for which I wasn't paid, and journalism, for which I was, I chose journalism."

Everyone refers to her as "the kid." Without makeup and in flat shoes, she looks even younger than her eighteen years. The others ride around on scooters, but she pedals her old bike around town, stopping at the police stations and hospitals every night, far from home. One winter she gets a cold on her way to the orthopedic clinic and the San Jacopino police station, and gets seriously ill. "There was such a strong wind that night and my old bicycle didn't advance. I had to pedal standing up in order to get anywhere. A few hours later I got an earache, an ear infection. By the following week I was being operated on for a mastoiditis that was beginning to develop into meningitis."

She's young but already shows enormous talent. She has an original take and the ability to describe what she sees in tightly worded prose. One of the pieces she writes during this period, about an experimental school, opens with this witty line: "When, on a recent morning, amid a fluttering of chickens, our car descended upon San Gersolè and unloaded three people, a camera, and flashbulbs at its flower-laden doorstep, the school was a hive of activity." A profile of a Franciscan friar from Pisa who has founded a refuge for street kids begins with this cinematic image: "Look closely at this portly man, gray haired and gray bearded, who moves with the slow, lumbering steps of a tired lion. Look at him, and if you have the good fortune to cross his path, answer his greeting, a robust pat on the back, with deference. Look closely, because there are not many like him in this world."

Reading through these early articles, it's hard to believe they were written by a girl barely out of high school. In June 1950 she reports, with great intensity, on the trial of a gang of smugglers trafficking in stolen Jewish artifacts. She describes the methodical, painful testimony of a series of witnesses — relatives of people deported to the camps and in some cases the victims themselves — who are forced to restrict their accounts to descriptions of the thefts without making reference to their personal tragedies. She writes an unforgettable portrait of one of them, a man from whom several safes have been stolen. She deploys considerable storytelling gifts: "The judge says, 'You must restrict your testimony to the theft.' The man shakes his head, mumbling, 'What did they steal?' adding, too softly to be heard by the people in the rear of the courtroom, that yes, he had been robbed: of his daughter Matilde, of his brother-in-law Vittorio, of his grandchildren Amiel, thirteen, and Lia, twelve. All had perished at Auschwitz. As he spoke, he played with his hat in an attempt to calm his nerves. When he departed, supported by his son and a family member, his shoulders trembled. 'Safes?' he repeated, 'What safes?'"

A colleague recalls their first meeting, in a courtroom where several people are being tried for the summary execution of some Fascists. He notices her in the group of journalists, blonde and slight and decidedly pretty. But when he approaches her, attempting to make a joke, she puts him in his place with a dirty look. "Young man, this isn't a party. Three men have been killed. Yes, they were Fascists, but they were also human beings." She's young but very firm. She understands that in order to succeed in a field dominated by men, she must prove herself to be the best. She rewrites every article dozens of times, obsessively refining her prose. She studies each topic in depth. She reads the great writers, hoping to learn from the elegance of their style.

The widow of a colleague recalls that Oriana visited often to borrow a book or ask for advice: "Sometimes in the morning we would find notes she had slipped under the door overnight. She worked and smoked constantly." She realizes that she is practically a kid, but she is determined to take on whatever comes her way. "I think success is a gift that becomes the young," she will write later, when she is famous. "Napoleon was already Napoleon at twenty-seven. Alexander the Great was dead at thirty-two. Rimbaud had written his two finest works by the age of sixteen."

When veteran reporters treat her with amused benevolence, she loses her temper. She wants to be taken seriously despite her age. "Once, they sent me off to cover the trial of a man accused of indecent acts. I felt uncomfortable, but I didn't want to leave the courtroom because I had to write the article. At the juiciest point in the trial, the judged yelled, 'Send that girl out of the courtroom!' 'I'm a reporter!' I yelled back. 'Don't be ridiculous!' he insisted. 'Get out of here!' The usher escorted me out."

In time she becomes close to two fellow journalists, Mario Cartoni of *La Nazione* and Elvio Bertuccelli of the *Nuovo Corriere*. "Since we were all assigned to cover the Assizes Court, Cartoni came up with the idea of taking turns. When I was there, they didn't have to come, and vice versa. Later we would share information at the bar over a Cinzanino. We were always together, like the Three Musketeers." Among her papers, there are a few photographs of those evenings at the trattoria. She is the only woman sitting with a large group of men at a table. None seems to draw her attention. "Of course, I was looking for my Jack London, perhaps a Jack London who didn't realize he was a Jack London, or who might one day become a Jack London. But it was like searching for a butterfly in winter. That period of my life was, in that sense, a long winter spent waiting, in vain, for a bit of warmth."

She says, with pride, "I never took off Sundays because on Sundays I got a bonus of almost a thousand lire. In a sense I was like a doctor on call who goes off with his little buggy wherever he's needed, without a thought for holidays or mealtimes." She writes on a wide array of topics: fashion, human interest, crime. She works every day, without schedules or distractions.

One day in April 1951, she comes upon an intriguing story. A Communist Catholic has died in Fiesole and has been refused Catholic rites by the local priest. In reaction, his fellow party members have stolen the church vestments and candles and celebrated the funeral on their own. Oriana writes an article describing the sequence of events. She knows she will never be able to publish it in *Il Mattino*, because of its close relationship with the Christian Democrats, a party with strong ties to the Church, and so she sends it to Arrigo Benedetti, the editor of *L'Europeo*, the most prestigious and liberal weekly in Italy at the time. The journal looks like a newspaper but comes out once a week and is known for its innovative layout, prestigious contributors, and aggressive style of journalism.

"I had no illusion that he would publish it. But the following week, at the newsstand on the corner of Via Cavour and the Piazza del Duomo, there it was, *L'Europeo*, with a huge picture of Oriana Fallaci on the front page. Beneath it, the headline 'Even in Fiesole, God Needs a Little Help.'" The first person to call her is Uncle Bruno, almost irritated by her success. "He was a famous journalist and he was afraid I might eclipse him. He called me up and said, 'Who do you think you are, Hemingway? Fool,'" and hung up. I grew up at a time when young people were treated with great firmness, at home, at school, at work. And that firmness did me good."

Arrigo Benedetti, too, calls her, curious to learn more about the author of this brilliant article. "'You're very good, you know. But tell me, are you related to Bruno?' 'Yes...' 'Good, then write something else for me. I'd like a long interview with Professor Cocchi.' Cocchi was a famous Florentine pediatrician. He received me, I wrote up the interview and sent it to Benedetti with a note: 'Mr.

Benedetti, my uncle Bruno complained last time that my name was written in overly large type.' 'So this time we'll put it in even bigger type,' answered Benedetti. As you can probably tell, he wasn't a fan. The feeling was mutual. The Cocchi article filled the entire third page; with that, my entry into the world of weekly newspapers was complete."

A few months later, the editor in chief of *Il Mattino* asks her to attend a speech by the leader of the Italian Communist Party, Palmiro Togliatti, and write a nasty, funny piece about it. "I wouldn't dream of it," protests Oriana. "First I'll go hear what he has to say and then I'll write a piece about it." Shortly thereafter, she is called to the editor's office. He's an old-fashioned boss who expects complete obedience from his writers. Oriana has already raised eyebrows by addressing him with the familiar *tu* rather than the more formal *lei*. "Don't spit into the wind," he warns her. She balks and is fired. "I had to face the tragedy of explaining to my parents what had happened. This was worse than failing my exams. It took me a week to find the right words."

Bruno Fallaci saves the day by inviting her to write for *Epoca*, a new weekly based in Milan that models itself after the most prestigious American magazines. He is editor in chief. "He respected me a lot even then. He said I was good because I 'wrote like a man.' And even though I didn't like that description very much—what did it mean to 'write like a man'?—his words soothed my wounded pride. The trouble is that he didn't want to be accused of nepotism, so he barely used me. What did I write for Uncle Bruno? An article about the mosaics of Ravenna, or rather about the Galla Placidia mausoleum, which was beginning to crumble. Another on the history of ice cream, for which I was paid by the ice-cream producer Motta. A piece about an Henri Cartier-Bresson show. And one on Michelangelo's *David*, which a Christian Democrat assessor

With her uncle Bruno Fallaci (*top left*) and other colleagues from the magazine *Epoca*.

wanted to cover with a fig leaf because a group of students had covered up its privates with a pair of women's lacy underwear."

On the occasions when he lets her write about politics — like the election of a new mayor of Florence in 1951, Giorgio La Pira, one of the most important Catholic figures of his time and a Franciscan tertiary since his school days — Oriana is able to deploy her talent. With her very first line — "The Honorable Giorgio La Pira didn't want to cause any trouble" — she plunges directly into the story. She describes this unlikely politician, a mystic who lives in a monastery and gives away all his worldly goods to the poor, like a character out of Dostoyevsky. She describes his eccentric manner: "After taking in the entire piazza, he made the sign of the cross, leaned into the microphone, and said: 'in the name of the Father, of the Son, and of the Holy Ghost . . .' His invocation shocked many of the Communists who had gathered there." And his outwardly gentle but stalwart antifascism: "His strength is hidden behind apparent submissiveness. Thanks to this sweet disposition, during the Fascist period he was able to lead several rabid Fascist *Federali* [local officials] by the nose. When he was sent to stand guard at the Fascist cemetery in Santa Croce, he said, 'Yes, yes, I'll go. Poor souls. But I don't need a rifle. I'll take my rosary and say prayers.' The Fascists, unconvinced, never sent him back." Oriana is only twenty-two but already shows a great gift for storytelling. She writes about politics in a way no one has before.

After less than a year, Bruno Fallaci is removed from his post, and she is fired along with him. "I had committed the unforgivable crime of being my uncle's niece. My uncle and I have never been well loved by the Italian journalistic establishment. I suppose that is because we are in the habit of calling a spade a spade, a fool a fool." Luckily she has the backing of Arrigo Benedetti, the editor of *L'Europeo*, who admires her writing and her determination. "Once, he said to me: You're good, but you won't make many friends in our world, which is full of prima donnas and has little consideration for women. None, in fact. You have a way of taking what you want without waiting for things to be given to you, and this will rub many people the wrong way." He tells her that if she moves to Rome, home of the movie industry and the center of celebrity culture, she will have more opportunities to write for *L'Europeo*.

She decides to follow his advice. In 1954, she leaves Florence with a suitcase in which she has packed her few belongings. In her pocket is the address of a friend of Benedetti's, fellow journalist Nantas Salvalaggio. "Nantas found me a room to let in the Parioli neighborhood, and that's where I set up shop. It was the start of what I call the Hungry Years. How hungry I was all the time! I was always famished. I ate only bread, sometimes crackers, which the landlady would find in my closet. She used to scold me: 'They attract ants! They attract ants!'"

5. THAT PEN OF ORIANA'S

It is the early 1950s, and the era of great Italian cinema is just beginning. Oriana writes for *L'Europeo*'s entertainment and society pages on subjects that she cares little about. Her natural severity and Leftist background have not prepared her for the Roman scene. She dreams of writing about politics, the only topic that really interests her, but she is not yet able to articulate this out loud. She's young, and a woman, so she goes where she is asked. She has only one friend at *L'Europeo*, bureau chief Renzo Trionfera. "A lovely, generous man. I was so scared of him! But he encouraged me. He would say, 'That pen of Oriana's...' Or, 'Written in Oriana's pen...' As if he were equating my pen with Marcel Proust's. He fought for me to be hired."

There are very few female journalists in Italy. "I felt as lonely as a bastard dog. I defended myself like a bastard dog and attacked like a bastard dog, and that's how I became the equivalent of a black man invited to the White House. I launched a new trend of women journalists in Italy." She still dreams of becoming a writer, but in the meantime she must make a name for herself and build her résumé. She knows that being a journalist can help her.

"I owe everything to journalism," she will say years later. "As a child I was poor; because of journalism I didn't grow up to be poor. I was full of curiosity, hungry to see the world, and I was able to do this because of journalism. I had grown up in a society that oppressed and mistreated women; because of journalism I was able to live like a man."

She knows she is beautiful and that this beauty can open many doors. It helps to shield the sharp edge of her intelligence so that her interlocutor will lower his guard. She's not intimidated by anyone, a quality she demonstrates again and again. A disagreement with one of her senior colleagues, Davide Lajolo, quickly becomes legendary. Oriana shows up at his office to challenge him for a comment he has made about her. Lajolo, who also fought in the Resistance, under the battle name Ulisse, jokingly places a revolver on the desk between them. Without blinking an eye, Oriana places her lipstick next to it. They become friends. Later, Lajolo will say of her, "I just had dinner with Oriana Fallaci. She is vivacity personified, a woman with an uncommon intelligence and a capacity for work greater than most men. A journalist and commentator with a grasp of every detail, but also an overarching understanding of every subject. With that delicate silhouette of hers she has traveled the world. If you look into her pupils, you will understand how much strength and energy lies under the surface, ready to explode. One doesn't converse with Oriana; one debates, one argues with her. She has the arrogance to show she knows as much as her interlocutor but is seeking something else, something that nobody knows, the secret implications, the unspoken motives, the revealing details beyond the obvious facts within which they are contained. After she has assailed you with her insistent questioning, she smiles at you and seduces you all over again, only to begin again, attempting to get you to say whatever you had sworn to keep to yourself."

Incurably curious, insistent to the point of insolence, in 1954 she manages to work her way into a press trip aboard the first flight from Rome to Tehran. It is her first foray out into the world. As she boards the flight, she is as excited as if she were climbing onto a rocket to the moon. The plane takes off at one in the morning from Ciampino Airport: "Rome glittered beneath us like a scattering of lightning bugs, palpitating with light. Soon it was just far-off glimmer, like a star, fallen from the sky." She doesn't sleep, determined not to miss a single detail. While her older colleagues snore or drink, she sits with her nose stuck to the window, taking notes. The sunrise over the Bosphorus blinds her: "The sky was still dark around us, but to the east, over the Sea of Marmara, the horizon was on fire; red, purple, and yellow bursts ripped through the blue, softening along the edges into glowing pink plumes." She watches as Anatolia is replaced by the mountains of Armenia and finally by an immense desert: "There are no trees, no grass, no rivers, no lakes in this deserted plain. It was like flying over a desolate lunar landscape. That was Iran. After three hours of brown, hilly earth, we were rewarded with our first sight of the Tehran plateau." Iran, ancient Persia, the land of the *Thousand and One Nights*, which she had dreamed of as a child, unfolds beneath her like a promise: her first taste of the East.

The trip is carefully planned, with tours of the city and its museums. After procuring a black chador, Oriana manages to sneak into a mosque. Later, she is received by the empress. Soraya is the shah's second wife; already, rumors are swirling because of the delay in producing an heir to the throne. She agrees to meet with Oriana because she is the only woman in the Italian delegation. Her conditions are that Oriana will not ask indiscreet questions or bring up politics. Oriana accepts and asks no political questions. But her article begins with a description of the coup a few months earlier, an attempt to overthrow the shah. She subtly infuses the article with politics, down to the last line.

The resulting piece is a perfect example of journalism Fallaci-style. She describes her arrival at the palace dressed in black, as per her minders' request — the court is in mourning for the death of the shah's younger brother. A servant mistakenly leaves her alone in the empress's dressing room, where she catches a glimpse of satin lingerie and rows of riding boots. A breathless lady-in-waiting then leads her to the correct meeting place, a sitting room that Oriana evokes in a few vivid strokes: crystal chandeliers and a carpet so lush that her high heels sink, as if into a mound of sand. A woman arrives; she could be one of the many ladies of the palace but turns out to be the empress herself. (Oriana forgets to bow as instructed, which makes Soraya laugh, and this breaks the ice.)

With the same nimbleness she will later exhibit during her great period of political interviews, she encourages the empress to speak. The pauses become as articulate as her words. Oriana describes her silences, her glances, the movements of her head. The monotony of palace life is inferred from a slight grimace that appears on Soraya's face as she describes her daily routine. She suggests the empress's anxiety at being childless by describing her reaction to the news that the actress Silvana Mangano is pregnant: "'She's having a baby?' the empress murmured, and her expression suddenly darkened." Oriana has decided to push her to admit that the motive for her upcoming trip to the United States is the desire to meet with a famous gynecologist, rather than the official reason, which is to visit Hollywood. She does this by describing the empress's body language, despite her denials: "She slowly lowered her teacup and looked down, and when she looked up again she had a lost expression, like a child who doesn't know what to say. Then, in the quiet, uncertain voice of a person who is ashamed to tell a lie, she said, 'No, it is a pleasure trip.' And she quickly changed the subject."

Oriana's ability to expose the personality of her interviewees is already apparent in this first piece of international reporting. If the world leaders she would lay bare in her famous political interviews twenty years later had read this interview, they would have

At the headquarters of the newspaper *L'Europeo* in 1955.

been warned. It is not what they say or don't say that has the most impact, but the careful way she layers each detail. Even at this early stage, her intuition and interpretative skill lie at the heart of the interview, leading her interlocutor in a predetermined direction. There is no escape. She also shows great storytelling skill: Instead of merely laying out a series of questions and answers, she constructs a narrative with a beginning and an end, and in the middle, a real tension that carries the reader through to the final words.

After her return to Italy, she continues to write about the film industry and high society for *L'Europeo*, under a new editor. Arrigo Benedetti has left to found *L'Espresso*, replaced by Michele Serra. In 1955, Oriana is hired full time and moves to Milan, where the newspaper is headquartered. When she arrives at the offices of the most prestigious weekly in Italy, she still has the look of a young girl. She's twenty-six, doesn't know anyone, and has no idea how to dress. She always wears trousers, unusual at the time for a woman, and prefers the color black. Michele Serra teases her, saying she looks like a chimney sweep. The reigning woman journalist at *L'Europeo* is Camilla Cederna, who is extraordinarily elegant and well connected. (Soon she will leave to join Benedetti at *L'Espresso*.) Oriana admits, "I was a child of the proletariat; my parents didn't even know the meaning of the word 'parlor.' And I was young. I lacked the courage to seek out Camilla's friendship or even her indulgence; I knew she had no interest in me. I remember the humiliation I felt one day when Emilio Radius, the lead editor and a friend of hers, came to me shamefacedly and gently chided me for 'imitating Camilla's style' in an article. (In reality, I had merely opened my article with an adverb, as she often did.) I was told that 'la Cederna was offended' and that I should find my own style."

And so she does, rather quickly. She writes about anything and everything, because she is convinced that it is only through practice that she will become proficient. She writes about a father's attempt to bring back his son from the Foreign Legion; about a young man who commits suicide for no apparent reason; about a scam artist who takes advantage of the orphans in her care; about an Englishman who has a sex change. She continues to cover Roman society, particularly film stars. She has the boldness required to smoke out celebrities and the tenacity to lie in wait for hours. She writes about the love affairs between foreign actresses and Roman princes and the private lives of Italian starlets, the Capri vacations of the rich and famous, and Audrey Hepburn's honeymoon in the Roman hills. Maria Pia of Savoy's wedding gown, and the Sanremo song contest. In time, the interviews become more frequent and her technique more refined. Oriana begins to find her stride. Her narrative verve makes up for the often very limited information at her disposal. When she is denied entry at the Venice Film Festival, she doesn't give up and instead writes a brilliant lead based on the comments about the stars made by people around her.

She works hard, but she's bored. The only thing she enjoys is the travel. She accepts every out-of-town story that comes her way. In April 1955, the weekly asks her to cover the impossible love between Peter Townsend and Princess Margaret, a huge embarrassment for the English royal family. She flies to Belgium where, for months, Townsend has been living in exile, refusing to speak with journalists. She shows up at the range where he rides every day. She waits for him outside his home. She manages to procure his phone number. She gets no information out of him, but out of that nothing she builds a perfect little story. More than an article, it's a screenplay, based on a few words exchanged on his doorstep. "Townsend smiled: 'You don't give up easily.' 'Nor do you, Captain.' Another smile. He tapped his riding crop rhythmically against his boot. 'I'm sorry I can't give you what you want. I wish I could.

After all, you've earned it.' Another smile. Then I asked the question that, deep down, mattered the most to me: 'Would you deny that you intend to marry Princess Margaret?'" Townsend denies it, but Oriana's description of how he swallows hard and raises his face quickly, tightening his jaw, turns his no into a yes.

Oriana's style, the style that will make her famous around the world, is already perfectly formed: her tenacity in pursuit of a story, her ability to build a narrative, and her decision to include herself in that narrative. She asks the photographers who work with her to include her in their shots of the interviewee and writes in the first person. She describes her feelings and addresses the reader directly: Do you see? Understand? Let me explain. It is as if each article were a conversation.

The Hungarian Revolution marks a decisive turn in her career. On October 23, 1956, Budapest rises up against the Communist regime. Oriana pesters her editor into sending her over to write a colorful piece about the uprising after Budapest has been freed. When she lands in Vienna on November 2, she discovers that, over the course of just a few hours, the situation has changed. The Soviets have invaded, the borders are closed, and the capital is cut off. She ignores the recommendations of the Italian embassy in Austria and decides to enter the country secretly. She hires a taxi, which is forced back. Then she manages to hitch a ride with a Red Cross convoy, which is stopped just a few kilometers from the border by the invading army. In her article for *L'Europeo*, she describes a snowy, muddy night in a Soviet camp. Suddenly, she finds herself traveling back to the Second World War, when her elders spoke of the famous Turkestan Legion, composed of Soviet prisoners from central Asia, sent by Hitler to fight against the Italian Partisans after September 8, 1943. Nothing has changed, except the guttural words of the soldiers as they attempt to convince her to turn back.

Before returning to Austria, the Red Cross convoy pauses at an outpost held by a group of insurgents. Their commander is an old man. He holds the position with a group of thirty young men, even though they know they have no hope of surviving. Oriana notes his tired demeanor, his long beard, his hollow eyes. He reminds her of her father when he was taken by the Fascists, his heavy-lidded, downcast eyes. She feels she could listen to him for hours, but as they hear the rumble of approaching tanks, the Red Cross convoy prepares to depart. She too must leave, abandoning the old resistant to his fate. He prepares a final coffee and then says his goodbyes with a gentlemanly bow, a gesture from another time. "Dear sirs, we all have to die someday," he says. Later, Oriana hears that he has been killed. The one thing she can do for him is tell his story, and she does, writing an extraordinary piece that will make him live forever.

On her return to Austria, she asks to visit the refugee camps in order to speak with some of the people who have fled Hungary. She is devastated by what she sees. She transcribes clandestine radio messages, translated by her interpreter. "How can you ignore the cries of our women and children who are being murdered? People of the world! Hear the desperate cries of a small nation!" She lays out the horrifying stories of the refugees in a series of articles. The last one ends with a powerful image: the disfigured face of a student whose tongue has been cut off because he refused to name his comrades. "He'll never speak again," a woman tells her, "but you can. Speak of this, tell his story when you return to Italy. Tell everyone you see." Recounting the scenes of the Hungarian Revolution, Oriana's journalistic voice acquires a new dignity. She's not there to entertain with her narrative abilities. She becomes a witness, a soldier, fighting on the front lines for freedom and justice, the two ideals that have marked her since childhood.

The trip to Hungary marks her profoundly, and she does not hide this from her readers. "As men and women who are aware of what is happening around us, I think it is out of place to speak of celebrity love affairs, society scandals, and film premieres attended by stars dressed in tuxedos and revealing gowns," she writes in an article from Vienna. Her emotions and indignation spill out onto the page, unfiltered. She seeks to move the readers, to shake them, even if it means writing with brutal honesty: "Those who are still able to enjoy frivolous things and ignore the agony of an entire people should come to Vienna and see what is happening here." She can't imagine going back to writing about gossip and the high life. But that is exactly what will happen upon her return. Less than a month later she is in London, covering a scandal at Buckingham Palace. From the first line, her frustration is evident: "And now, let's turn our attention to Margaret's latest crush…"

To Michele Serra, Oriana's wish to travel to Hungary had been merely a whim. He had sent her only because he knew all too well how pointless it was to try to stop her. For her, it had been a point of no return: "It was an important experience, like a trip back in time to the period of the Resistance. I could almost smell it." The war correspondent is born. Vietnam is not far off. But first, she must convince her editor to send her there. And for that she must become one of *L'Europeo*'s top reporters.

6. DISCOVERING AMERICA

It is in America that she has her first chance to make a name for herself. She has dreamed of that country from an early age: "I was brought up to love America, even when the Americans bombed us and killed a thirteen-year-old boy who sat near me at school. On August 11, the Americans arrived in Florence. For me, in my child-like fantasy, Americans would always be those angels dressed in khakis. They were fantastic. I began to dream of going to America, and many years later I went there and fell in love with the physical place, with my dream."

In December 1955, she takes part in a press trip to inaugurate the first direct flight between Rome and Los Angeles. She travels with a group of Italian journalists. Once again, she is the only woman. She visits Hollywood, Washington, and New York. Half a century later, Giovanna Govoni Salvadore, the interpreter on the flight, still remembers Oriana clearly. She was the youngest and the small-est person there, she says, but not easy to overlook: "She had a big personality and didn't mince words." She kept photos of the trip. In one, she and Oriana walk down a New York street; in another, they visit a graveyard and Oriana jokingly makes a gesture for good luck. She's wearing a coat that's too big for her; her plump face is framed by short bangs. Hat, gloves, purse, a string of pearls, and low heels. She looks like a young teacher.

"She didn't speak English well, so she asked me to translate for her during her interviews," Giovanna remembers. When the group stops over in New York for a few days, Oriana announces that she intends to interview Marilyn Monroe, the most elusive star in American movies. Monroe has been in hiding for almost a year. She has broken her contract with her film studio and left Hollywood and is living in New York. No one knows her address. She barely leaves her apartment, and when she does, it is said that she wears a wig. Giovanna accompanies Oriana on her hunt. "Everyone said we were crazy. One time we went to a premiere of a movie starring a friend of hers, thinking we might find her there. We stayed at the theater for a long time, searched the dressing rooms, and, in the end, were locked in. We made the best of it and slept on the chairs in the theater; at dawn, the guard threw us out."

The search soon becomes frenetic. Over two evenings, Oriana visits twelve restaurants, eighteen nightclubs, eight cinemas, and fourteen theaters. The other correspondents tease her. Forget it, one of them says, I've been looking for her for six months. At the offices of 20th Century Fox, where she calls asking for an address, the secretary jokingly says, please let us know if you find her. Soon, news of the young Italian journalist on the lookout for Marilyn Monroe gets out. Her American colleagues call her to find out how the search is proceeding. They make bets. She returns to Milan empty-handed, but she doesn't give up. She writes a piece about not interviewing Marilyn Monroe, placing herself at the center of the story. It is brilliant and her editor is pleased.

A year later, in 1957, she convinces him to send her to Hollywood. At the time, such a trip is an extravagance for an Italian newspaper. "He sent me there with five hundred dollars, an inadequate sum to cover a month in Los Angeles. I got by because of the hospitality of an Italian American woman who let me sleep in her garage. The garage was empty, except for a bed, a table, and a bathroom. The trip went well and I managed to interview a lot of actors." Again, she requires help with her English. She chooses Paola Brandt Kennealy, an Italian living in Los Angeles with her husband, Bill, a journalist and screenwriter. Paola remembers that month in Hollywood in Oriana's company. She can't recall the garage, but confirms that Oriana was living with an Italian American family. "They would tell her all the Hollywood rumors to help prepare for each interview, and gave her tips on where to ambush each actor."

Oriana gets around in Kennealy's Cadillac. She doesn't know how to drive, so she lets Paola do the honors. Paola remembers her fondly. "She was like a frightened bird, very young, very graceful, with an expressive face. But her eyes revealed a bewildered soul." She knows nothing about this large country; she doesn't understand the language well. But she is determined not to fail. As her parents always said, she has to be the best. She puts her head down and charges forward, pretending she has no fear. Giovanna, the interpreter from her first trip, also remembers her complex nature: "She was fragile, but she used aggressiveness as a shield. She attacked first. As a result, Americans were often terrified of her."

That month in California allows her to study the world of American movie stars up close. Hollywood is just over half a century old. In 1887, when a Puritan pioneer from the Midwest, Daeida Hartell Wilcox Beveridge, decided to move there to get away from the corruption in Los Angeles, it was still a plain covered in wild orange trees and holly. Mrs. Wilcox named her ranch, simply, "Hollywood," forest of holly. Little did she know that soon the mayor would allow William Selig, a "motion picture salesman," to shoot movies nearby. And that three young rebels — Samuel Goldwyn, Jesse Lasky, and Cecil B. DeMille — seeking to avoid the fees imposed by the Motion Pictures Patents Company in New York, would rent a part of the ranch to make a film. The rest is history.

Oriana observes everything with a critical eye, discovering the reality of America alongside the readers of *L'Europeo*. As usual, she says everything that is on her mind, with great sincerity. The capital of world cinema appears to her as "stupid and brilliant, corrupt and puritanical, fun and boring." Oddly, it is overrun by rats who live in the trees of Beverly Hills and scratch around at night, even more noisily than the cicadas in Florence. She observes everything with an air both amused and severe, and without missing a single detail. She makes friends with Jean Negulesco, a Romanian exile who has lived as a painter in Paris and is now a director in great demand. Every day, in order to remind himself that he is rich, he buys art, compulsively. She visits Greta Garbo's villa; one day, many years later, Garbo will be Oriana's neighbor in New York. She visits one of the last remaining prewar stars, Mary Pickford, who speaks to her in French, convinced that it is the only language spoken in Europe.

Her notebooks, filled with notes, reveal a talent for finding flourishes of color. She writes about a young taxi driver, a third-year student at the University of California, who surprises her with the question: When will the Italian Socialist leader Pietro Nenni make peace with Giuseppe Saragat? And about a Catholic priest in Hollywood who delays the start of Mass in order to accommodate late-arriving actors and then begins by exclaiming, "Okay!" And about a guide at a local cemetery who shows her a reproduction of Leonardo's *Last Supper*, boasting of its superiority to the original in Milano: "This one is bigger, and it's new!"

In the evening she goes out with Paola and Bill. She wants to see everything. She visits fashionable spots like Mocambo and Romanoff's. She constantly asks questions, exhausting her guides. Whenever she can, she invites herself over to actors' homes, has dinner with their families, swims in their pools. During an evening at the home of the director Henry Hathaway, she becomes bored with the wives, who talk only about the help and recipes, and joins the husbands, who are watching a boxing match on TV. The world of American celebrities suits her. She recreates each character in minute detail. She senses, intuitively, a certain emotional fragility in many of them. In Judy Garland she can still see the young girl who just wanted to sing and instead was forced to become a star, her life a perennial diet. In Loretta Young she sees a lonely woman who keeps a rosary in the car, hanging from the rearview mirror, in order to pass the time at traffic lights.

In a few cases, she allows herself the satisfaction of a small vendetta. She gets back at Elvis Presley, who refuses to see her, saying, "You came from Italy to interview me? So what? Others have come from China." She describes him as an idiot with a mouth shaped like a rosebud, who travels with a group of kids who yell, "Elvis is coming! Elvis is coming!" wherever he goes. She is kinder to others. A few years earlier, Frank Sinatra had flatly refused to meet with her in Rome, where he was traveling with Ava Gardner. Oriana had sworn never to speak to him. One night in Hollywood he is seated next to her at a film opening. "I stared at the screen, pretending not to see him. But just before the lights dimmed, Frank Sinatra, who has a memory like an elephant, taps my arm and asks, 'Are you still mad?' with a smile. A smile that could enchant a serpent. Forget a woman."

Just as in her articles about Cinecittà, nothing escapes her. A Roman friend who had introduced her to the Italian jet set writes in a letter, "We've lost sight of you, Oriana. People are relaxed; no one is upset, no one complains about the infernal Oriana who makes us all look like a band of idiots. What a shame." The actress who impresses her the most is Jayne Mansfield. She has the quality that Oriana admires above all others: courage. "She is the nicest, most sincere, and most criticized girl in Hollywood. The only one who never disappointed me," she will write of her. Impressed by Mansfield's lack of tact, she does a long interview with her in which the actress recounts her success story, based not on talent but on her desire to become a star.

She detests the falseness and arrogance that abound in Hollywood, in other words, almost everything. She says this in so many words to her readers: "When I approach a 'star,' I try to understand whether he or she is sincere. They rarely tell me about themselves. Unless they are very stupid or very desperate. There is a falseness in their way of speaking and moving that fills me with suspicion and makes me uncomfortable. They are too used to coming across as something other than who they really are and can't be spontaneous when they're not standing in front of a director." Whenever she senses falseness, she identifies it and then ridicules it. The highly mannered Yul Brynner, who invites her to his set, comes across poorly in her article. "He lit my cigarette with studied slowness. Then he blew out the match with his full lips. His breath was simultaneously violent and delicate. Mr. Brynner would be disappointed to hear that this action did not produce in me a delicious frisson. It did not."

She describes the process through which film studios create stars, using Kim Novak as an example. The actress, an insipid big-boned girl of Czech extraction, had been remade from head to toe and transformed into a diva. She poses in front of Oriana in a red dress: "smooth and round as the California apples being sold at the Farmers Market in Los Angeles." Oriana gets all the details from the agent who created her and, with a hint of amusement, passes them on to her readers: "She used to walk like a duck and didn't know what to do with her hands. She would squeeze a handkerchief between her fingers and burst into stupid giggles in public. She had no sense of style. We had to teach her everything." Even so, Oriana can't understand why Kim Novak has become so famous and picks her apart in her article, which culminates with Novak's trip to Europe, an obligatory passage for any aspiring star: "Kim showed up at Cannes with nineteen pieces of luggage and a complete incomprehension of the practice of hand kissing. 'Whenever a man kissed my hand, I would do the same,' she says. They thought it was a joke, and laughed. But now I know better.'"

It is in Hollywood that she comprehends the nascent power of journalism. In this tiny city, there are nearly a thousand reporters writing for dozens of publications devoted to the movies, which sell millions of copies nationwide each week. Reporters follow every detail of the actors' lives, sharing them with the reading public. Stars fear them, and because of that, treat them with great deference. Oriana studies the working methods of Louella Parsons, Hedda Hopper, and Sheilah Graham, who write syndicated gossip columns for hundreds of newspapers across the country. She even meets with one of them, Hedda Hopper, noting her advice: "Don't spare anyone. Speak ill of everyone. Take pleasure in being known as a snake."

In her investigations, she relies on the help of the Italian American community. She becomes friendly with the Pierangeli sisters, Marisa and Anna Maria, the latter having become famous as James Dean's great love, the one who got away. Gregorio Bernardini, a young man who directs the Fiat offices in San Fernando Valley, helps her approach William Holden, a car enthusiast. She turns to Valentina Cortese, the wife of Richard Basehart, to receive the honor of being the only journalist invited to Joseph Cotten's yearly party. It is a very exclusive party, but Oriana is bored and leaves early with Orson Welles and his Italian wife, Paola Mori.

With Paul Newman during a 1963 interview.

Naturally, she writes about this first meeting with Welles. "I found him so unpleasant that, just to annoy him, I dove into the pool only a few feet away from where he was sitting. It was a spectacular belly flop — plop! — and I sprayed water all over his beautiful silk suit. You know what he did as I splashed about like a duck? He erupted in laughter and removed his jacket and trousers, carefully hung them up to dry, and then jumped into the pool, turning it into a churning ocean. With one finger he plucked me out of the water like a flea, saying, 'I hate women. They're sensitive, realistic, practical, unpredictable, and as inscrutable as animals. I love animals because they make me laugh. Would you like to join me for dinner?'"

After that season in Hollywood, her trips to the United States become more and more frequent. She has an open-ended visa and is determined to use it. With the regularity of a metronome, she takes the flight to New York, always carrying a small embroidery project and a long list of story ideas: "Something on Elizabeth II's official visit to the States, something on gangsters, something on Mickey Spillane, a story about Broadway, one on Christmas, and an article about the Miller couple."* She returns often to Hollywood, where she has developed certain routines: "I can't complain about how I am treated in Hollywood. They treat me very well indeed. All I have to do is call, and people say come on over, bring your swimsuit. I'm several shades darker than Sidney Poitier, and my bones ache from swimming." By now, her English is excellent. Many actors become friends.

Years later she will go on a road trip with Shirley MacLaine. They plan to cross the country from west to east, but the trip has to be cut short because they are constantly at each other's throats. The actress remembers, "I had explained to her that Native

---

*Playwright Arthur Milller and his wife, Marilyn Monroe.

Americans think that taking their picture is like stealing their soul, but she didn't pay me the slightest mind and took all the pictures she wanted. We had a big argument and went our separate ways. Oriana didn't understand. It was supposed to be a pleasure trip, but to her everything was work." The notebook she takes on the trip is full of notes. In Texas, a state trooper arrests them for speeding; they spend a night in jail. Oriana is amazed by the seriousness with which traffic laws are observed: "No one passes in America. They wait, even if the car in front of them is five miles away, or even ten miles. They say, 'It's dangerous.' I don't know how they manage to have accidents." In the desert, they get a flat tire. "Emptiness, silence. I see a car in the distance and run, run, run toward it. It's an old gray-haired woman in a Renault. 'Don't ask me for help,' she says, 'I'm lost too.'" On the border of Nevada and Arizona, they're stopped by the police. "They ask us if we are carrying fruit or vegetables. It's customs. No, I say, like a good Italian. If they had decided to investigate further, they would have discovered that our car was full of oranges, bananas, grapes, peaches. And also carrots, celery, and the green peppers Shirley loves to eat with salt." In Alabama, they stop in a small town called Florence, a detail that amuses her to no end.

Her articles detailing the lives of the American stars are published in *L'Europeo* during the fall of 1957. The series is titled "Hollywood Through the Keyhole." It is a big success. Italian readers are not used to celebrities being written about in this way. Oriana is not intimidated by them, a fact her readers enjoy. She is funny, exuberant, and curious. She takes the readers by the hand and leads them into the celebrities' homes. And she always writes herself into her articles. She becomes a character, someone her readers remember and feel affection for. Her irreverence makes the readers feel better about their gray, humdrum lives.

During the spring of 1958, the Longanesi publishing house offers to publish a collection of her articles. The proposed title is *I sette peccati di Hollywood* (The seven sins of Hollywood). For Oriana, who has always dreamed of being a writer, it is a decisive moment. "Already when I was a little girl, I wanted to write books. Not just to be a writer, but to write books, because I love them, I love the feel of the pages. At least this paper is not used to repair shoes. Once, I brought a pair of shoes to the cobbler to have the heel repaired, and the cobbler returned it to me wrapped in one of my articles. It is unpleasant to know that after a week you've already expired."

Books always held a central place in her dreams about the future. "I will never forget what I felt when I held my first book in my hands. It was as if I had given birth to a child. I started to tremble and ran to the bathroom to cry." She asks Orson Welles to write an introduction. He cannot hide his admiration for the young Italian journalist who has laid bare the lives of the stars, with talent and insolence. "Oriana Fallaci has a sharp, Tuscan eye; it was a clever idea to embed her in our Hollywood caravan for a little while." Welles is the first to decode one of her secrets — her ability to conceal sharp journalistic instincts beneath a deceptive mask of femininity: "Mata Hari, too, was beautiful. Each of these two skillful spies has, in her time, taken advantage of men's well-known bias. She knows that men believe that intelligence is reserved for the less-attractive members of the so-called weaker sex. In Hollywood, there are plenty of beautiful women. Oriana Fallaci's fascinating loveliness made it possible for her to disappear into the crowd."

She dedicates the book "To my mother and father." Sales are good. Oriana's name, already familiar to readers of *L'Europeo*, begins to spread. She is interviewed by her colleagues, who are amazed at the sudden success of this young woman with teased hair. A few of them still joke about her meek appearance; one describes her as "the pale blonde special envoy with rosebud lips."

Quickly, though, they begin to realize that their rival will soon eclipse everyone else and become the only Italian journalist — male or female — to be recognized and read all over the world. Giorgio Fattori, the new editor of *L'Europeo*, knows well that sales increase whenever her name appears on the cover. Oriana has achieved fame on a national scale. This should be a happy time. But in reality she is going through one of the most difficult periods of her life: an unhappy love affair that will change her forever.

7. FIRST LOVE

His name is Alfredo Pieroni and he is the London correspondent for the now defunct *La Settimana Incom Illustrata*. They meet shortly after her return from Hollywood, when she is in the process of finishing her book. She is six years younger and much more famous. Until that moment she has thought only about her career, but her encounter with this colleague causes her to pause. For the first time, she is deeply affected by a man. She is not prepared for what she is about to experience and finds herself at a loss.

Love reveals a new Oriana, fragile, tender. It is almost hard to believe that she is the author of love letters to Alfredo, drafts of which she keeps among her papers. The woman who writes them dreams of a shared life, says she is willing to give up everything, even work, to fulfill this dream. She is a woman begging to be loved, who forgives everything and justifies anything, who abases and effaces herself before the man she loves. For perhaps the first time, Oriana is completely vulnerable. She will be deeply wounded by this relationship. She will lose a child and, almost, her own life. The experience will deeply affect her personality and the way she sees her own existence.

In her early letters to Alfredo, she attempts to make light of the situation and play the flirt. In one she includes a drawing of a besotted young girl with a bow in her hair, who asks where she can find Ms. Fallaci. In another letter she explains that she wants to put in a good word for Oriana, who is suffering from lovesickness after their latest meeting. Soon she begins to write more openly, without filter. She declares herself to be in love — irreparably, obstinately, tenderly, she says — and does everything she can to bridge the distance between them. She deluges him with letters and spends her days next to the phone waiting for his calls. The truth is that their relationship isn't quite real. Alfredo doesn't return her feelings. It is a monologue, a long letter addressed to a person who does not respond.

At first Alfredo is intrigued by his colleague: pretty as a doll, tough as a man, and more talented than most. Everyone is talking about her, some with admiration, some with envy. Flattered by her attention, he is open to a dalliance but nothing more. Very soon, the intensity of Oriana's feelings begins to frighten him. The more love letters he receives, the more he tries to tamp down her ardor. He asks her not to mention their relationship and invites her to London only at her insistence. He never writes. Once in a while he makes the mistake of promising to call, and then forgets. Oriana spends entire days sitting next to the phone. He doesn't deny having other liaisons. She is extremely jealous but accepts even this. There is nothing she will not accept from Alfredo.

The hunting ground for her society reporting for *L'Europeo* has always been Rome and Paris. But now she makes continual attempts to dig up stories that will take her to London. Any excuse will do: a scandal involving Princess Alexandra of Kent, Ingrid Bergman's newest love affair, an Indonesian witch doctor who cures celebrities with meditation. Traveling to London for work means visiting Alfredo, even for a single night. Oriana, who will later tout the values of long-distance love, wants just the opposite with Alfredo. She dreams of a home, a shared life, children. In other words, the bourgeois dream desired by every woman of her generation.

She loves to do a million small things for him. The few nights she is able to spend at his place in London, she is the happiest woman in the world. She cooks and cleans house, wishing he didn't have a housekeeper so she could do everything herself. She says she would like to be related to a pilot on the London–Milan route so she could wash and iron his shirts and return them to him the following day. She barrages him with packages: a small basil plant, a Pierre Balmain tie, a focaccia from the Caffè Cova in Milan, a silk bathrobe, an umbrella for the famous English rain, medicine when he is sick, a gold pocket watch from her favorite jeweler on the Ponte Vecchio. Fabrics for his tailor, or even samples so that he can make his own choice.

Alfredo is an elegant man. Thanks to him, Oriana learns how to distinguish between a grisaille and a tweed, a waistcoat and a double-breasted suit. She has always valued practicality over style, but during this period she spends a fortune at the seamstress. Every letter brings news of a new dress — usually blue, because it is Alfredo's favorite color. She knits him a sweater, dreaming that the mannequin she uses to calculate the size is him. "I've become faster at knitting than I am at writing," she proudly writes in one of her letters.

She accepts an assignment to travel to Paris and work on a series of stories about the great designers of the time. As usual, her interviews are irreverent. She describes the young Yves Saint Laurent as a shy kid, terrified of the press. "'*Enchanté*,' said the boy king with such effort that I feared he might faint. He didn't faint, but he did falter slightly." Coco Chanel is a forbidding — if miniature — devil in a short skirt: "She was so tiny, so very tiny, you could lift her with your pinky." She tears them to shreds, showing sympathy only for Pierre Balmain, who is lively and seductive: "He is the only tailor who doesn't act like a tailor, amid all these gentlemen who live by doing women's work." The world of fashion appeals to her even less than the film industry.

The fashion houses come across as austere as government ministries; the models look like piteous, undernourished creatures; the clothing is scandalously overpriced, especially to someone who has grown up in poverty. Each time she is received by a designer, she feels as if she is being judged: "It's always embarrassing for a woman to undergo the judgment of a great couturier," she confesses to her readers. But she remains true to herself always, ending the series with a plea for independence: "Now you know who they are, and what they think. Each of them has his own philosophy. Be sophisticated. No, be simple. Wear black. No, wear red. Place the pocket in the right spot. No, place it above the rear end. Be slender. No, be normal. The most logical conclusion, dear ladies, is the following: Wear what you like."

The thought of Alfred follows her everywhere like an obsession. She realizes from the start that it is an unbalanced relationship. The idea of losing him is deeply distressing. She has terrible thoughts. When the newspaper sends her to Paris to write a piece about a novelist who has killed herself for love, she is profoundly shaken. The idea that Alfredo might break off their relationship destroys her; she fears it would be the end. She doesn't want to appear hysterical and so she apologizes in every letter, but then she admits that he is the center of her existence.

Nothing else exists. Her work, which until then had been the center of her existence, seems to have lost meaning. Once again, the newspaper sends her to Tehran because there are new rumors about an impending divorce between Soraya and the shah, but everything about the trip irritates her. She claims to have lost interest in journalism, to hate traveling and the people she meets. On her return to Italy she writes an angry article about the Iranian couple. She begins with a line that could just as easily refer to Alfredo and herself: "Their love has ended. Maybe it never existed."

———

That spring, she realizes she is pregnant. She knows that Alfredo has no desire to have a child with her and that her pregnancy may well drive him away definitively. She finds herself in the situation of being forced to decide, alone and quickly, what to do. This is a very delicate chapter in the life of this woman who, years later, will not hide her deep sadness at having never had a child. She will admit to more than one interrupted pregnancy, all of them miscarriages.

In a letter to Alfredo she appears to consider having an abortion. She makes inquiries into who might be willing to come to her aid in London or Paris. Even in England, abortion is still illegal and performed in secret, but there at least she would be shielded from the curiosity of her colleagues and parents. She explains to Alfredo that her plan is to undergo the procedure in London and then travel to Paris, the only city where she can convalesce for a few days without causing suspicion. She says she has found two or three addresses, and that the decision must be made soon: "I need to do this as soon as possible because if not it will be too late and too dangerous. It hardly seems right for me to go to hell so young, and in these circumstances." An abortion violates her principles and instincts, but at the time she can think only of Alfredo: "I know, quite certainly, that I must do this — if I didn't, it would ruin, or at least disrupt, your life."

The information in Oriana's papers is not detailed enough to reconstruct a precise account of what happened next. The only thing that is certain is that in May 1958, Oriana faints just steps from her hotel in Paris, on Rue de Berri. The fetus has died; without immediate surgery, she too will perish. A German friend who is aware of her situation organizes Oriana's admission to a hospital and explains her condition. Oriana receives emergency surgery. She will need a second operation a month later, because the bleeding has not stopped and there are complications. The doctors tell her that this incident may prevent her from having children in the future.

It is a terrible trauma. In a letter she explains that she can't imagine returning to Italy, now that she is all sewn up and resigned to her fate, and being forced to lie to everyone. She has a nervous breakdown but hides its cause from her colleagues and family. She is unable to sleep and begins to take large amounts of sleeping pills; she tinkers with sedatives and antidepressants. Many days she is confined to bed with a fever, and she has terrible headaches and finds it difficult to write. She is often on the verge of tears. The editor of *L'Europeo* puts her on medical leave for a few months and forces her to rest. He thinks Oriana is working too much. To outsiders, she appears to be the same driven young woman as always, but inside she is a wasteland. "How I've changed!" she writes in a note. "I feel old, but no one believes it because I'm small and have this body and this face."

The relationship with Alfredo becomes even more difficult. Perhaps alarmed by the incident, he avoids her. Oriana attempts to bind him to her with a professional project so that she will have more excuses to write and call. In the fall, she convinces him to write a book about Italy's professional class, elaborating on his articles. She finds his writing to be exceptional. When she is alone, she reads and rereads his articles as if they were love letters. She promises to take care of everything: to obtain a contract from her editor, do research, share her contacts. For months this is all she does. She even conducts a few interviews on his behalf, sending him the full transcripts. She taps her connections and networks for him. In her constant letters to Alfredo she includes a complete list of the tasks she has undertaken on his behalf, like a faithful secretary: an appointment made with the directors of the Montecatini chemical plant; a report on the Mediobanca located with the help of a friend who works in the stock market; an interview with the mayor of Florence, Giorgio La Pira. She offers to type the entire text. She types quickly, she assures him, better than a typist, without typos.

During that same period, the newspaper commissions a long series of articles on the movie business in Rome, hoping to repeat her Hollywood success. Titled *Dietro di luci di Cinecittà* (Behind the Lights at Cinecittà), the series sputters on for months. Oriana's heart isn't in it. All she can think about is Alfredo's book. She has only one desire — to erase her own career in order to dedicate herself fully to him. "I don't want to be good at what I do anymore," she writes. "You're really good, and that makes me happy."

The ambitious Oriana seems to have disappeared, along with the combative, intractable, and irascible one. After every argument, it is she who writes a letter of reconciliation, apologizing and seeking compromise. She inundates Alfredo with letters. She writes letters that she later regrets, and then writes more letters asking forgiveness. She feels silly and doesn't understand what is happening: "What can I do if I love you and I think you are the best, and I think there is no one but you, and for this reason I'm willing to be mistreated, without fighting back? I've never said this to anyone. I've never felt it, and couldn't have."

Increasingly, their long-distance relationship follows a vicious cycle. She knows he doesn't love her and cries. He detests her tears and avoids her. The final letters, from the spring of 1959, are dramatic. Alfredo doesn't want to see her. He doesn't answer her calls. He doesn't bother to hide a relationship with another woman in London. Oriana calls repeatedly, even at night. She has lost all reason. She has lived for two years with the conviction that Alfredo is her life partner and is unable to accept that it was all a fantasy. Her final letters are desperate: "You were my reason for living. I asked nothing of you. It was enough to know that I existed for you and

With her younger sisters, who also became journalists; (*top to bottom*) Oriana, Neera, and Paola.

could talk to you, see you once in a while, be close to you, help you. Now I have lost even this. This decision is too heavy a burden. It's killing me."

On June 28, she stops over in London during an assignment for *L'Europeo*. She has written to Alfredo, informing him that she will be at the Normandie Hotel for twenty-four hours before traveling on to Brussels. She does not leave the hotel, hoping he will call. The following day is her birthday. Even though they are finished, she implores him to spend a final evening with her. She lies there on the bed next to the phone, which remains silent. Then she takes a bottle of sleeping pills out of her bag and swallows the whole thing. Alerted by the hotel, her family sends one of her sisters to take care of everything, quietly, in order to avoid a scandal.

8. AROUND THE WORLD

The unhappy love affair with Alfredo represents a turning point in Oriana's life. She will never mention him again. Only a few clues will filter through in interviews about her youth. "Obsessed with the fear of being put on a leash and muzzled, for years I existed like a dog without an owner: free and unapproachable. I rejected anyone who fell in love with me, and did not allow myself to fall in love. I suffered and made others suffer, but I refused to drop anchor. Nor did I drop anchor when I was swept up in my first love. Which, by the way, was not a happy love. It helped me see that falling in love is giving oneself over to another, hands tied."

It takes her a long time to recover. After returning to her family, she spends time in a psychiatric clinic, a traumatic experience that she will speak of many years later in a letter to a close friend. She describes the leather straps on the beds and the bars on the windows. She also describes her depression, the recurring thoughts of death, the impression of having been cast aside by Alfredo, along with the child they might have had together. She recalls the terrifying sight of the fetus, as small as a walnut, discarded amid bloodied gauze and glass vials. The image stays with her. It is as if she herself had died, she confesses, as if all the tenderness and warmth she felt inside had died with the fetus and her love for Alfredo.

She stops working for four months. But she knows that writing is the only way to stay alive. When she returns to work, in October, her first article is a highly personal and caustic guide to the art of living in hotels. One of her first pieces of advice makes clear reference to her own experience: "Don't commit suicide in a hotel. People will get very annoyed." The old Oriana is back and has decided to announce her return in her own way. By acting tough.

In order to boost her morale, the director of *L'Europeo* proposes an investigation into the conditions of women around the world. At first Oriana resists. She has never enjoyed writing about women's issues: "Women aren't a special fauna, and I don't see why they should be seen as separate, particularly by newspapers, with their own section, like sports, politics, and the weather." A dinner with a successful friend who cries when she speaks about her life awakens something in Oriana: "I was like a person who has forgotten she has ears until she gets an ear infection. That day I realized that while men's problems are born out of economic, racial, and social circumstances, women's problems stem from one issue: being a woman."

She leaves during the winter of 1960 with the photographer Duilio Pallottelli. The idea is to travel around the world meeting non-European women. They will visit Turkey, Pakistan, India, Indonesia, Malaysia, Hong Kong, Japan, and Hawaii. They take with them ten cameras, a typewriter, four suitcases, and a fur for Oriana to wear in Japan, where they will encounter cold weather. The first stop is Turkey, where Oriana meets women whose lives have been transformed by the reforms of Atatürk. She meets female judges, soldiers, and pilots, who seem to her much more emancipated than her fellow Italians: "They are Muslim women who no longer wear the veil and are respected and free, but also unhappy, just as we are in the West. But it is worth noting that they are aware of this, which is already an advantage."

With Duilio Pallottelli, the photographer who accompanied Oriana during her 1960 trip to Asia to research the conditions of women.

In Pakistan, she has her first painful encounter with Islam. She comes across a wedding procession in Karachi. The crowd carries a figure hidden behind a pile of red fabric, like a package. Who is that? she asks. Nothing—a woman, she is told. Shocked by these words, Oriana asks to interview the bride. The guests oblige, even though they cannot understand what could possibly interest this foreign journalist. They unwrap the bride. She is a young girl with a pale face; her eyes are closed and coated with silver dust. She's crying. Oriana tries to console her: "I told her there was nothing to cry about. I had seen the groom and he was handsome, and seemed kind." She is lying. The groom is a smarmy man who has already tried to seduce this Western journalist who goes around with her arms uncovered. But Oriana is deeply moved by the child bride's sadness and wants to help. The women in the wedding party do not understand her attitude. "All brides cry," one of them tells her. "I cried for three days."

It is here, face-to-face with this human package, that Oriana begins to form her first doubts about Islam and the way it treats women. She writes, "This strip of land where there are no unmarried women, or love matches, and where mathematics are considered an opinion, includes six hundred million people, half of whom, more or less, are women who live behind the darkness of a veil. More than a veil, it is a sheet that covers her from head to toe like a shroud in order to hide her from the eyes of all but her husband, her children, or a feeble servant. This sheet, which is called purah or burka or pushi or kulle or djellaba, has two holes for the eyes, or a fine mesh opening two centimeters high and six centimeters wide. The wearer gazes out at the sky and her fellow man like a prisoner peering through the bars of her prison. This prison reaches from the Atlantic to the Indian Ocean, and includes Morocco, Algeria, Nigeria, Libya, Iraq, Iran, Jordan, Saudi

Arabia, Afghanistan, Pakistan, and Indonesia. It is the immense reign of Islam."

She continues: "The first thought a Western woman has when she arrives in a rigorously Muslim country like Pakistan is that she appears to be the only woman to have survived a tsunami that has washed away all the others." Oriana does not follow rules and insists on going everywhere, causing unrest and protestations. She is pushed off the tram because she has dared to use the men's entrance. She is forced to wait for hours at the bank until her photographer arrives, because the bank teller refuses to hand money over to a woman. She knows that men notice her and is used to being complimented. But in Pakistan the attention of men disturbs her deeply. She detests being mentally undressed. Her voyage of discovery of the female condition has only begun, but she is sure that she has encountered the worst possible case, that of women in Islam: "These veiled women are the unhappiest women in the world. But the paradox is that they don't know it because they don't know what exists beyond this veil that imprisons them."

India is next. In New Delhi, she discovers that alcohol is banned and people drink in secret. She is struck by the number of people who sleep in the streets in Calcutta. After that, she visits Jaipur, which has been described to her as the Florence of India. She meets the elderly Rajkumari Amrit Kaur, the only daughter of the Raja of Kapurthala, and is reminded of her grandmother, who went to the beach "dressed all in white, with a white handkerchief on her head to protect her from the sun." She tries on a sari, which, for the rest of her life she will consider simultaneously the most beautiful and the most impractical garment in the world. She is struck by the progress achieved by Indian women, who have been in positions of power for years. While interviewing a group of contraception experts, she is shocked by one detail. They tell her that the women who have been sterilized leave the clinic in tears because, as they put it, "What is the use of a tree that can no longer sprout leaves?" This comment reopens a hidden wound.

After India, she travels to Kuala Lumpur, where she meets with matriarchs from the Malaysian jungle, where land is passed down from woman to woman, and men are simply a means of reproduction. In Singapore she interviews Han Suyin, a writer and doctor with a Flemish mother and Chinese father. Though she is still young, she already has many adventures behind her. Her first husband was killed by Communist fighters in China, and her great love, a Western journalist, died in the Korean War. Now she is married to a Briton. She looks after her patients and continues to write. Oriana listens for a long time, taking notes, and asks her to speak about the lives of women in China, where she is planning to travel next. Han Suyin talks for hours. Even though she has unfinished business with the Communist regime, she does not hide her admiration for what Mao's regime has done for women: "This is probably not what you would expect a Catholic woman to say about China. But I'm a doctor and I see the truth. Like surgery, it hurts, but it heals."

Oriana is denied a visa to enter China, so she settles for Hong Kong. She travels to the border to gaze at the forbidden land beyond her grasp. Returning from the border by train, she sees an old Chinese woman with bound feet. She stares at her in horror as she hobbles on her stumps like a wounded bird. "'In my day, our feet had to be as small as possible, no longer than nine centimeters,' the woman told me. 'Mine are longer because I haven't bound them in forty years. We used to start binding them when we were five years old, using cotton strips one centimeter wide and two meters long. We would bind all the toes with the exception of the big toe, and tighten the bindings every day until the bones broke and the toes bent under. We did it in bed, and the pain was

Standing in front of Japan's famous Kamakura Buddha.

unbearable. One night it hurt so badly that I undid the bindings. But my mother beat me and I never dared do it again. 'You'll never find a husband if you have big feet,' she warned me. Before making a marriage proposal, men used to ask, 'How long are her feet?'"

In Hong Kong she goes to clubs where a young woman can be bought for a few dollars. She visits Shau Kei Wan, a bay where women live in houseboats and work with their babies strapped to their backs and toddlers attached to their ankles with rope. The local newspaper, *The Standard*, interviews her as if she were a celebrity on world tour. While answering questions, Oriana removes the wig she is wearing and tosses it distractedly into a drawer. The shocked journalist asks her why she wears a wig. "Because I like it and it makes my hair look tidy," she answers, without the slightest embarrassment. Before leaving for Japan, she orders a cheongsam — the traditional narrow Chinese dress — and buys gifts for her family: chopsticks, statuettes of Buddha, embossed stationery.

Japan poses the greatest challenge. There are too many contradictions all at once. Japanese women are among the most emancipated in Asia and yet they maintain the traditions of their ancient society. She interviews an elderly imperial princess who has lived through the changes the Americans have brought with them and defends them vividly: "Please write that out of the ruins of our cities has risen a new generation of women and that these women are no longer merely an aesthetic symbol or elegant objects but individuals capable of deciding their own destiny. Write that the women of Japan today know how to read and write and that they edit all the best sellers in the country, whether the traditionalists like it or not. Write that all this happened because of the war. Japanese women are the winners in this war."

The last leg of the trip takes them to Hawaii. Oriana discovers that Hawaiian women were once the freest in the world, that they did not know jealousy and made love without shame, even outside of marriage. She is particularly struck by Mary Kawena Pukui, who runs the local anthropological museum and tries to teach the traditions to new generations: "She was upbeat but a bit mad. Suddenly, she got up and started dancing the hula. 'You see this? It means I love you,' she said, crossing her arms in front of her chest and wiggling her fingers. 'And this means child,' she said, moving her arms as if rocking a newborn to sleep. 'This is the sign for tree,' she said, raising her arms to the sky and bending her wrists. 'The stuff they do for tourists in Honolulu isn't real hula. Hula is set to slow music and tells stories through movement; how can you tell stories to the rhythm of modern music? All poetry is lost.'" Oriana departs, her suitcase filled with exotic flower bulbs, forbidden by law, for her father.

After her trip, she doesn't hide her perplexity from her readers. "From one end of the earth to the other, women, like men, lack the equilibrium of justice and common sense. Either they are segregated like animals in a zoo, left to peer at the sky and their fellow man through the prison of a veil, like a shroud over a corpse, or they are like lion trainers, costumed in red jackets, whip in hand. I don't know whether I felt more pity for the Muslim woman begging for a place to sleep in a hospice or for the female soldier in Ankara competing against men for medals on the shooting range. I don't know if I was more taken aback by the Indian doctor who helps women in her country to have fewer children or by the geisha in Kyoto, elegant as a butterfly pinned to the wall. It goes without saying that slavery is deadening and terrible, but freedom, misunderstood, can be just as deadening and terrible. Often in my travels it has been difficult to determine which was worse."

Before returning to Milan, she makes a stop in New York, a city she has always loved but that this time disgusts her. She finds the

In Japan with a group of geishas.

skyscrapers dirty and the streets deafening; the women are constantly in a hurry and constantly at war with men. The depression caused by her separation from Alfredo has not yet lifted. When she's unhappy, she gets no pleasure from travel, she writes to a friend. She feels lost in a country where nothing is familiar. Everything looks the same. Her surroundings, her emotional life, and her condition as an independent woman feel like the detritus of her childhood dreams, a screen to shield her sadness. This somber mood pervades her reportage for *L'Europeo* and the book that follows.

The Useless Sex is published in 1961; she dedicates it to her sister Neera. It is not one of her best. Nevertheless, it signals two important milestones: her transition from the society pages to more weighty subjects, and the moment she becomes an international celebrity. The book is translated into eleven languages and sells extremely well. Oriana's name transcends Italy's borders. Thanks to her global view of the profession and the many contacts she makes on her reporting trips, her articles are reprinted in all the important European newspapers.

Her most pressing goal is to be published by American newspapers. "You are the most powerful press in the world," she will say later in a speech before an association of American journalists. "Because you belong to a powerful country, because you have the benefits of everything money can buy, but also because English is spoken more widely than Italian or French or German. When you publish a story, it becomes *the* story. I can contest it a million times in Italian, German, or French, but if my version isn't published in English, it will never be read outside of Europe."

One of her colleagues describes her as "the most turbulent journalist in Italy." She receives interviewers in her Milan apartment, a place she uses only between one trip and the next. An interviewer writes, "She lives on a little street that no taxi driver knows, in the former attic of a small building from which one can see the roof-tops and trees. There is no elevator because Fallaci, a world traveler who spends most of her time on planes, is afraid of them. The apartment lies up two flights of steps behind a door with the following sign: "Please place telegrams and express mail under the door and leave packages with the downstairs neighbor." One imagines an orderly young woman, but instead, beyond that door, lives the messiest young woman in Italy. She lives in a confusing pile of books, suitcases, newspapers, shoes, bottles, and strange objects. She compulsively collects precious, useless items: Etruscan vases, antique clocks, swords, revolvers, broken telephones, medicine bottles, ugly dolls, Napoleonic prints, Oriental garments."

She is always in a hurry, absorbed by work, and exhibits almost no common sense. An interpreter who helped translate her Hollywood interviews remembers, "We used to work in her Milan apartment, and there was this little dog who wouldn't stop barking. Finally, I asked her, 'Have you fed him?' The poor thing was starving; she had forgotten to feed him." When journalists come to interview her about the book, Oriana poses for photographs with her hair down and a malicious look. "Why did you choose the title *The Useless Sex*?" they ask her. "In order to sell more copies," she answers, throwing back her head nonchalantly to exhale cigarette smoke. She enjoys playing a character, especially a controversial one.

9. PENELOPE'S REVENGE

At this stage, Oriana is frequently contemptuous of the subjects she is asked to write about. She often signs her articles with a pseudonym. The world of cinema now bores her. She has attended the Cannes and Venice festivals too many times, and visited Hollywood too often. She feels like she knows everyone already. At parties, she wanders from room to room, drink in hand, with a bored air. Angelo Rizzoli, a producer and the owner of the publishing house that publishes her books, holds her in high regard. In jest, he refers to her as "the cutest ass in the business" and insists that she should write a screenplay.

But Oriana dreams of something different. When she does celebrity interviews, she reveals her contempt by writing articles that are masterpieces of cruelty. More and more, she has become the central character of her articles and refuses to hide her disapproval. "I never get nervous before doing an interview," she writes. "My state of mind beforehand is one of indifference or boredom." The only thing that amuses her is the opportunity to turn a meeting into a story, combining theater and satire. It is what she has always dreamed of: being a writer.

A routine piece about the pop singer Claudio Villa becomes a self-portrait of Oriana, who feels no curiosity regarding this star everyone is talking about but is moved by the enthusiasm of her friends. She hosts a dinner party. When she mentions that she will interview Villa, a scene erupts, like something out of a play. Her maid screams and drops her tray, and with it the pheasant, a gift from the actor Vittorio Gassman. Her friends jump to their feet, exclaiming, "'For God's sake, why didn't you get your hair done this morning? At least wear a hat. You're not planning on wearing that sweater, are you? Quick, help her dress!' Walking all over Gassman's pheasant—as if it were a carpet—they proceeded to dress me with the same care lavished on a bullfighter before a fight or a princess on her way to the opera. By ten, I was ready, even though the appointment wasn't until eleven. At ten fifteen, we were downstairs, headed toward the Fonit recording studios on Via Medea in a long caravan of cars, like a wedding cortege."

She openly mocks celebrities. Cary Grant, who has the ill fortune of sitting next to her on an airplane, is described as a funny middle-aged man who attempts to convert her to healthy living through hypnosis. "'Of course, it takes willpower,' he says. 'You can't do it on your own. Would you like me to hypnotize you?' Without waiting for an answer, he began to stare into my eyes. 'That's it. You will no longer drink, smoke, or wear sunglasses. Relax. You feel confident and sure of yourself, without these poisons. Relax...' Why disappoint him? His desire to help is so great and his expression is so friendly."

She ridicules Salvador Dalí—who makes the mistake of threatening Oriana's dog with a toy pistol at a hotel in Venice—from the first page to the last, concluding, "I forgot to mention that he is a close friend of Franco's and a very unpleasant man." She starts an interview with Gina Lollobrigida by saying, "I don't think you're as stupid as people say." And then asks her, "Don't you think it's immoral to make millions just for appearing in a movie?"

She prefers to write on more serious subjects, particularly politics. She writes a profile of Antonio Segni, leader of the conservative wing of the Social Democrats, who has just been elected president. And a story about the wedding of Anna Maria Fanfani, daughter of Amintore Fanfani, secretary of state and one of the most respected leaders of the Social Democrats. She interviews Nilde Iotti, a Communist member of the House of Deputies and one of the first women elected to an important government post. A few years earlier it had been revealed that Iotti was having an affair with the leader of the Communist Party, Palmiro Togliatti, who had left his wife and child for her, causing a huge scandal. When the paper sends Oriana to Athens to cover the wedding of Juan Carlos of Spain and Sofia of Greece, she starts her article with a description of a workers' strike in Asturias. When she is assigned to interview the actor Maximilian Schell, most of her questions are about his family's antifascism and escape from Vienna when he was a child.

When she goes to Monaco to cover the fiscal dispute between the kingdom and France, her article is written in the style of an ironic war dispatch from the front: "Here I am, in the most exposed location should a war break out between France and Monaco: a room on the second floor of the Hôtel de Paris... I feel just as I did six years ago, when I was covering the Hungarian Revolution — this is a war, and we are war correspondents — and we feared that the Soviets might invade at any moment." She deflates the pathos with which the situation has been described in the press: Rainier at war, Princess Grace taken hostage in Paris, where she has actually gone to do some shopping. Oriana ends with these words: "I should have stayed on the Via Veneto."

She wants to write about other things, to return to the heroic times of the war. She needs a subject that will distance her forever from the society pages. The space race, a different kind of war, will supply the excuse she has been looking for. But first, she must find a way to forget Alfredo and close this painful chapter of her life.

———

She does this by writing a novel, *Penelope at War*, which is published in 1962. She had written it quickly in 1959, after the breakup, in less than a month. She rewrites it a year later and then revises it once more, definitively, in 1961. "I needed something, I was looking for something. So I flew to New York and stayed there almost two months."

Penelope at War is the story of a woman who discovers New York and, at the same time, finds love. The protagonist, Giovanna, or Giò, is a screenwriter, who goes to America to gather ideas for a movie. While there, she bumps into Richard, a man she fell in love with during the war when she was a young girl helping her father in the Resistance. He was a soldier in hiding. She tries to win his love but fails, because Richard is gay. It is a novel, but as usual for Oriana, a novel in which most things are true.

Every page of *Penelope at War* is about Oriana. Giò is the same age and shares her directness and her passion for writing. Like Oriana, people notice her. She describes Giò as "a strange girl, charming in her way. She doesn't talk much and has beautiful eyes. She becomes ferocious when she's angry." The book is a novel-manifesto, in which Oriana makes sense of her life. She's thirty-three years old and has survived an unhappy love affair. This is her way of fighting back, by becoming "La Fallaci."

The novel describes two love affairs, one with a man and the other with New York. The first is doomed to fail from the beginning, while the other will last her whole life. The perspective on the city reflects Oriana's own on her first trip to the United States. She is overcome: "New York is a miracle that surprises me more with each passing day. There are no statues on this island that has been sliced into perpendicular, regular rectangles, nor domes or gardens. This gray, angular concrete jungle rises up, without a curve or an unexpected spiral, or a wisp of green. Wherever you look you find hard edges, geometric steel fire escapes, stone cubes. Despite this lack of grace it has a certain magic, which emanates from the skyscrapers that rise up like petrified giants and from the terror that quickens your breath as you walk down its endless avenues. At the end of each avenue, a patch of blue liberates you from fear. The sun, reflected against the windows, gleams brighter than diamonds. And at night, the windows burn hotter than stars."

She recounts more personal details from her first visit to New York. She describes her nervousness at customs, where every bag is opened, and her relief when everything is in order and the customs officers greet her with "hearty handshakes and sweet names like honey, sweet cheese, and sugar." She describes the city that seduced her in just a few sleepless days spent rushing around to see as much as she could. The lights that flutter in the breeze at night; elevators that upset your stomach; Times Square, with its homeless men and Salvation Army and toffee and shooting galleries. The big yellow taxis, the Sunday papers as thick as books, the giant steaks, the clattering subways.

Penelope at War is a book about love, colored by personal experience. It is a feminist book, a label that, at the time, she embraces. Above all, it is a book with a thesis: that the relation between the sexes has changed and women have taken on the male role. The story of Giò and Richard, of "the love between a woman-man and a man-woman," is based on her own experience.

Every phase of her unhappy love affair with Alfredo is included in the book, in distilled form. It begins with the romantic illusion that overwhelmed her when she met Alfredo, the belief that "the only way to become somebody, if you are born a woman, is to love a man. I am a normal being. I want what normal women want: a husband and children." This is followed by the willful blindness that shields her from every negative sign: "A quick scan of the letter was enough for her to sense that she had been put out to pasture. A closer reading revealed the enormous effort behind the writing of the letter. A third, even closer reading revealed what the letter didn't contain and which she had so fervently hoped for." She describes the long wait, day after day, for a phone call: "That silent telephone with its numbers, unmoving, peeking through the little openings, was transformed into something cruel and alive, bearing down on her."

Then there are the long sleepless nights: "These thoughts tormented Giovanna at night, as the glowing tip of her cigarette trembled and extinguished in a cloud of tiny sparks. Then the flame of another match illuminated two burning eyes, two hollow cheeks. She was tormented by angry thoughts, by her own wounded pride, by the realization that she had been emotionally robbed, by the misery of having invested her emotional capital in an enterprise that was destined to fail." Oriana includes a dramatic description of her surgery, the extraction of the fetus, a story she has not mentioned until that moment. The burning words spill out on the page: "It was Easter Sunday and there was a church across from the clinic. The bells were ringing, ringing, ringing. An old man with a tanned face and hands puffy with veins came into my room and said: "I'm your surgeon. Let's go, my dear."

It's not until the very end that Oriana's stubborn heroine is able to accept the truth, that Richard doesn't love her, and get on with her life. First, she has to hit rock bottom. Trapped in a room with Richard, she sees the absurdity of the prison she has made for herself: "All at once she felt herself suffocate. How small her world had become! When she was thirteen, the world seemed huge; through the window of her emotions she could observe a boundless landscape." It is Oriana, finally free of her obsessive love for Alfredo, a love that has pushed her to the verge of death. Instead, she has turned back and decided to pursue her dreams.

"Giò, the protagonist, was a stand-in for me at the time. There is an episode in the book that is drawn straight from my life. It's the moment she loses her virginity. It happened precisely in this way. When he realized I was a virgin, he started to cry. I consoled him, saying, 'It doesn't matter! It doesn't matter! Don't cry!'" At the time, losing one's virginity was a serious matter in Italy. The heroine of Oriana's novel does so almost as if ridding herself of a nuisance. "Giò is struggling for something greater than the right to live and work on an equal footing with men. She's fighting for the refusal to see virginity as a virtue, for sexual equality," Oriana declares in an interview. "She decides to sleep with a man as an act of will, even an act of freedom, and not out of love. He is the one who cries after the deflowering, not the woman."

In the book, Giò insists on going upstairs with the man, pushing him to the door. She sits next to him on the sofa and, looking straight into his eyes, declares, "I don't want to go home and I don't want to watch TV." "The act" — as Oriana writes in the book — is quickly accomplished, without drama. It is only when the protagonist returns home that she realizes what has happened. "First I felt a sense of wonder, and then a great fear, as if the room were teetering on the edge of a cliff, threatening to tumble directly into hell. She touched her sex to see if anything had changed. It was the same. Then she asked herself a worried question: What do I do? Nothing, she said out loud. I'll take a bath."

These are extraordinary words for the early 1960s. The book is controversial. An interviewer, a woman, asks Oriana whether she feels that women are happier when they are subservient to a man. "Not on your life! Are you kidding me? Those are silly stories for stupid men and stupid women. Subservience is a mortal sin. Whoever is subservient will go straight to hell, and the same goes for those who seek to dominate others."

One can see how far Oriana has traveled since her desperate letters to Alfredo just a few years earlier. *Penelope at War* is a summation of everything she has learned about love. It is a difficult lesson, but one based on reality. When someone asks her whether love is useful or damaging for a modern career woman, she answers, "It's simply inconvenient. It complicates life, distracts from your successes, seeps energy. But still, it's indispensable. Work fulfills many needs, but not that one."

Penelope at War expresses how Oriana would like to experience love, and the reality she will have to accept in its place. She is romantic, excessive, and naturally passionate, but she learns her lessons quickly. After this great disappointment, she forces herself to look at love in a new way, as a fever that eventually goes away. She claims the right to have sex with whomever she likes, without commitments. She admits having "sexual organs and desire, like a man." If a breakup hurts her, she keeps it to herself. She has discovered this secret: that internal wounds are the hardest for people to accept. As the heroine of her novel says, "It's incredible how deaf people are to non-physical pain. If you have a stomachache or a sore foot, everyone tries to help and treats you with respect. But if you're miserable, no one can help you."

This conviction stiffens the already prickly personality she uses as a protective shield. In a letter, she explains that to protect herself she cultivates her nastiness as if it were a virtue. It is an attitude she will embrace her whole life. Later she will tell a friend who accuses her of being hard, "I'm not nasty, it's life that is nasty to me."

She resists settling down. "For years I refused to let anyone be my jailer; airplanes were my most faithful accomplices. It was easy, even painless, to flee. For all their fame and reputation, none of these men counted much." She admits, without hypocrisy, that she doesn't like to sleep alone, especially when she is working in another city, and that she enjoys male companionship. Colleagues, actors, photographers — the list of men she takes up with and then abandons is long. Sometimes, as she writes in a letter, she can barely remember them.

She hardens, becomes almost cynical. A man can be good company, and if he's intelligent he can become a friend, but love is out of the question. In a letter she writes, "I'll tell you something terrible: I've never been in love. What can I do? I'm just not capable of it. Sometimes I pretend, but after a while the man in question realizes I'm pretending and gets upset. Is it my fault?! It's like whiskey: I drink it to be polite, but I don't enjoy it. If I enjoyed it, it would hurt me. Falling in love hurts, and I don't want to suffer."

In 1963, a year after *Penelope at War* is published, she moves to the United States. "I closed up my Milan apartment, a charming four-room attic, packed all the essentials into two small trunks, and, just as I had when I left for Rome, set off without knowing where I would live." New York City attracts her like a magnet. In an article she confides, "I have a burning need to see New York, this bridge between old Europe and the mind-bending mystery that is America." She rents an apartment in a Manhattan skyscraper on the East Side, tiny but with a view of the city. A friend who knows of the lingering sadness left by the separation from Alfredo calls it a "cage for a crying bird."

This life choice is dictated as much by instinct as by reason. Even at thirty-four she has begun to think of her career in global terms, beyond the borders of Italian journalism. New York is the launching pad she needs. "I live in New York because it is an international city, just as Paris was in our grandparents' time. It is a maelstrom of cultures, ethnic groups, points of view, opportunities. And, whether we like it or not, the new imperialism is the imperialism of the English language. English is the language of science, of contemporary culture. In order to be read widely, an author must write in English or be translated into English. At the time of the Roman Empire, the lingua franca was Latin; earlier, it had been Greek. If I had been born in Carthage, sooner or later I would have moved to Rome."

She doesn't like everything she sees and she doesn't hide this. She notices a certain dangerous shallowness: "Americans don't believe in any happiness beyond the happiness of material comfort. Like gourmands, they would like to share this happiness with the rest of the world, as if happiness were something that can be consumed." She notes the febrile rhythm of the city, which never slows down and runs over anyone who stumbles: "The days here are shorter than in any other part of the world. Life is harder than anywhere else in the world. You have to be a soldier like me, rough, thick-skinned, to survive. New York and I are at war, and I have no intention of losing. If you lose here, you die." Her relations with the United States will always be fraught. But something draws them together. America is the place where a person can be reborn, which is precisely what she needs at this moment in her life.

After a decade at *L'Europeo* and three successful books, her fame is vast. She is more comfortable in the world of actors and celebrities than any other Italian journalist. Some become close friends: Ingrid Bergman, Anna Magnani, Sofia Loren, Sean Connery. From them she learns the secrets of being a star, which she will one day become in the realm of journalism.

A few friends try to convince her to become an actress. In 1965, when the producers of an American film about Michelangelo, *The Agony and the Ecstasy,* come to Italy to begin shooting, the producer asks Oriana if she'd like to play the role of a Medici noblewoman. He says she has the right face. Oriana considers his offer, but the editor of *L'Europeo* refuses to let his most famous journalist take a month's leave of absence. In the ensuing years, she will turn down several offers because she is too involved in her own work to take a break. These include Luchino Visconti, who asks her to play the Nun of Monza in his film of Manzoni's *I Promessi Sposi* and who refuses to take no for an answer: "You're an actress. I can't understand why you've never worked as an actress."

Her envious Italian colleagues refer to her as "*la strega di Piazza Carlo Erba*" — the witch of Piazza Carlo Erba — riffing on the address of *L'Europeo*. They gossip behind her back about her love life. She pretends not to care. She has decided that she wants to be a modern woman and free herself of the past. When an American journalist asks her what she would change if she could go back in time, she answers, "'First of all, I'd ignore all the taboos I grew up with.' 'What kind of taboos?' 'Social, religious, sexual . . . all of them. Do you know what it's like to be a Catholic girl born in a country where everything is a sin, everything is wrong? Sex is a sin, unless you're married, after which it ceases to be a sin. You grow up without understanding whether love and sex are two different things or one and the same.'"

She lives the life of a free woman, declaring far and wide that love is a trap designed to control people and upholding her freedom and right to privacy. "I am very discreet regarding my love life, my relationships with men. I've always been that way. Only rarely has it been made public whom I loved or who loved me. When I was interviewed for *Life* magazine, the journalist wanted to know if I was a lesbian."

Solitude is good for her writing: "I have trouble writing when someone is hanging around. Men know how to isolate themselves to write because their wives don't dare disturb them. But it's different for women because men are always interrupting them, asking for a kiss or a cup of coffee. You're in the middle of something, and he comes in to ask you for a cup of coffee, with the excuse that you need a break. If by some miracle he's quiet — it almost never happens — you can feel his presence. Even when it's quiet, you're not alone. And in order to write, I need to be alone."

She lives her relationships with the knowledge that they will end. Sometimes they end dramatically. But she knows now that unhappiness doesn't kill you, no matter how much of yourself you put into it. She knows that if a man hurts her, she can tell him, "I don't need anything, or anyone." And that she can fill her solitude with the work that has formed her identity: by feeding a sheet of paper into the typewriter, lighting a cigarette, narrowing her eyes to protect them from the smoke, and beating down hard on the keys.

10. CONQUERING THE MOON

In 1963 she publishes another book, *The Egotists*, a collection of interviews with celebrities known for their unpleasant personalities. It is commissioned by Rizzoli, which published *The Useless Sex* and *Penelope at War* and will publish all of her books. Oriana is not particularly interested in the project but allows herself to be persuaded. She thinks of it as a leave-taking from the world of celebrities, which she frequents less and less. Instead, she interviews Senator Lina Merlin, a politician who fought to close the brothels in Italy; the Nobel Prize winner Salvatore Quasimodo, whom she dislikes; and Cesare Zavattini, the neorealist screenwriter and a longtime friend.

One particularly engrossing interview describes her meeting with Natalia Ginzburg, who has just won the Premio Strega for her novel *Family Sayings*. She is one of the people Oriana most respects. She had exhibited great dignity after her husband, Leone Ginzburg, was tortured to death by the Nazis. She had spoken at meetings of the Partito d'Azione and written books Oriana greatly admired. Oriana even praises her looks: "the masculine, sad face that looks almost as if it had been carved out of wood."

Ginzburg agrees to talk about her husband's death. Leone Ginzburg, a Russian Jew who grew up in Italy, had been one of the most promising young intellectuals of his generation, one of the founders of the Einaudi publishing house and of the Giustizia e Libertà antifascist movement. After being jailed by Mussolini and freed after the fall of the regime in 1943, he joined the Resistance and became one of its leaders in Rome. He was arrested there by the Germans and, after refusing to collaborate, died in the Regina Coeli prison in February 1944 as a result of the torture he had received. It is something Ginzburg seldom discusses. "Leone had no hope of making it out alive. He received a second beating from the Germans, and this time they broke his jaw. That night, he fell ill and asked the nurse to call a doctor. But the nurse didn't call anyone; she just gave him some coffee. And so Leone died there, alone. The janitor found him there, dead, at dawn."

She agrees to read from "Memory," her poem about her husband's death:

Men come and go through the city's streets.
They buy food and newspapers, they have their jobs to do.
They have rosy faces, rich, full lips.
You lifted the sheet to look at his face,
You leaned down to kiss him in the same old way.
But it was the last time. It was the same face,
Just a little more tired. And the suit was the same.
And the shoes were the same. And the hands were those
That would break the bread and pour the wine.
Today, with time moved on, you still lift the sheet
To see his face for the last time.
If you walk along the street, nobody is beside you.
If you are afraid, nobody takes your hand.
And it isn't your street, it isn't your city.

Oriana tapes the interview, her throat tight with emotion. "I listened in silence," she writes, "and for the first time since I started doing interviews, I found it hard to hold back the tears."

But she is rarely impressed by her subjects. She needs a project that will take her out of the day-to-day work for the newspaper. She considers writing a book about the heroes of her youth, the Partisans of the Partito d'Azione, a small utopian group that rose out of the Fascist Resistance but unraveled after the war because of internal disagreements. She searches out several surviving members but soon realizes it is a mistake. Reality is always disappointing. The heroes of her youth have gotten fat and old; they are less impressive than they seemed when she was a little girl.

One of them, the writer Carlo Cassola, invites her to sign an appeal for unilateral disarmament by the West. She responds categorically: "The reason I can't accept your invitation isn't...that I disagree with your ideas about unilateral disarmament. It is the reasoning you lay out in your letter: 'At the worst, what could happen? An invasion? In the face of annihilation, it makes no difference whether we are free or in chains. It will not matter whether we continue to enjoy the benefits of liberty or live under the boot of Fascism.' I've read a lot of terrible things, but I have seldom read anything more horrid, more dismal, more morally suicidal than this." The only member of the resistance for whom she feels undying veneration is Pietro Nenni, a passionate politician from Emilia-Romagna who speaks frankly and who, as secretary of the Socialist Party, consistently fights for an alliance with the Communist Party. During the war, he had lost a beloved daughter, Vittoria, an anti-Nazi Partisan. At the age of twenty-eight, she had been deported to Auschwitz and died there. "You charm me effortlessly," she writes to him, "you are part of my education, part of my culture, part of my emotional makeup."

In the end, she decides, instead, to seek out the heroes of her time: the American astronauts who are racing to reach the moon before the Russians. In 1957, the USSR had launched Sputnik, the first satellite to orbit Earth. From that moment, the two superpowers have been engaged in a space race. It is a war, and Oriana wants to meet the men who are fighting it. Everything about the project excites her. She believes fervently in progress: "The only thing in this world we live in that fills me with hope is the conquest of science," she says, recalling the days when she was an avid reader of Jules Verne.

She asks the director of *L'Europeo* to send her to the United States to do a reportage. She spends two lengthy periods at NASA, one in 1963 and the other in 1964. In all, she spends almost a year with the astronauts. She writes a series of articles and a book on the subject, *If the Sun Dies*, which is published in 1965. The dedication is longer than usual: "To my father who doesn't want to go to the moon because there are no flowers or fish or birds on the moon. To Theodore Freeman, who was killed by a goose on his way to a space flight to the moon. To my astronaut friends who want to fly to the moon because one day, the sun may die."

Like her other books, *If the Sun Dies* is autobiographical. It is constructed as a dialogue with her father, a man from another time who cannot understand the desire to travel in space. Edoardo Fallaci is utterly uninterested in these newfangled inventions. Oriana never manages to convince him to get on a plane. She almost succeeds only once, by describing the beauty of the Royal Botanic Gardens at Kew, outside of London. But in the end, he changes his mind and Oriana takes her mother instead. During the entire flight her mother repeats, again and again: "Your father was right. What's the rush?"

During this long, eventful year with the astronauts, Oriana feels, for the first time, removed from her past. Face-to-face with the rockets that will one day send a man into space, she thinks of her grandfather Antonio. During the bombings, instead of going to a bomb shelter, he would put on his cap and go out into the streets, wave his cane at the sky, and yell, "Animals! Animals!"

She interviews famous writers, including Ray Bradbury and Isaac Asimov, and reads many books on the space program. She watches NASA documentaries. She wants to see everything, meet everyone, experience everything. She asks to be lifted up to the tip of a rocket, in order to get a sense of its size. She tries on a space suit. She undergoes personality testing with the mission psychologist in San Antonio. She receives a terrible score: She's too creative. When the NASA psychologist shows her a series of inkblots, she frustrates him by imagining a million things: "a girdle, a mouse, my grandfather's pipe, the pearl earring I lost in Paris, a .22mm bullet, an anemone, a chicken."

She visits NASA headquarters in Downey, California, the first time she has traveled to California to write about something other than the movie industry. The pilots who are preparing to conquer space are the new stars. An Italian friend who works in the movie business in Hollywood complains, "You too! That's all anyone wants to write about. No one gives a fig about actors anymore."

She is given permission to interview a few astronauts in Houston. They live in neat little houses lined up one next to the other, like the cells in a convent. Each has a wife and kids, closely cropped hair, clear ideas. She meets with seven of them—Alan Shepard, Gus Grissom, John Glenn, Scott Carpenter, Wally Schirra, Gordon Cooper, Deke Slayton—for a series of interviews, timed by the NASA press office. She has very little time with each; to her they seem almost like clones. It takes all of her talent to find a distinctive quality in each of them. But as with every subject she writes about, this is what fascinates her the most: the human element.

She approaches each astronaut with her tape recorder in her bag, microphone in hand. She offers each a cigarette to break the ice. She asks them whether they are afraid, adding, with a laugh, "Whenever I'm in a plane, I think about plane crashes." She is friendly, because she loves people with courage. But she hasn't

With the astronaut John Glenn in 1965 during her research into space exploration.

shed her impertinent streak. To Alan Shepard, the first American to leave the Earth's atmosphere, she says, "You appear to have some sort of complex, Commander. The 'first man' complex."

In January 1964, she receives a telegram informing her that Tosca has suffered a heart attack. She interrupts her visit to NASA and returns to Florence, where she finds her mother in bed, alive but suddenly aged. As soon as it is allowed by the doctors, she takes her mother to the countryside to rest. A few years earlier she had used her royalties to buy a farmhouse in Casole, near Greve in Chianti, a quiet place for her parents to retire and a home base for her. This is where she will retreat with the people she loves whenever she is in Italy.

Like all nomads, she is obsessed with her roots. She chooses an area she has known since she was a little girl, the place of origin of the Fallaci family. She loves the little town of Casole, and all of Tuscany. "My country house is very beautiful," she writes, "like a Leonardo da Vinci landscape. From my house you can see hills, mountains, and cypress trees." There is a detail that delights her: Giovanni da Verrazzano, the explorer who sailed up the Hudson and discovered what would become New York Harbor, was a native of Greve, as was Amerigo Vespucci, after whom the New World was named.

Over the years, she adds to her property and it becomes a compound, with a large house of twenty-two rooms, a mill, a few buildings in need of repairs, and lots of land. The house has a tower, which Oriana reserves for her own use. She wants the property to be self-contained, so she builds a pool and digs a lake, filling it with fish. The garden contains every kind of tree: oaks, strawberry trees, cypresses, lemon and other fruit trees. She loves trees for their silent stoicism and because they consume only water and sun and are completely benevolent. "There is a tall, gorgeous cypress tree in the garden of my country house. He loves a female cypress, also tall and gorgeous, on the other side of the road, and she returns his love. At night, they whisper to each other and sprinkle seeds into the woods and meadows, and in spring we always have two or three baby cypresses, born of their love."

Autumn is her favorite time of year in Casole, when the woods are ablaze with color, although she is annoyed by the waves of city folk who set out on Sundays and steal her grapes, chestnuts, and mushrooms. Her family makes pot after pot of preserves; they produce olive oil and wine, as expensive as champagne but made in the traditional manner. After closing his shop in Florence, Edoardo Fallaci enjoys playing the farmer and raising animals no one has the heart to butcher. They live out their lives peacefully on the farm. There are rabbits, chickens, beehives. A rose garden, a vegetable garden, lavender and rosemary, which are dried and placed in wooden chests.

There is a hearth in the kitchen big enough for a man to stand in. The house begins to fill up with furniture and mementos of Oriana's travels. It is full of mice; at night they nibble on everything, even the books, but she refuses to set traps. She likes to hear them scurrying about as she lies in bed. She imagines they are the spirits of the dead: "Maybe they really are ghosts. I love them because they don't bother anyone; they just scamper up and down, reminding you that they were here first. We need ghosts; you can't just live oblivious of the fact that there were other people here before you."

During Tosca's convalescence, Oriana sits with her in the garden and tells her about the space race. She describes every detail, every twist. She loves to see her mother open her eyes wide, like a little girl. She has brought packages of dehydrated astronaut food, but her father gets rid of them one by one, feeding them to the animals as a way to show his contempt for the whole idea of space travel. Oriana has to order more, which her mother keeps in a locked cabinet. Over the years, she will keep all the trophies her daughter brings back from her trips in that cabinet: a rock from the Parthenon, a doll from Kyoto, a piece of rubber from Malaysia, a topaz from Brazil, a ring from Calcutta.

When Tosca begins to feel better and makes her first timid forays into the kitchen, Oriana sits with her, gazing out at the leaves fluttering in the wind. She is enchanted by the trees: "Have you noticed how beautiful our cypresses look through the kitchen window? You want touch them; if you reach out, you can almost feel the tips of the branches, like paintbrushes, soft as velvet."

She stays in Italy for four months. Every so often the newspaper sends her on a reporting trip, always within Europe. She writes a series on the Scandinavian royal family. When she writes about the elderly King Gustav VI—who spends his summers in Italy to indulge his passion for archaeology and Etruscan tombs—she hearkens back to an encounter years earlier: "He was visiting the Uffizi Gallery and I was following him, with my photographer. Suddenly he stopped and said in a booming voice, 'Do you know that I work?' 'Yes, Your Majesty.' 'And that this is my vacation?' 'Yes, Your Majesty.' 'So leave me alone.' 'No, Your Majesty.' Did he lose his temper? Not on your life. He gave me a surprised, bemused look, and exclaimed, 'Boh!'"

For a profile of King Olav V of Norway, she goes to a ski race, even though she hates the cold. She buys boots, a coat, and a fur hat. His son-in-law owns a clothing store, and in order to meet him she torments the saleslady, asking to see every fabric until he comes out to see who is causing a commotion. No matter how hard she tries, nothing in Europe excites her. "It's 1964," she writes in one of her articles. "Other planets await us."

Once her mother is feeling better, Oriana has a burning desire to return to her astronauts. She has decided to write a book about them and needs more material. A Ford Foundation grant to cover her travel expenses encourages her to depart. But her enthusiasm is short-lived. After one too many bureaucratic questions — Do you believe in God? Do you follow a particular diet? Do you suffer from any contagious diseases? — she tells the interviewer to go to hell.

Most important, she refuses to be assigned a travel companion or to provide an itinerary. "I never know when I will arrive or when I will depart," she explains in a lengthy irritated missive. "I may find myself in Saint Louis and decide, on the spur of the moment, to take a quick trip to Mexico City to buy a sombrero. You may find that bizarre, and my father says it's mad, but writers are always a bit mad." The grant is withdrawn.

11. MISS ROOT BEER

She returns to the United States in May 1964 and meets a second group of astronauts in Houston. Following the protocol, she interviews them in a small, bare room. Eight astronauts, ten minutes each. She has to plead with the press representative to get a few more minutes: "An interview is an extremely difficult thing, a mutual examination, a test of nerves and focus," she explains. Each astronaut walks in, says hello, sits down. As with the first round, at first they appear almost identical. At last, one of them refuses to go into the little room. It feels too much like a dentist's office and, as he points out, he has already been to the dentist. Oriana intuits that she has found a kindred spirit.

His name is Charles Conrad, but everyone calls him Pete. He's brave, athletic, and sure of himself, as they all are, but also a bit wild and filled with an infectious joy. The two quickly become inseparable. He appreciates that she's not just another admirer, like the women who want to marry the astronauts, even though they're all married. He can't understand why this pretty Italian journalist isn't married. Doesn't she get bored being alone? he asks her. "I'm always alone, even when I'm with other people," she answers.

They make each other laugh. They launch Project Cheese, a chain of drive-ins on the moon, which, they joke, will most likely turn out to be made of cheese. They go out in the evening to drink and dance the twist. She can keep up with him. "I can drink anything," she says, "even whiskey, even though I think it stinks." The only thing she can't stand is root beer. He christens her Miss Root Beer.

The months she spends with Pete and his colleagues are a happy time, a celebration of the youth they all share. "Our thirties are a fabulous decade. They're free, rebellious, rule-breaking years, because the years of waiting are over but the melancholy of decline has not yet set in. Finally, we're perfectly lucid. We are a field of full-grown wheat, neither unripe nor yet dry." At night, they walk along the beach, shoes in hand. They practice what Pete will say when he walks on the moon. Oriana is happy because she feels like one of the guys.

Many years later, Pete's widow, Jane Dreyfus, will recall Oriana's time with the astronauts: "She used to come over to our house all the time. She would sit on the edge of the pool and relax. She could talk for hours, about her childhood and the war. She had been very brave. I think she liked to be around the astronauts because she shared their attitude toward life, their courage. It's what drew her to them." She explains that the other wives were often suspicious of Oriana. It's not difficult to see why. Oriana is a woman with a free love life, not one to mince words. ("She used to curse so much!" Jane says with a laugh. "It was in Italian, but we knew what she was saying.") She carries her freedom like a banner. "Regarding sex, I'm completely free, and have been for many years," she tells a newspaper. "Sex is so damned important. It's not indispensable, like intelligence, but if you don't have it, you become less intelligent. It's a kind of sustenance, like food, like sleep."

Jane has kept Oriana's upbeat letters, full of descriptions of the packages she regularly mailed across the Atlantic. She remembers that Oriana loved to laugh and to give presents. She would overwhelm her friends with gifts, sometimes lighthearted, sometimes significant. She sends Pete hat after hat—they are both collectors — and a toreador outfit, because she finds that the process of dressing the astronauts is similar to the preparations before a bullfight. "The sadness grows, as well as the fear." She sends Jane an expensive Pucci outfit to wear to a party in Houston. "It's gorgeous but I'm not sure the size is right. It's made of velvet, the special Florentine velvet Emilio invented years ago. The colors are bright, perfect for you, and it has long sleeves. If it doesn't fit, we can cry together and I'll take it back to Florence." She confesses that for the first time, she feels at home: "Your friendship means a lot to me. In the States, through my friendships with the astronauts, I've found something I had never found before, in Europe or anywhere else."

Jim Lovell, who in 1970 will command the ill-fated Apollo 13 flight, goes to Casole for a visit. Half a century later, he describes how the NASA community had embraced Oriana: "When she was with us, she was one of us." He remembers an evening when they went out looking for a restaurant for dinner. "Oriana kept saying, 'I'm hungry!' with that funny Italian accent of hers." He imitates her loud voice, and her manner, each syllable distinct. "Everything was closed. Finally we found a hamburger place. She looked at us, perplexed. 'How am I supposed to eat this?' she asked. 'Well, you pick it up with your hands and eat it.' And she screeched, 'I don't eat with my hands!' There were some toothpicks on the table, and she ate the whole thing with those. We couldn't believe our eyes." She has an explosive personality and never holds back. "I'm a pain in the ass, I know," she tells a reporter years later. "You know what the astronauts used to say? One way to be sure we'll come back from the moon is if we take Oriana with us."

When she learns that one of her friends, Theodore Freeman, has died in a training accident, she is distraught. She goes to Washington for his funeral. The astronauts at the ceremony are all calm. No one cries. Oriana is upset and hurls insults at them. Finally,

Pete speaks up, teaching her a lesson she will never forget: "Do you really think we're not moved, seeing him in that coffin? Tomorrow, when they lower him into that grave, each of us will think, it could just as easily have been me. If I could bargain with death, maybe I would trade places with him. I haven't asked myself, but maybe I would. But, since you can't bargain with death, I'm still alive. And since I'm alive, I don't waste time wailing like a character in a Greek tragedy. And since I don't waste time wailing, now I'm going to have a martini. A double."

In the fall of 1964, her lengthy stay with the astronauts comes to an end, and Oriana returns to Italy. A letter from her father awaits in her apartment in Florence. "I bought you a tree. Remember the oak above the spring? The big one, with the exposed roots, that you used to climb when you were a kid? The owner wanted to chop it down. I bought it from him, so it would stay where it is. Mamma was against it; all that money for a tree in someone else's field. But I knew you would be unhappy if I let him chop it down, so I bought it, as a present to you. You'll find it there when you return, waiting. In the same spot, near the spring." It is like a letter from another world.

She returns to the newspaper and starts writing her book about the astronauts, whom she speaks of with admiration and regret. "I've met so many people in America, but I think the astronauts are the best people I've met. I grew up in Italy, with great respect and admiration for courage, sacrifice, and discipline. When the war was over, I searched for these qualities in the people around me. I've always had a test I used to evaluate people. I would look at a person and ask myself, 'Would this person have talked if he had been arrested and tortured by the Fascists?' Often the answer was yes. The reason I like these young men is that I found an entire group of people who would have remained silent."

She would give anything to go to the moon. In one of her notebooks, she records the following conversation: "Dick [Gordon]
walks me to the hotel. 'Too bad,' he says, 'we can't take you up there
with us. You would go, wouldn't you?' he asks. 'In a heartbeat,' I
answer. 'But you could die,' he says. 'Of course,' I answer. 'But
everyone has to die and this would be a fun way to go. It's worth it.'
'Thanks,' Dick says. 'That's the nicest thing anyone has ever said to
one of us.'"

If the Sun Dies is a big success, in Italy and abroad. Oriana is invited
to speak on TV. No one else has described the astronauts with this
combination of camaraderie, admiration, and irony. She is not shy
in front of the cameras. She feels like an ambassador speaking on
behalf of her friends, whom she praises tirelessly: "First, they are
researchers. They do research during the day, at night, at home, in
their training. They are all engineers, with degrees in aeronautic
engineering. They study geology, chemistry, math, physics, biology.
Not only do they do research, but they undergo intensive training,
in the desert, in the jungle. Their work hours are like forced labor."
    On the day of the first lunar landing, July 20, 1969, she is at Cape
Kennedy, with thousands of other journalists, to report on the
event for her newspaper. The first man to set foot on the moon is
Neil Armstrong, whom Oriana knows only by sight. Pete will lead
the next mission, which will land on the moon a few months later,
in November. He won't receive the same acclaim, but he will carry
with him a photo of Oriana as a baby, in her mother's arms. He
has promised to take her for a walk in his space suit. The picture is
among the papers found at Oriana's house after her death. There is
a message on the back, in Pete's hand: "Dear Tosca, we carried this
photo aboard the Yankee Clipper to the Ocean of Storms, on the
Moon. November 14–27, 1969, for Oriana." The note was signed
"the Commander of Apollo 12."

Pete's mission touches her directly. Oriana enjoys getting a few personal objects past the NASA controls. In addition to the photo, she gives Pete a pendant. And she makes him promise to bring her back a few lunar rocks. On his return, Pete drags his feet. When Oriana reminds him of his promise, he changes the subject. Distributing lunar material is against the rules and Pete is a rule follower. One evening, after much cajoling, he lets her touch a few fragments in a cabinet at home, still covered in a light dust. Then he locks them up again. It's a terrible disappointment.

That same evening, they argue bitterly over politics, an area where they have very different ideas. She is a progressive and critical of American policy. He is a patriot and a conservative. The dinner devolves into a battle of wills. Pete says that if she detests American foreign policy so much, she should pack her bags and go back to Italy. Oriana leaves, slamming the door. The following day, she calls him. He is in a meeting, but Oriana insists on speaking with him. She asks him whether he truly believes what he said to her. When he says yes, with a note of irritation in his voice, she hangs up the phone.

"She wrote him a furious letter, which he ripped into tiny pieces," Jane Dreyfus recalls. She too had experienced Oriana's ire. Afterward, Oriana had written, "Don't be too upset when I write hard things. I'm a hard person; it's not my fault, it's how I'm made. But there's an equal amount of gentleness in me. It's just that I don't show it. Otherwise, in my line of work, I would be eaten alive." They will never see each other again.

Years later, when Pete dies, she does not attend the funeral. When she is disappointed by someone she loves, she erases that person from her life completely: "I don't know how to forgive. I can neither forgive nor forget. It's one of my greatest failings, the hardest to live with. Especially when pain is inflicted by someone from whom I expected affection or tenderness, or whom I admired.

I don't declare war against those who have offended or hurt me. I just liquidate them. I erase them from my thoughts. There is not a single man or woman who has hurt me who has not ended up in the Siberia of my emotions."

In those years when she is researching NASA, she goes back and forth between Italy and the United States, unable to choose between the two. She misses Florence, which she considers her real home: "I speak Florentine, I think in Florentine, I feel Florentine. My culture and education is Florentine. When I'm abroad and people ask me where my home is, I answer: Florence. Not Italy. It's not the same thing." In 1966, when the city suffers a devastating flood, she rushes home. She stays a few months, gathering funds from her American friends. She arranges for her royalties to be donated to the city.

In long letters to her American friends, she describes everything she sees. The shortage of drinking water: "What a paradox. Everything is covered in water, and there's nothing to drink." A couple of boutiques on the Ponte Vecchio that have managed to escape the waters: "A silver merchant and a tie shop. The silver shop has been cleaned. There are a few pathetic pieces laid out, and a sign that reads, 'Sorry this is all we have, please buy it,' in English. In the tie shop, a pile of wrinkly ties is displayed in the window, with another sign, also in English: 'Please buy this floaded merchandise, thank you.'" The people of Florence, whom she loves: "At ten or eleven in the evening, they're still there, cleaning, washing, scrubbing. Men, women, children. You see them on ladders scrubbing the leftover oil on the walls, the ceiling. They're obstinate, silent, stubborn; they have a will to live, to survive. You wouldn't believe your eyes. I mean: the city is dead and they act as if it were alive. Their courage and strength are breathtaking."

With her keen eye she captures intimate scenes, revealing

details, witty exchanges. Like this one, at the doors of the Battistero, black with mud: "Someone has cleaned the head of Lorenzo Ghiberti, which is carved into the third panel of the Gates of Paradise. In the middle of all that black mud you can see one tiny head, Ghiberti's, staring out with a look of shock. An old man walks by. He stops, looks at the head, and says, 'See what the heavenly Father has done? You put in all that hard work to sculpt Paradise and he gave you the Inferno. Damned fool!'" She intends to write a book about the flood, but work takes over. There are the assignments for *L'Europeo* and her second book on the space race, which comes out in 1970, *Quel giorno sulla Luna* (That day on the moon). In it, she calculates the price of America's dream of conquering space: at the time, $23 billion — a huge sum, but far lower than the cost of the Vietnam War, which, between the years 1966 and 1970 had cost the United States $71 billion.

Between her first and second book about the space race, something significant has changed. The United States has allied itself with South Vietnam against its neighbor to the north. It goes without saying that Oriana requests to be sent to the war zone. The editor in chief of *L'Europeo* at the time is Tommaso Giglio. More than his predecessors, he has learned that it is easiest to let her do what she wants. "He never played the boss with me," she writes. "He understood that I worked better when I was given a wide berth. If they tried to rein me in, I became a stubborn mule. 'I want to go to Vietnam, Giglio.' 'So you'll go to Vietnam.' 'What kind of reportage would you like me to do?' 'Whatever seems best to you.' That was the kind of relationship I had with Giglio."

The Vietnam War marks the beginning of a new chapter in Oriana's life. It leads her back to war and into the orbit of François Pelou, the great love of her life, who will teach her to see power with new eyes. The happy-go-lucky years spent in Houston and at Cape Kennedy come to a definitive end. Oriana Fallaci the war reporter is born. Angry at the injustices of history. Curious about the mystery of power. "The moon was shining, that same moon that men desire to travel to in order to enhance their greatness. And I remembered something François said to me yesterday: 'The moon is a dream for people who lack dreams.'"

12. SAIGON AND SO BE IT

She leaves for Vietnam in November 1967, with the photographer Gianfranco Moroldo. When she arrives in Saigon, everyone tells her that the person to know is François Pelou, the bureau chief of Agence France-Presse. She goes to his office on Rue Pasteur and, from the first, is impressed. "A handsome young man with gray hair and an athletic build, a hard, attentive expression, eyes that miss nothing, simultaneously melancholy and ironic. He impressed me right way. You know that kind of person you turn back to study again and again, because he stands out, because there's something about him? His gestures were brusque, unfriendly; he wasn't ingratiating, and wasn't looking to be charmed."

Many years later, François Pelou will describe that first meeting: "She burst into the offices of Agence France-Presse, in the heart of Saigon, during a torrid afternoon in the fall of 1967. She arrived without an appointment, as if she had blown in with the wind. We introduced ourselves — I didn't know who she was. She made a seemingly superficial observation about the city and its inhabitants. A moment later she was gone, only to return soon after, dressed in a way that was calculated to enhance her attractiveness. It was clear that she had decided to take possession of my office and its staff."

At forty-two, François is four years older than Oriana and a veteran international journalist. In the 1950s he had covered the Korean War and led the France-Presse offices in Hong Kong. He has traveled extensively in Asia and spent time in Vietnam since it was a French colony. In 1963, he witnessed the killing of Lee Harvey Oswald, the accused killer of John F. Kennedy, shot by Jack Ruby while being transferred from the Dallas police station to prison.

Oriana has already encountered him — though she doesn't know it — in Han Suyin's novel *A Many-Splendored Thing*. In the book, François Pelou is the protagonist's French colleague, described as a man of superior intelligence and elegance, who observes war with honesty and objectivity. The protagonist writes in a letter from Korea:

> Some GI remarks I overheard:
> "... What the hell are we fighting for anyway?"
> "I wish someone would sit down and explain to me what this god-dam war is all about."
> It is as François said:
> *"Il faut dire aux hommes pourquoi ils doivent se faire tuer."*
> (You have to tell men what they're dying for.)

François is never hostile and is willing to talk to anyone: South Vietnamese, Americans, Vietcong. Especially if it will save lives. Every life, to him, has immeasurable value. It is the first thing he teaches Oriana, on the day of their first meeting. While they're talking, he receives an urgent phone call. His expression changes. An informant has just told him that the authorities will execute three Vietcong prisoners the following morning. This means six people will die, explains François, because the Vietcong kills one American for every one of their own killed. The war, which had begun quietly at the end of the 1950s with the arrival of American military advisers to help the South Vietnamese government

The French journalist François Pelou at the headquarters of France-Presse in Saigon in 1968.

defend itself against Communist guerrillas from the North, is now full-blown. There are Americans on the front lines. François alerts the American embassy so that it will pressure its South Vietnamese partners to halt the execution.

A long wait begins. Oriana is reminded of the time, long ago, when her father's life hung in the balance. The office waits in silence. François sits perfectly still with his feet propped on the table, arms crossed, lips tight. Oriana is unable to sit still. She goes out to gather news from the JUSPAO — the American information service — and returns to her hotel, then comes back to the office. Around eleven o'clock that night, the phone rings, with the news that the execution has been halted. Oriana erupts in relieved laughter. "Thank you, François, thank you!" she repeats over and over as she bounces up and down around him like a young girl. The French journalists are amused by her antics. They are convinced that in just a few weeks she too will be inured to the ugliness of the Vietnam War and will became cynical, like them. They don't know that Oriana is incapable of becoming used to death.

François is the same. He has been writing about war for years, but he is still disgusted by the absurdities of conflict and infuriated by the waste of human life. He and Oriana meet often to chat at the end of the workday. Oriana pelts him with hundreds of questions. She trusts him blindly and asks his help to understand every angle of the war. She quickly grows tired of staying at the hotel listening to the chatter of the foreign journalists. She wants to go to the front. With his help, she sends a request to the American commander. She is invited to visit the army base at Dak To. She buys a uniform and signs a paper releasing the U.S. Army from any liability in the case of her death and detailing where her remains should be sent. The night before her departure, she receives a note from François at the hotel: "Have fun in Dak To. And don't be afraid."

——

More than a military base, Dak To is an isolated landing strip on a hill, surrounded by Vietcong. The trees are carbonized stumps rising up toward the sky. The ground is littered with bomb craters. Oriana steps out of a military transport, weighed down by her backpack. She looks around, reflecting that, before the war, those hills must have been beautiful, a succession of jade, blue, and emerald hues. During the day she keeps occupied, interviewing soldiers, taking notes. But at night the mortar blasts become more and more frequent; the base is attacked for hours. In the darkness and confusion, she feels isolated and exposed. A French journalist takes her by the arm and pulls her to safety. François has alerted him that an Italian colleague will be on the base and asked him to protect her.

She stays three days, but it feels like an eternity. During the day it is hot, especially with the helmet on. But François has told her never to remove the helmet: "Protect your head as if it were your only concern," he insists. At night it's cold, and she has nothing to cover herself with. Again, François's friend comes to the rescue, with a sleeping bag. She washes herself with a glass of water, sleeps in her clothes. The commander allows her to share his field toilet, since she's the only woman. One day, sitting near a truck, she glances at a mirror and at first she doesn't recognize the dirty-faced stranger with tired eyes who stares back at her.

She's happy to return to Saigon. Even though bombs are clearly audible in the distance, in the capital it is still possible to attempt a normal life. To go to the races, the pool at the Club Nautique, dancing. Increasingly, François accompanies her. Oriana realizes that her admiration for this gruff, sensitive journalist, who speaks little but seems to understand everything, is growing with each passing day. "I would often go to the office on Rue Pasteur to ask him for advice or help, or simply for relief from my bewildered state. And even though he was not directly involved in my reporting, he guided it. Slowly, he became my guide, my conscience."

In the evenings, they meet in his office. The slow-moving fan barely stirs the hot air, and his colleagues depart one after the other, to rest or seek out company. François waits for the last calls from his correspondents in order to forward them to Paris. She asks questions and learns from him all the lessons he has picked up in years of covering wars. For example, that war is like boxing, brutal but fascinating, because it reveals man in his purest state: his courage and his fear. When the night shift comes, he walks her back to her hotel.

"I had gotten behind his brusque exterior, and his freedom of thought had seduced me. Our bond was becoming more and more important to us." François becomes her confidant and guide. No door is closed to her. He helps her obtain permission to interview two Vietcong prisoners. Oriana goes to the main jail in Saigon. When the guards bring the first prisoner, a young woman, Oriana offers her a cigarette and explains that she will tell her story to the world. "There is no need for the world to know anything about me," the prisoner responds. She has cracked under torture and can't forgive herself. After saying this, she shuts herself off in a hostile cloak of silence.

The second prisoner she interviews is a man. He has been arrested for placing a bomb in a restaurant in Saigon that killed many people, among them four friends of François's. He smiles at her and gives her a great interview. Afterward, he bows deeply with his hands together over his heart and wishes her "happiness, health, and a long life." Then he waits for the blindfold to be placed over his eyes before being led back to his cell.

Oriana wants to meet with General Loan, the chief of the South Vietnamese police and the most powerful man in Saigon, who generally refuses to be interviewed by Western journalists. Again, the meeting is facilitated by François. "There is only one foreigner in Saigon who can see Loan at any time and speak openly: Pelou. The reasons for this friendship, if that is what it is, are unknown to me. But as soon as I mention Loan, François says, 'We'll see.'" Many consider him merciless and bloodthirsty, but François has a deep respect for Loan and considers him courageous in battle and firm in his convictions. He explains to her that Loan has a more complex view of Vietnam than she suspects. Oriana is perplexed: "His ideological independence sometimes drove François to paradox, or to what I believed to be a paradox."

When she asks to ride in an American fighter-bomber, he accompanies her to the military airport. "François arrived at six, half asleep. He opened the car door with a yawn and invited me inside. On the way, he talked about this and that, without mentioning the Vietcong or airplanes at all, just to stay awake. At Biên Hòa, he noticed I was wearing loafers rather than military boots, and he woke up completely. He kept yelling that if had to jump out of the plane with a parachute, I would break my legs into a hundred pieces; that women and idiots shouldn't be allowed anywhere near war zones; that it was too late to go back. And he left me there without even saying goodbye." After the mission, Oriana asks the pilot to give her an official statement of their top speed, so she can show it to her astronaut friends in the United States. All the Western journalists compliment her on her courage. "But François said nothing. In his way of measuring the world — courageous people on one side and cowards on the other — my act of bravery barely registered."

Many years on, François recalls the episode: "Oriana was a lion, prepared for any experience. But she also had an irresponsible, impractical side. That time, when she wore loafers, I got angry because it was dangerous to get into a military plane with those shoes. Oriana used to tell me about the bombings during the war when she was a little girl, about her father who had been a Partisan, about her activities as a courier for the Resistance. But in reality she knew nothing about war. She learned everything here, and her reporting was exceptional."

They often disagree and engage in intense discussions. François is disgusted by the Buddhist monks who light themselves on fire to protest the policies of the South Vietnamese government, which supports the Catholics and persecutes the Buddhists, accusing them of sedition and of collaborating with the enemy. The first immolation is performed by Thích Quảng Đức. On June 11, 1963, he sets himself alight in a street of Saigon, surrounded by praying, chanting monks. The scene, captured by an American photographer, is seen around the world. It shocks people and provokes copycat suicides. From 1963 to 1966, at least thirty-three monks set themselves on fire in public places. François argues that the monks are manipulated by their leaders, who are trying to draw the attention of Western journalists. He is convinced that they are drugged when they burn themselves. "There is no willpower in the world that can make a man sit still when he's on fire. Not to mention another drug: brainwashing." Oriana would like to witness an immolation. François refuses to help her. He says he saw one, two years earlier, and that it is a disgusting sight and nothing more.

"It's difficult to say when love awakens. One day you feel it in your body, like an illness. You don't realize you've been infected until the symptoms appear, like a dizzy spell." When Oriana returns to Italy for Christmas, and then travels to New York, she realizes that what she misses most is François. The day she leaves Saigon, she gives him a flask, a camouflage blanket, and a waterproof poncho. She even opens a bottle of champagne in his honor.

He writes first, a "brief, clear letter, just like him." When she receives it, she cries tears of joy. This has happened only twice before, she writes in her response: the day she heard her father would not be shot, and the day she learned that her mother had survived her heart attack. She realizes she is in love, and therefore terribly vulnerable. "When I'm in love, I become as tender as a lamb," she writes in a notebook, almost angry at herself. A colleague who knew her at the time confirms this: "Confronted with love, Oriana lowered her defenses and became helpless. I witnessed her relationships and her suffering and was never able to understand how a woman who was so strong could be so fragile in love."

In another letter, François tells her that Saigon is quiet, too quiet. He has the feeling something is about to happen. But for the time being the city is preparing to celebrate Tet, the Vietnamese New Year. A few weeks later, Oriana hears on the radio that during the night of January 30, 1968, at the start of the Tet celebrations, the Vietcong has attacked Saigon and various other parts of the country. It is the start of the Tet Offensive which will last two months. It is the first time the war has come to Saigon and the first time that the enemy has so openly challenged American supremacy on the ground.

Oriana takes the first flight back to Bangkok, via Hong Kong. She carries a bag, a camera, and a voice recorder, along with a bottle of Chianti from her farm for François. She travels from Bangkok to Saigon on an American military plane, the only way to fly into the city. As the plane circles above the city waiting for authorization to land, she sees flames and smoke rising from many parts of the city. There is fighting in the streets. In a few places the Vietcong flag is still flying.

As soon as she lands, she heads to the France-Presse office. The office is surrounded by barbed wire and guarded by two soldiers, who fire three warning shots as she approaches. "*Bao chi!* Press!" she yells, showing her badge, and is allowed to pass. François is out, at a press conference being given by the South Vietnamese army.

His officemates don't know when he'll be back. She sits down to wait. "At a certain point, the door opened and there he was. Dirty, with a long beard, thinner. His khaki pants and light blue shirt hung limply, as if they belonged to a larger man. His cheeks were hollow, his nose seemed longer, sharper. When he saw the bottle of Chianti, his lips curled up into a strange smile. Then he saw me; all I remember is a hand ruffling my hair and his booming voice: '*Bravò! Bravò!*' I don't remember anything else because at that moment I started to cry, like a child." In the arms of her exhausted colleague, speaking a language that is not hers, she finally feels at home. For Oriana, who has sworn never again to fall into the trap of love, it is like the end of an ice age: "You can't live without love. I tried, but I couldn't do it."

François recounts the events of the night of January 30. The Vietcong had entered the city in groups of three, dressed as farmworkers. There were many of them, between six and ten thousand. Their weapons had been delivered weeks earlier, disassembled and hidden in the wagons of flowers that were delivered daily to the market. Every so often, when he describes one of the atrocities that took place during the attack, he loses his composure. He turns away and dries his eyes. During the counteroffensive, General Loan is photographed shooting a prisoner whose hands are tied. The photo circulates the globe, creating a wave of indignation. François is distraught and refuses to meet with him.

A few days later, Loan is seriously injured. There is talk of amputating a leg. Oriana visits him and sits for a long time at his bedside in bewildered silence. Finally she manages to ask the burning question: Why did he shoot a man whose hands were bound? Loan answers that the Vietcong fighter had just killed some of his policemen and their families, and that he was fighting without a uniform, so as not to be recognized, something he considered an act of cowardice. Then he turns toward the wall and cries. As she's leaving his hospital room, Oriana notices a pile of Western comic books on

his bedside table. She realizes that François must have left them.
"He's an odd young man, isn't he?" Loan says. "But a good kid. I
think he stole them from his son to give them to me. Years ago I
mentioned that I liked them."

When she's not reporting in the streets of Saigon, Oriana works in
François's office. On the door there is a sign: "No admittance." But
people come and go, and the office is so chaotic that sometimes,
in order get work done, Françios has to bang on the table and yell,
"Everyone out!" Oriana has added a feminine touch: a small bird-
cage with a bird inside who twitters whenever the teletypewriter
goes off. Digging through Francois's papers, she discovers the diary
of a Vietcong fighter, translated into English. She reads it cover to
cover. She is particularly moved by the soldier's account of his love
for a distant comrade. Her colleagues poke fun at her and call her
a romantic. François defends her. "It's not easy to cry when you've
seen war," he says tenderly.

She visits the rest of the country. She wants to describe what has
changed since the Tet Offensive, now that she has seen guerrilla
warfare on a massive scale. She is full of admiration for the Vietcong. Like most European journalists, she considers them to be an
army of Davids engaged in a war against the American Goliath. In
her articles, she denounces the massacres committed by American
soldiers and their South Korean allies, whom they use for the dirt-
iest jobs. But in reality, the more she sees in Vietnam, the more she
understands that crimes are being committed on both sides.

Her most traumatic discovery happens in the imperial city of
Hué, famous for its exquisite palaces, which for weeks has been
besieged by the Americans and South Vietnamese and defended by
the Vietcong. It will become one of the worst massacres of the Vietnam War. When Oriana arrives, the city, which has been retaken
by the South Vietnamese, is a pile of rubble and corpses. There are

tens of thousands dead. It's hard to say what has killed more people: the American bombings or the Vietcong mass executions.

One scene in particular upsets her. A group of children laughs as the gravediggers toss bodies into communal graves. Each time a body arcs through the air before falling, they jump up and down chanting, "One, two, paf! One, two, paf!" Seeing Oriana blanch, a priest who is accompanying her explains, "Madame, it's their only source of entertainment. The dead are their toys." Suddenly, Oriana feels weak. She is ashamed to belong to the human race, a race capable of such things. She wants to adopt one of those children. She wants to talk to François about what she has seen. Like never before, she wants him at her side. "I don't understand anything," she writes. "I feel so alone, so unprepared. I wish François were here to help me, to explain things to me."

In May, François announces he will soon leave Saigon to become the chief of the Agence France-Presse bureau in Brazil. They know they will continue to see each other. Before leaving, he gives her a gift. "He smiled his beautiful, indulgent smile . . . He grabbed the bag he always carried with him, like a backpack, containing his camera, paper, rolls of film, and all the spent cartridges he picks up on the street. He dug through it and pulled out a book, covering the title with his hand. "I brought it for you." It's a book by Blaise Pascal. Rereading a famous passage, he had thought of her, always searching for purity in heroes, always disappointed. "Man is neither angel nor brute, and the unfortunate thing is that he who would act the angel acts the brute . . . It is dangerous to make man see too clearly his equality with the brutes without showing him his greatness. And it is also dangerous to make him see his greatness too clearly, apart from his vileness."* They have often discussed this

*Blaise Pascal, *Thoughts*, Harvard Classics, volume 48, part 1. Translated by W. F. Trotter (NY: P. F. Collier & Son Company, 1910).

topic. François, who always speaks his mind, accuses her of seeing things in black and white, of being an extremist. Oriana accepts his criticisms without protesting.

Soon, she too has to leave Vietnam for New York. But she will return many times. She has become *L'Europeo*'s war correspondent. On each trip she fills notebooks. She will use all this material in her articles and later a book. *Nothing, and So Be It* is published in 1969 in Italy and is quickly translated into several languages. The Italian reporters in Vietnam treat Oriana with respect, often tinged with fear. Stories of her skill, but also about her nastiness, abound. Oriana is a battering ram; if she wants something, she gets it. And if someone gets in her way, she flies into a rage, hurling violent insults. In the evening she meets up with other journalists at he Hotel Continental, an old colonial building she loves for its old-fashioned atmosphere, its iron elevator and the grand wooden staircase that creaks underfoot. The manager is a Frenchman from Corsica. Years later, he still remembers Oriana and the fear she inspired in her colleagues: "One day, it must have been 1968, I see four or five journalists arrive at the hotel for a drink, and I ask, 'Are you celebrating something?' 'No,' they say, 'we're scared.' Oriana had arrived."

Nothing, and So Be It has a unique, highly personal structure. It is constructed as a dialogue with François. Through their relationship, she has rediscovered the political dimension of life. They discuss war, social justice, power. François has a deeper political understanding, has seen more. He helps her to see that the world is not black and white, that every political position is true only in part. Oriana matures quickly. She learns to look at war and heroism — her obsession — in a new way. "I experienced that period with a feeling of equilibrium I had never known before. That sense of equilibrium did not diminish my passion but weighted it with a new, painful feeling, the suspicion that it was all pointless."

François is quiet but direct. He always says what he thinks, even

With Pelou and Otto Preminger at the launch of Oriana's book *Nothing, and So Be It.*

when it causes pain. One day he recounts something he saw in Korea when he was embedded with the French troops. They were supposed to gather corpses and place them in coffins. It was very cold and the bodies were frozen in strange poses. They had to be bent and twisted until they broke, making horrifying noises. It was terrible work, but there was one soldier who didn't seem to mind. He didn't try to lay them out flat, didn't hesitate. He would take the bodies and beat them until the arms and legs broke and they fit into the coffins. Meanwhile, he sang a song. Oriana listens in silence. "François never tells stories just to tell stories. He's always preparing you for something. There's always a moment when the meaning becomes clear or you realize he was trying to explain something."

Half a century later, François recalls her great capacity for listening: "Despite her reputation and her exuberant temperament, Oriana listened quietly and often asked for advice. She accepted suggestions and ideas for articles, almost with docility." He has beautiful memories of the moments they shared in Saigon, suspended outside of time. "We would bring her with us whenever we went out on a reporting expedition. And we always ate together, in one of the tiny restaurants in Saigon. We had wonderful moments together. There was a lot of adrenaline in the air; during war, you feel that more than in any other setting."

He still has great admiration for Oriana. He describes the perceptiveness with which she captured each nuance of the war. "Oriana chose to focus on the human aspects, which always — but especially in a Buddhist country — accompany a conflict. General Loan, the chief of police who became notorious because of that photograph in which he was captured shooting a Vietcong in the temple, is a perfect example. It was so simple to judge him by that image. But Oriana managed to dig into his psyche and bring to the surface the circumstances and emotions that might explain his action. Nothing is ever simple at war."

With the photographer Gianfranco Moroldo (*right*) near Hué, Vietnam, in 1968.

13. BACKPACK AND HELMET

Each time Oriana returns to Vietnam, she visits the front lines. The first few times she is accompanied by the newspaper's photographer, but now she travels alone, with her camera hanging from her neck. "Taking pictures gives me something to do during battles and helps keep the fear at bay." She asks to ride in an American bomber during a mission. She describes the experience in interviews: "It was a small A-37, carrying two napalm bombs and four fifty-five-pound bombs. I was sitting right next to the man dropping the bombs, shoulder to shoulder. I felt like I was doing the bombing. That's all. Then they machine-gunned the Vietcong. It didn't feel right. I didn't feel like a witness; I felt responsible. The experience still turns my stomach." She is very superstitious. In her pocket, she always carries an old coin from the Vatican, a family relic that belonged to an ancestor who fought at Porta Pia during the capture of Rome in 1870. They say it cures headaches and protects the wearer from bullets.

According to the Geneva Conventions, journalists should not be armed, but it's not unusual for them to be given a weapon when they follow the U.S. Army into combat. Oriana tells the *Time* correspondent, "I carried any weapon I could get my hands on...I wouldn't have known how to shoot any of them, but if you had seen me walking toward you, you would have been scared to death." One of her colleagues adds, "I learned that, even as a reporter, you were never a simple bystander. At times like that, you might find yourself picking up a rifle, transporting wounded or dead, helping to gather water. You might even find yourself killing someone." Near the end of her life, Oriana will write out a confession and a letter that she'll never send. It will be discovered among her papers: "One time, in Cambodia, in 1973, I was with a company of South Vietnamese soldiers surrounded by Khmer Rouge guerrillas. The South Vietnamese commander, a young captain, handed me an M16 and munitions, saying, '*Je vous prie, il le faut*' [I beg you, you must]. For over six years I had refused many similar offers. But that day I accepted the weapon, and I used it."

She enjoys the company of American soldiers. She likes listening to their stories about their far-flung families, about their fear of dying. As usual, she easily gains their confidence. The chief of a battalion with whom she is embedded writes her a letter: "Let me know if you come back. Everyone talks about your time here. I've never seen a woman be so easily accepted and loved by all the men before; you worked your way into our memories and hearts. Thank you from all the men of the Third Battalion of the 12th Infantry Regiment. You have given us something we won't forget: Your sense of humor and the real concern you have for all of us who are fighting in Vietnam."

She is used to living rough and has no trouble adapting. "Early on, when I was with a company of soldiers, I didn't know where to pee. So I would call Pip, a sergeant who was often with me, not too smart but nice, and ask him to shield me. Pip would stand there with his rifle so no one could see me while I peed." She had grown up among men in wartime and hadn't forgotten what it was like. Her first period had arrived when she was with the Partisans on the Monte Giove. "I didn't know what was happening and got really scared. They said, 'Don't worry, it's a beautiful thing, you're a woman now.' And they gave me cotton."

She carries her own backpack and gets offended if anyone offers to help. This is her stuff and she can carry it, she insists. She considers herself one of the guys, as she had when she was with the Partisans and with the astronauts. "On the front, when I slept on a cot or on the ground in the woods next to the soldiers, the only woman among a hundred or two hundred men, I never felt like a female among males. When they shoot at you, it makes no difference whether you're a man or a woman."

Away from the front, things are not so simple. In *Nothing, and So Be It*, she describes long waits at the airport surrounded by tired soldiers leaning on sandbags, "all staring at you because you're a woman." In *Un cappello pieno di ciliege*, which will be published only after her death, she describes an attempted rape in Vietnam. It is 1970. Saigon is dark and the streets are empty because of the curfew. "The young woman is there as a war correspondent. She's back from the front, wearing a backpack. A pickup truck has just dropped her off on Rue Pasteur and she's walking back to her hotel. She's lost in thought, exhausted by the horrors she has seen in battle. She feels a great pity for all humans and in particular for those in uniform. 'Poor kids. Tomorrow they'll have to go on killing or be killed,' she says to herself as she passes a bivouac full of South Vietnamese soldiers. She greets them with a slight nod of the head. A few of them come out of the bivouac. Two by two, they jump on scooters, which she hadn't noticed before. They start to encircle her, enclosing her in a moving fence with no way out. Meanwhile, they sneer: '*Regarde ce que nous avons ce soir. Où vas-tu, jolie femme? Viens ici, laisse-toi baiser*' [Look what we have here tonight. Where are you going, pretty lady? Come here and let me give you a kiss]. Then the moving fence becomes a fixed one. They climb off their scooters and begin to touch her, grab her, push her. Their hands and arms are like the tentacles of a hungry octopus. She defends herself with punches, kicks, and a rage born of fear and anger. The backpack weighs her down, but she can't take it off. And even if she could, she wouldn't; it contains all her work—recordings, pages of notes, photos. But it makes it hard to fend off the tentacles of the hungry octopus, and there are too many of them. They surround her, block her path, knock her to the ground, and try to undress her. Two Americans patrolling Rue Pasteur in a jeep save her. Sheer luck."

Oriana's femininity is part of her, along with her curiosity and her impertinence. She doesn't use it against others, nor does she brandish it like a shield. It is simply part of her. Her appointment books are filled with references to vaccines against cholera and reports of trips to the front, but also hair appointments, fittings, and reminders to buy stockings and pick up blouses, nail clippers, little silver clutches. François recalls this aspect of her personality with an indulgent smile, as if once again seeing her slender, elegant silhouette: "Oriana was at home in any setting, no matter how extreme, but one thing she never forgot, no matter the situation, was her femininity. She was very pretty and she knew it. But she didn't use her allure to ply information out of the soldiers, as did many of her colleagues. She was different, better than that. She wanted to know and to understand."

Her face is expressive and always in motion, illuminated by her curiosity and inner vitality. Her elongated eyes are rimmed in black eyeliner. Her hands are always manicured, the nails always painted red, and she has beautiful lips, quick to curl into a laugh, despite her increasingly bad teeth, the result of excessive smoking. Her voice is low, slightly hoarse from cigarettes, and her physique will remain slender throughout her life, without the need for dieting or exercise. "I gave up sports at twenty-three, when I broke a foot skiing at Abetone. I never got over the indignity of it."

———

She is not the only female reporter in Saigon. During the Vietnam War, 467 women are accredited, more than half of them American. A female war correspondent isn't a novelty in the American press. The first had reported during the Second World War, and one of them — Marguerite Higgins — had been allowed to embed with the troops in Korea. But in Vietnam, their numbers multiplied. This is a result of the civil rights movement. After the passage of the Civil Rights Act of 1964, a few female reporters had filed a discrimination suit against their newspaper, which refused to send them to Vietnam. And they won. Female journalists are finally allowed to go to the front. First come the veterans of the Second World War, then the militant anticommunists, and, from 1966 onward, many freelancers.

Although the presence of women journalists isn't an anomaly among the American press, it is certainly so in the Italian press corps. Oriana is the only female Italian journalist to cover the conflict and is able to make the most of this in her articles for *L'Europeo*, at times, in fact, exaggerating the challenges she faces. In Vietnam, the American armed forces give the press free rein; it is a reporter's paradise. An American journalist who was there at the same time remembers, "No location was out of bounds, and there was no one we couldn't reach for an interview. Looking back, it was incredible. You only had to pull out your credentials and they would let you board a bomber. I broke the speed of sound on an F-6. I participated in bombing raids. I went everywhere in Vietnam. I was on board aircraft carriers. You name it, I did it. No one ever said: Who is this? Whom do you write for? What are you doing here?"

Nevertheless, it is dangerous work. In the two years before Oriana's arrival, ten foreign journalists had been killed and at least thirty injured. "I had met the photographer Catherine Leroy who, a few months earlier, had been hit by seventeen pieces of mortar shrapnel. She was a young blonde, twenty-three, with a girlish

On Y Bridge in 1972. Oriana was taking a picture of a Vietnamese woman crying over the body of her dead child, when she was surprised by shots fired by the Vietcong.

body and the face of an old woman. Her right arm, right leg, and right cheek were covered with scars, and she had a limp because the wound on her leg refused to heal. I asked her, 'Why don't you go home?' She just shrugged her shoulders."

While Oriana is in Saigon, a group of her colleagues is murdered in cold blood by the Vietcong, in Cholon. She is close to one of them and knows that his wife is pregnant. She stares at the photo of his corpse, disfigured by machine-gun fire, hands tied behind his back. She is distraught: "Maybe it's small-minded to bring up the issue because they have killed only five of us. But the issue must be raised. How many of these crimes have been committed by the Vietcong and have not been captured on film? Each time a Vietcong prisoner is executed, his throat cut, a photographer is there. But who is there to capture the execution of an American or the decapitation of a South Vietnamese prisoner?"

After a flight on an American warplane, she suffers palpitations. The doctor says she's fine, that the symptoms are the result of a sudden change in air pressure. Later, she sees a doctor for acute bronchitis. The doctor gives her a pill and says, in a tired voice, "You're the first patient I've seen in six days who doesn't have a bullet wound or who isn't in a coma after a suicide attempt. Everyone in Saigon is committing suicide." Oriana's health has always been delicate. In letters to her parents, she writes of terrible headaches and exhaustion that keep her in bed for days. She gets malaria and every possible tropical fever. At these moments of weakness, she feels unable to face the trials of war. "My God, I had forgotten what war is made of. And suddenly I ask myself, what am I doing here, why did I want to come here? Out of rage, curiosity, dissatisfaction, unhappiness? Happy people don't come here unless they're forced to. And nobody forced me, quite to the contrary. I feel a kind of astonishment, mixed with regret."

ORIÀNA FALLACI

On April 4, 1968, Martin Luther King Jr. is assassinated, and race riots erupt in many American cities. Oriana flies to the United States to write a reportage for *L'Europeo*. But less than a month later, she returns to Asia. She stops in India because the editor of the paper has asked her to interview the Beatles' guru, the Maharishi Mahesh Yogi, whom she considers a fraud and attacks from the first line in her article. She also interviews the Dalai Lama, whom she likes immensely. She spends a whole day with him and is struck by his cheerfulness and his pacifism. When she asks him to comment on his enemies, the Chinese, he answers, "As a Buddhist, I can't accept the word 'enemy.'" After what she has seen in Vietnam, such a statement seems miraculous.

A year later, in March 1969, she returns to Asia. This time she goes to North Vietnam with a delegation of Communist women. This, too, is a coup; the country rarely allows entry to journalists who are not allied with the regime. She stays twelve days. She is given two translators, who follow her everywhere, like shadows. "I realize I won't be able to work as I do in Saigon, with the same freedom of movement granted by the Americans, even to those who are critical of them." She stays in an old French colonial hotel in Hanoi, now rebaptized the Reunification but still known by all as the Metropole. There aren't many journalists there, just a few Russians, some Cubans, a couple of French. The delegation follows a tight schedule set by the regime: a meeting with a fighter who has spent time in captivity in the South; another with a Catholic priest allied with the Communist government; a chat with the editor in chief of one of Hanoi's five newspapers; a visit to the Museum of the Resistance. After much insistence, Oriana is granted a meeting with General Võ Nguyên Giáp and with two American pilots who are prisoners of war.

Giáp, a commander since the time of the anticolonial wars

against the French, is a living legend. Oriana manages to get forty-five minutes with him. As always, she prepares carefully, reading interviews and a biography. Giáp has been a fighter from his earliest years. He has fought the Japanese, the French, and now the Americans. She is struck by one detail. His first wife and comrade, Minh Thai, deflected attention from Giáp's escape to China in 1939 by getting herself arrested. She died a few years later in a cell infested with mice. Oriana is convinced that this is the reason for his legendary tenaciousness; in her view, he is driven by the desire to avenge her death. During the interview, Giáp does not allow her to use a tape recorder. She takes notes, as do the interpreters. The published text is the result of a comparison of the two sets of notes. After she has written her article, she is handed three sheets of carbon paper containing the text she is authorized to use. She does so, alongside her own article.

The interview is widely discussed. After it appears in *L'Europeo*, it is reprinted in all the major newspapers in Europe and the United States. This happens more and more frequently. Oriana has managed to meet one of the most mysterious men of the period, a living legend who rarely agrees to interviews, and to get him to say things he has never said before. It is the first of her major political scoops. François recalls: "One of her most successful interviews was the one with General Giáp. He admitted that the famous Tet Offensive was actually a mistake and that he, General Giáp, had no responsibility for it. It had been started in error by the Vietcong embedded in South Vietnam."

She also obtains a meeting with two American pilots being held as prisoners of war. She is highly frustrated by the interview, because she is convinced that they have been forced to give predetermined responses imposed on them by their jailers. Major Roger Ingvalson, captured recently, is still robust and tan. He answers like a robot, without showing the slightest emotion. The other pilot, Lieutenant Robert Frishman, moves her deeply. He has been held for a year and a half and looks gaunt and scared, almost resigned to his fate. Before leaving, Oriana writes down his wife's address and promises to meet with her and update her on his situation, and to tell her, as gently as possible, about the injuries he sustained during his capture. One of his arms is deformed. Her interview, which is reprinted in the American papers, elicits solidarity in the reading public.

When Frishman is released a few months later, Oriana is at the airport to meet him. She calls out to him, attempting to break away from the other journalists. Frishman's wife points her out to him, but he limits himself to a brief nod of acknowledgment. He refuses to meet with her. She insists, and, a few times, he sends his wife in his place. Then nothing. Oriana reacts by writing an uncompromising open letter in which she criticizes not only his lack of courtesy but also, and especially, the fact that he has changed his story about his experience in captivity. In other words, she accuses him of what, to her, is the gravest fault: a lack of courage.

The articles she writes about North Vietnam are all critical of the Communist regime, a fact that is much criticized in Italy. The Leftist press accuses her of sympathizing with the United States, forgetting that in her articles about South Vietnam, she has been just as critical of the Americans. "The fact that I'm against the Americans in Vietnam doesn't prevent me from speaking about all the terrible things I saw in Hanoi. The horrible Stalinism, the fear, the oppression, and my certainty that after victory these would be applied to the rest of the country and to Cambodia as well. I was the only journalist, the only one, who wrote the truth about Hanoi, back in 1969. All the others who went saw exactly the same things but didn't write about them. And, it goes without saying, I was pilloried for it."

She is an unmanageable journalist, who always says what she thinks. As a result, she eventually breaks with everyone. In the eyes of the Italian Left, she's a conservative; to the American government, she's a subversive. Barry Zorthian, head of the U.S. Army's press office in Saigon, calls her to his office several times. "He wanted to alert me to the fact that he had received a report about the articles I had written in Vietnam, and to inform me, as delicately as possible, of his displeasure. 'Darling, are you a Communist?' he asked. 'No, Barry.' 'Lots of people claim they're not, even when they are.'"

She reports on the Vietnam War until the very end of the conflict. In her letters to her mother, she admits, at times, to exhaustion. "Frankly, I've never felt this tired, this shattered. Maybe it is because of my visits to the front — twice with the South Vietnamese and once with the Americans. They were very trying. Bouncing around in military trucks, which is so hard on the body, and the nervous tension during helicopter rides in certain areas . . . it's inevitable. Maybe I'm just worn out. But the truth is I can't wait to come home and sleep in my own bed." No one is forcing her to return to the front. She is now rich and famous. But she was not raised to throw in the towel. To her, life must be lived with full commitment and idealism. "I don't know whether I'm good at what I do," she says, many years later, "but I work hard, and I work well. I have dignity. My life is proof."

On her way back to New York, she always stops in Italy, loaded with presents for her relatives: a plant for her father, a bolt of silk for one of her sisters, and always something for her mother: "I'm bringing a trophy, the most beautiful tablecloth you've ever seen." One time she carries a Vietnamese cabbage on her lap the whole way, so she can give it to her father for him to plant in Greve. "I carried it from Vietnam to Cambodia, to Phnom Penh, and from there to Bangkok, then New Delhi, Karachi, etc. With each leg, it stank more. So I added more plastic bags. When I arrived it was almost rotten and my father asked me if I had lost my mind. To make matters worse, that variety of cabbage is common in Tuscany."

While at the front, she exhibits courage and character. One day she and a colleague were both in a town taken by the South Vietnamese and Americans. There is a rare moment of calm after the battle, while the soldiers go door-to-door. They sit together next to a wall. They have bought drinks from a street vendor who stopped to speak to them in French. They smoke and drink, listening to him in silence. Suddenly, a group of American soldiers descends from a jeep and grabs the vendor. They insist that he is a Vietcong who has been feeding information to the snipers who are still hidden in the ruins. Oriana tries to stop the arrest. She argues with the soldiers and follows them to the command post. Her colleague remembers, "The officer was annoyed by our intrusion, but he knew who Oriana was. He knew her articles and her relationship with the South Vietnamese command and with France-Presse. And they tried to be nice. But she kept yelling and screaming. She called them slave drivers and torturers. The captain tried to placate her by promising that the prisoner would not be mistreated. They were only going to interrogate him. And she said, 'Fine, interrogate him, but don't lay a hand on him. I'll come back tomorrow and the next day and the day after that, and if he has one scratch on his body, one bruise, you'll be sorry. Typical Oriana. She couldn't stand injustice or prevarication."

François is no longer at the France-Presse offices on Rue Pasteur. The new director is Jean-Louis Arnaud, who has less patience with Oriana. "One day, I kicked her out," he says, "I literally showed her the door. She had brought her article to transmit through the teletypewriter and of course she insisted hers should go before all the others. At one point I lost it and yelled, 'Oriana, get out!' It must have made an impression, because a few days later she said, 'You know, no one has ever thrown me out.'" Arnaud smiles as he recalls the episode. "She could be insufferable, but she was an interesting person, never boring. And she obtained whatever she set her mind to. I think that she did everything she set out to do in Vietnam."

In 1970, U.S. troops enter Cambodia, opening another front in the war, and once again begin to bomb Hanoi. Oriana is indignant and says so in her articles. She asks for permission to travel to Cambodia to witness this never-ending war that spreads like a cancer. She writes of the soldiers' distress, of how they smoke pot in order to distract themselves from the horror. She accuses the army of sending draftees, rather than volunteers, into battle. She does a long interview with an American lieutenant who allows her to use his name and record his words. "If I get out of here alive I'm planning to make things difficult for the U.S. government. I want to get back at them for sending me here," he promises. She interviews two North Vietnamese prisoners; she finds them particularly moving because, given that the North Vietnamese government denies having troops in Cambodia, no one intervenes on their behalf. "They are among the most victimized victims in Vietnam."

When Secretary of State Henry Kissinger begins peace negotiations with the North Vietnamese, Oriana reports on the negotiations with brio and effectiveness. Kissinger meets with the North Vietnamese in Paris and reaches an accord that includes the removal of American troops, a cease-fire, the return of prisoners, a transition to free elections, and the presence of the North Vietnamese in the South. Oriana explains every detail of the resolution of the conflict and, especially, the uncomfortable truth that it represents an American defeat. "Kissinger knows perfectly well that he has surrendered, because there was no other option but to

surrender. Kissinger knows he has accepted all of the North Vietnamese demands. He knows that in five or six years at the most the
Communists will rule Saigon."

That is exactly what happens when the North Vietnamese enter
Saigon in April 1975. Oriana isn't there. She has returned to Italy
because her mother is very sick and she is afraid of being stuck in
Vietnam. But in her articles she recounts the events of the days
leading up to the fall of Saigon. She describes the city as it awaits
its demise. She writes of a friend who begs her to find her a foreign husband so she can get an exit visa. Of the ex–prime minister,
Nguyễn Cao Kỳ, who requests refugee status for two million people. Of travel agencies invaded by hysterical crowds seeking visas
and tickets. Most of the foreigners have already left. The embassies
are almost empty. There are only four news agencies left, plus sixty
or so foreign correspondents, but they have no freedom of movement. The final dispatches are dated April 28 and inform the public that the North Vietnamese troops are making their way up Tu
Do Street, Pasteur Street, Công Lý Street. Oriana has no illusions
about what awaits the city: "The Communists are splendid while
they fight, and intolerable once they have won."

14. A MAN OF FEW WORDS

"This man is the most wonderful discovery of my adult life," Oriana writes of François. The most valuable thing she gains from her time in Vietnam isn't fame — she's now an international figure — or the rank of war correspondent, which opens the way for her to interview the powerful men of the planet. It is this man of few words, almost gruff, who understands and respects her, and who could become the love of her life — if only he wanted to. Their relationship lasts five years, until 1973, and it is a great love, marked by one deep, fundamental problem: François is married and Catholic. In his family, divorce is not an option. In the long run, this will lead Oriana to separate from him. Interviewed forty years later, François admits it was a painful decision: "I regret not having gotten a divorce. Oriana wanted a family, children. She believed in the symbolism of the ring. If I had done it, her life would have been different."

In Saigon, where people live with the knowledge that they could be killed at any moment, the issue doesn't arise. "When you're facing down death, every small thing, every feeling becomes precious. Food tastes better, friendship is stronger, love is deeper, joy more joyful." But when François leaves for Rio de Janeiro with his family, things become more difficult. He and Oriana can't live together. They can't spend the holidays at Casole, where she gathers regularly with her family. On the few occasions when she is able to bring him to Tuscany, she is free of the tension she feels during the short pauses from work that she allows herself. To a friend, she writes, "My vacations are complicated because I'm torn between the desire to be in several places at once, with my mother, with the man I love."

Despite her declarations of freedom, marriage still represents something important to Oriana. During this period she writes in her notes, "I'm not married. I have never imagined getting married. Even if I consider myself truly married to the man I have loved for years." She has a romantic disposition despite all her ideas about being a free woman, and she is faithful by nature, despite her nomadic lifestyle. In François, as with Alfredo, she believes she has found a man with whom she could spend the rest of her life. A man who works in the same profession and thus can understand her life of constant motion. "I don't have a home. I have a place in America, a place in Italy, and places around the world, the many hotel rooms I have inhabited over the years. How does someone like me maintain a relationship, create a family? Some may say that even sailors have families. But that can happen only because somewhere there is an obedient, submissive wife who stays in one place. A man could never accept this role."

For the second time, she is surprised by the intensity of her feelings. He is always in her thoughts. She would cover him with presents if he let her. François recalls, "Once, she showed up in a Mercedes Spider and said, 'It's yours.' I was shocked. In my day it was men who gave presents, not women. But even in this respect she was her own woman, behaving outside of normal patterns of behavior, ahead of her time. She wanted to prove that men and women are the same." They see each other often, and jump around from one plane to the next. Oriana travels to him as often as possible, arranging to do stories about Brazil, because François has a bureau to manage and a family to look after. Only once, he's able to spend a few months in New York at Oriana's.

That will be their only experience of living together. Oriana is not used to sharing her space with a man and will always be very critical of cohabitation. "Living together with a man, the man one loves the most, the best of men, is an intolerable torment for a modern woman, a woman who is not a slave or, as people like to call them these days, an objectified woman. They don't know how to behave; they seek a mother in every woman, and especially in the woman they marry or live with."

When they are apart, she writes often. As always when she is in love, she reveals her hidden side, which is extremely tender. François recalls, "She was never aggressive with me. She was passionate, tender, sweet. She prepared her favorite Tuscan dishes for me and wrote me rivers of words, long, long letters that sometimes I couldn't even finish reading." She writes many poems for him, all in French. Many are preserved among her papers. A group of them is bound in a notebook, jokingly titled "Les pensées de la Falou pendant l'absence de le Pelou" (The thoughts of Falou during the absence of Pelou).

In her poems, she describes François as a very handsome man, with a delicious curve of the neck, an insolent forehead, stern but kind eyes, a perfect mouth, a straight nose. He is an angel, a miraculous figure who "opens the door to my soul / once under lock and key." In a photo taken during a visit to Casole, François sits on a garden chair while she sits on the ground at his feet, looking up as she listens to him with rapt attention.

In addition to her love for him, she feels enormous admiration. She considers him a journalist of the highest level. She describes that he works "crouched over his typewriter like a race car driver over the wheel of his car." She respects his independence of thought, his strong cultural background, his rigorous ethics. In one poem, she confesses having written twenty pages of an article before realizing she was citing his words: "I believe in you so much / that your ideas become mine. / You reveal me to myself."

Every night before going to sleep she writes a few lines for him in a notebook, almost as if she were speaking to him. She writes of her feelings: "I miss you like I miss the rain / falling on the vineyards in July." Of her fear that everything will come to an end: "I get scared when you're distracted / when you're silent / when you don't say sweet things / when you look at me without seeing." Of the desire to belong to someone: "I'm yours / Finally, I exist / Thank you." In one poem she confesses that she has kept a wad of his gum in her jewelry box, which she puts in her mouth from time to time to remember the flavor of his kisses. In another she explains that when they sleep in the same bed, she loves to hear him snore because it means he's sleeping soundly. Then she can caress his head and kiss his eyes without being afraid that he will wake up and protest. François recalls this passionate side: "Oriana was a woman in every sense. She often told me she loved me. But it took me a long time to say those words."

Over time, the poetry begins to reveal signs of strain. Oriana is often lonely. She complains that he is never there when she needs him. He always has something else to do and is bound by a thousand worldly considerations, which she lists, angrily: his bourgeois home life, his Catholicism, his uncertainty, his weakness. She complains that he always puts his wife and son first. She tries to obtain a definitive answer about their future together: "It's not working / It makes no sense / We have to decide if you're with me / Or if I'm just a treat." After every argument, she goes back to New York. François remembers the tensions around his marriage: "Oriana wanted me to get a divorce, but I kept telling her that the faithfulness I had sworn to her was more important than a piece of paper."

At the same time, many things bind them together. Oriana can talk to François about the things that interest her, about her articles for *L'Europeo*. The early 1970s are a period of rapid maturation, in which François plays a crucial part. When they met, in 1967, the world was about to change forever. The following year, Soviet tanks quashed the revolution in Prague, and French students marched on the Sorbonne. "A bunch of idiots with long hair who pretend to build barricades without knowing why," Oriana opines contemptuously, considering them rich kids who are playing at revolution. On the other hand, she has great respect for people who risk their lives, like the Mexican students who, in 1968, march against the Olympic games, organized at great expense to their country.

She travels to Mexico for *L'Europeo*. On October 2, 1968, she is in Mexico City in the enormous Plaza de las Tres Culturas where students and factory workers are protesting against the government. She is standing on the balcony of a building on the square with other foreign journalists. Suddenly, the army surrounds the square and begins to shoot. A group of plainclothes policemen pushes its way onto the balcony and orders everyone to lie down. Lying next to a German reporter, Oriana is hit by a barrage of shrapnel. A photographer from the Associated Press captures the attack in three dramatic images. In the first photo, the German reporter has raised his head to see where the shooting is coming from, and Oriana moves her hands, as if saying, "Are they crazy?" In the second, they lie with their heads down. In the third, both of them lie flat on the ground. He is dead; she is injured.

She is carried away unconscious and left in a filthy room filled with injured and dying protesters lying on the floor in puddles of blood. Every so often she wakes up and tries to explain that she is an Italian journalist and that the embassy should be informed. A policeman winks at her and says that everyone claims to be a foreign journalist. Finally, a nurse secretly makes the call, saving her life. An ambulance is immediately dispatched to take her away, and

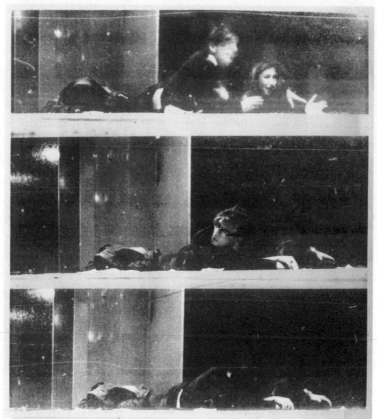

(MO-1)MEXICO CITY,Oct.2-(AP)-Civilians caught in crossfire
on a balcony at the Plaza of Three Cultures are shown as
they died during fighting between police and students in
Mexico City tonight.Person at left in the top photo is
dead as man and woman raise their heads calling for help.
In the center photo the man is still alive and in bottom
photo all three are dead.(AP Wirephoto)68 wwwww

The sequence of photos captured by Jesús Díaz of the Associated Press at the moment Oriana
was injured during the massacre in Plaza de las Tres Culturas in Mexico City on October 2, 1968.

a few hours later she undergoes surgery to remove the shrapnel. Two pieces have lodged themselves in her back and one in the back of her knee. As soon as the surgery is done, from her hospital bed, Oriana dictates her article on a recording device and meets with fellow journalists.

The world reacts vividly to her injury. Oriana's room is filled with flowers and telegrams. In the end, the Mexican government, irritated by the exposure, expels her, and Oriana travels to Rio to recover. She walks with a conspicuous limp, but in truth she is happy to spend time with François. "What joy it was to see him walk toward me with his brisk stride, his youthful, handsome face, his absurd gray hair, his brusque, rustic ways, like a peasant from the Auvergne. 'How are you? Always the lucky one. This time you really got hurt, hmmm?'"

She travels often to Brazil in those years to see François. Under his influence, she takes an interest in the political situation in Latin America. This only intensifies her criticism of the United States. Her articles denounce Washington's support of dictatorships in the region. "Isn't it terrifying and tragic that the happiest nation on earth, the richest, the most comfortable, the one in which economic equality has been achieved, should be so hesitant to turn its back on monarchs, dictators, and other cretins, and instead supports them, exports them? If only they mistreated me — it would give me more joy to insult them."

At François's suggestion, she travels to Recife to meet Hélder Câmara, a Catholic priest from the favela who is an exponent of the new liberation theology, which embodies the idealism of militant Catholicism that she too believes in. It is one of the few interviews in which Oriana refrains from asking impertinent questions. When she admires someone, she can be extremely respectful. "Rather than interview him, I listened," she admits in the ensuing article. He denounces the torture of dissidents in Brazil and the way the United States gets rich by supporting dictators. She listens rapt — despite her avowed atheism — as he describes his prayers. "Every night at two I get up, get dressed, and gather together pieces I've scattered around over the course of the day: an arm here, a leg there, my head who knows where. I sew myself back together, alone, and start to think and write and pray, preparing myself for Mass." She stays with him for three days and writes an emotive portrait.

She goes to Bolivia to interview the young French intellectual Régis Debray, jailed for taking part in the guerrilla campaign alongside Che Guevara. She visits the University of La Paz, where the students are involved in a hunger strike to obtain the return of the bodies of several guerrillas killed in the Andes. She travels to the difficult-to-reach mining town of Palca to interview a group of revolutionary priests fighting for human rights. She obtains a rare interview, via letter, with a group of sixty students and intellectuals who since 1970 have been engaged in guerrilla warfare in Bolivia and have recently attacked the headquarters of an American mining corporation in Teoponte and taken refuge in the jungle. Her fame can be a huge help to these disenfranchised victims. More and more often, she receives letters from political prisoners asking her to write about them.

She doesn't simply write about these issues. Often she gets directly involved. In order to obtain a pardon for the Bolivian guerrilla fighter Chato Peredo, she advocates on his behalf with the president, Juan José Torres. In order to meet, secretly, with the veteran Communist Carlos Marighella, long sought by the Brazilian government, she plays cat and mouse with the secret service agents who follow her around São Paulo. In order to raise international awareness about the case of Tito de Alencar Lima, a Dominican friar imprisoned by the Brazilian regime, she travels to the region to obtain a letter from the archbishop detailing the tortures he has been subjected to. Often, after interviewing political prisoners, she describes the location of their cells to their comrades so that they can orchestrate an escape. Whenever she can, she hides dissidents wanted by the regime in her hotel room.

She has never seen her work any other way. For her, being a journalist means being part of history: "What other profession allows you to write history as it is being made?" This is what she loves about journalism, a profession that in other ways she is beginning to find somewhat suffocating. She feels that this chapter of her life can't last forever, even on a personal level. François understands and admires her, but he is often far away. And he refuses to leave his family. His relationship with his wife, an American actress, has been strained for years, but he has a young adopted son and feels the responsibility to offer him as unified a family as possible.

Oriana is used to living and working alone, but in moments of fatigue, she dreams of having him at her side to look after her: "Sometimes I'd like assistance. I'm a very solitary kind of woman. Even when a man loves me, in some ways he is in competition with me. Maybe it's difficult to love a woman like me, a woman who doesn't inspire tenderness but is desperate for tenderness. At times I feel the need to justify myself or hide my success in order to obtain something more precious than success."

More and more, they argue about his refusal to divorce. After each separation, Oriana returns to him, driven by nostalgia. François is something new and precious in her emotional life, which for too long has been filled with one-night stands after which she wants only to light a cigarette and be alone in her hotel room. François is her equal, someone she understands. A complete human being whom she learned to admire in Vietnam, a man who recoils from every act of violence and fights against injustice, who conceives journalism as a mission, as she does. If he believes in something, he doesn't hesitate to fight for it. In 1970, he is arrested by the Brazilian government because he has dared to publish information without their permission. He is escorted to the airport and thrown out of the country. Oriana organizes a welcome party to meet him at the Paris airport.

In the 1970s, Oriana's journalism is politically engaged. She believes in women's rights and the struggle against oppression. She denounces the United States for its support of dictatorships in South America and the Soviets for their repression of internal dissent. Her upbringing in Italy during the period of fascism and the war has led her to react instinctually: "I was formed by the Resistance movement. It made me what I am. Despite my doubts and perpetual questioning."

For a long time she votes for the Socialist Party candidates, honoring her comrades in the Resistance — "Let's go vote for the dead, my mother used to say" — and in the name of social justice, a fundamental value. Then she stops: "As a young girl, I thought social justice could be achieved through socialism. After the war I joined the Partito d'Azione, which was a liberal Socialist party, in other words a party that sought to reconcile socialism and liberalism. Then the Partito d'Azione ceased to exist. I was on my own, and I began to reflect and grow, and gradually I realized I had spent my youth dreaming of utopia, of an impossibility. I became convinced that socialism was the brother of communism, another face of communism. I concluded that, despite its seductive aspect, socialism could not be combined with liberalism. And so I changed my way of thinking. But my attitude toward social justice didn't change. It stayed in me like a thorn in my heart. And I feel an instinctual hostility toward those who don't have that thorn in their hearts. I could never root for the team known as the Right."

Profoundly anarchic and antidogmatic, she soon breaks with the feminist movement, many of whose ideas she has shared and lived out in her approach to her private life. As a young woman, she had battled to find her own space: "The fact of being a woman has always seemed like a great burden. A burden full of rage, rebellion, and the will to show the world what I was capable of. At school I was the best because I wanted to prove that a woman can be just as good as a man. And the same goes for my newspaper work." For years she has stated that feminism was the only true revolution of her time. She has lived it in her own way, without subscribing to any particular group. She has liberated herself, pushed her way into the profession, accepted solitude, suffered for her choices. This does not prevent her from often arguing with the spokespeople of the official feminist movement, whom she finds dogmatic and shrill: "Feminists get angry when they see that you don't hate men as they do. Well, hell, I like men a lot."

Her attitude toward the Communist Party is also highly critical. She hates their party discipline and accuses them of being like a church. "I can't be a Communist because I'm not a Catholic," she jokes. "And because I'm anarchic." She often argues openly with the party, particularly when it attempts to take credit for the resistance against fascism and the Nazis, undermining the courage of the Catholic, liberal, and Socialist Partisans who fought at their side. But she recognizes their efforts in the battle against fascism and becomes inflamed when someone denies them. In 1976, she accepts an invitation to speak before the Partito Radicale, only to cancel when she discovers that one of the offices has chairs decorated with the hammer and sickle, so that people will sit on them, as a sign of contempt. "I got angry. How could they? People were tortured and shot because they believed in that symbol. I'm not a Communist. I've never been one, and I'll never be. But for God's sake! Pannella [Marco Pannella, the leader of the Partito Radicale] didn't fight beside us during the war—it was the Communists at our side."

She believes in politics; for her, the word is sacred. She cannot imagine a life without a political dimension. "I've always been political in my writing, actions, and life. I grew up in a political family, I was educated in politics, and I've always believed that one day I would enter political life. I would have very much liked to hold a post in Parliament because I believe in democracy, even the worst democracy. I can't imagine another way of governing. And I think I would have been an excellent parliamentarian. Undisciplined, of course, turbulent, irritating, but useful and honest. And I would add: If one could run for office without deploying millions and without joining a party, I would do so immediately." In the last years of her life, overwhelmed and confused by the polemic over Islam, she will be transformed into an icon of conservative thought and xenophobia. In reality, the only constant in her political worldview is antifascism.

"The risk of fascism is my fixation," she writes in a letter. The need to oppose fascism, of any type, on the Left or on the Right, is her line in the sand, the measuring stick with which she judges people and governments. Because Spain is governed by Franco, a Fascist dictator, she prefers not to go there. Or, if she does, she goes with the intention of denouncing the regime. In 1977, she places flowers on the tomb of Ramón García Sanz, an antifascist shot by the regime. She is struck by his story: "He died like a dog, alone. Before shooting him, they asked, 'Do you want to write a letter?' To which he responded, 'to whom?'"

She is willing to break off friendships over politics. She criticizes her friend Pete Conrad because he had dinner with Juan Carlos and Sofía of Spain during a trip to Europe: "I know those two imbeciles. I interviewed them in Athens before their stupid wedding, and they are on Franco's side." She turns her back on the journalist Indro Montanelli, whom she has admired since she was a child, because he criticizes the Resistance in a letter: "Don't sully the Resistance. It was one of our finest moments! I won't allow it, Indro, and if you do so in your history books, I'll tear you apart, I swear it."

In the early 1970s, her professional life is spent recounting the injustices and conflicts of the world. Her passport reveals just how much she traveled in those days: Lebanon, Israel, Ceylon, Trinidad, Thailand, Singapore, Vietnam, Bangladesh, Chile, Peru. After each trip she returns to New York, her city, even if her relationship with the United States has undergone a profound transformation. "America has disappointed me," she says to an American interviewer during the Vietnam War. "It's like when you're completely in love with a person, and you get married, and then, day after day, you realize that the person isn't as exceptional, as extraordinary or marvelous or good, or intelligent, as you thought. The U.S. has been like a bad husband. It betrays me every day." "But you like Americans," her colleague insists. "Yes, of course, I love children." She answers.

François is present in her life, but as time passes, Oriana loses patience. She wants to marry him, wants to have a child with him. Hearing him speak today, it's clear that this was an important love for him as well: "Oriana had such a strong personality that it was impossible not to succumb to her, not to love her. I remember her vitality, her exuberance. She was determined and proud, but also gentle." He is not forthcoming about the final breakup. It takes place in 1973, in Madrid. "She arrived one day, darker than usual and with a combative air. She wanted me to clarify the situation with my wife definitively, but I told her I didn't feel up to it. She left. We spoke the next day, and she told me she had sent all our love letters to my wife's address." Oriana is capable of terrible things when she's angry. Many years later, describing these events to a friend, she is still upset: "François had decided not to get a divorce. I made a package with all the letters we had sent each other and mailed them to his wife. Amen. We never saw each other again. Never." She resists speaking about him. To another friend who asks about the affair, she answers, visibly darkening, "Don't speak to me about him. I don't want to remember."

François's expression, too, darkens when he speaks of it: "It's a sad story. I would have wanted to continue, but it wasn't to be." In 1992, when he reads in the newspaper that Oriana has cancer, he writes her a letter. She returns it opened and without a word. "I knew she wouldn't answer," he says, "but I wrote anyway because I was also sure that it would matter to her that I cared, that she would be touched by my gesture." On the wall of his apartment in Paris he has a framed picture of Oriana, one that she had asked the astronauts to take with them to the moon, along with the picture of her mother. Her pretty mouth is twisted in a bitter smile. "If she had answered me, I would have done anything to help her. I've always felt the guilt of having caused her to suffer when we separated. But I wanted to respect her choice. The gesture was typical of Oriana: fragile, romantic, absolute."

15. INTERVIEWS WITH HISTORY

In Vietnam, Oriana had emerged as a political correspondent, which led to a period of interviews with the powerful men of the world. She uses the same techniques that she had perfected during her first visit to Hollywood. These are the "Fallaci Interviews," which will be studied in journalism schools thereafter. It has taken years to get to this point. "At first they didn't allow me to write about politics because I was too young and because I was a woman, but in the end I imposed my will."

Now that she has become a famous journalist she is able to invent a new way of talking about politics — irreverent, direct, and personal. "I kept arguing that 'we need to talk about politics in a different way.' People don't read political articles because they're boring. But politics isn't boring; it's entertaining, even funny. So why write about it in a boring way?"

L'Europeo considers her its star reporter. She covers the Indo-Pakistani War and the Maoist uprising in Hong Kong. Then she travels to the Middle East to cover the Israeli-Palestinian conflict and to South America to write about guerrilla groups fighting against various dictatorships. She quickly becomes famous for her courage and her combative spirit. A colleague remembers: "During the war between India and Pakistan, while we were following the Sikh troops and the Gurkhas, she took a different route. She got on a rickety boat and sailed up the Brahmaputra and arrived in Dacca at the moment the dictator's troops were killing their prisoners and burying them in common graves. Some were still alive. She made such a fuss that it was a miracle they didn't shoot her."

She inaugurates her series of political profiles in the Middle East. In March 1970, during a pause in the Vietnam War, she begins to work on a series of articles about the Palestinians. She has always avoided the topic because her heart, since the Second World War, has been with the Israelis. She writes, speaking of herself, "You know the Jews. You suffered with them, even as a child. You saw them being arrested and murdered in the thousands, in the millions. You defended them, helped them, loved them. You dreamed they would find a place to live, the ability to defend themselves; you were glad that they took possession of the Promised Land, finally. A country called Palestine."

She travels to Jordan, where the Palestinians have secret bases along the border with Israel. She sits down to talk with them for a long time. She writes about the war she had experienced as a child. "When I was a little girl I loved one of my teachers, the sweetest girl in the world. Her name was Laura Rubicek and she lived with her mother, a sweet, pale elderly woman. One night the Germans came and took them away, because they were Jewish. And they never came back." She interviews the leader of the PLO, Yasser Arafat, whom she dislikes because he comes across as profoundly insincere. As she always does when she meets a political leader, she tries to put him on the spot with the most challenging questions: What are the borders of Palestine? How can he speak of a pan-Arab union when even the Palestinians are divided? But Arafat eludes her questions. Oriana concludes, bitterly, "The meeting between an Arab who believes unreservedly in war and a European who no longer does is an immensely difficult meeting. In part because the latter is informed by her Christian background, by her hatred of hatred,

With a group of Palestinian guerrillas on the Israeli border in 1970.

and the former is bound by the law of an eye for an eye, a tooth for a tooth."

When she leaves the Middle East, she is filled with doubts and confusion, which she shares with her readers: "Like all wars, the Palestinian resistance movement inspires, alternately, admiration and indignation, sympathy and refusal. It all depends on the events before you, and on whom you encounter. If you go to the front with a group of fedayeen who cross the enemy lines and die, you can't help but fall in love. If you interview a young girl who sets off a bomb in a supermarket...you can't help but hold these people in contempt. It's true that getting to know them doesn't necessarily help you understand them. All this, while being attacked from all sides at the slightest pretext and while being violently denied the right to say, 'I don't believe in violence, I don't believe in guns, I don't believe in men killing men.' On a human level and on the level of history, the Palestinians are right; they are the new Jews of the planet. But, for this same reason, the Jewish people, who cannot and will not become Palestinians, are also right. But woe to you if you say this! You're asking for a bullet in the head, a bomb in your bed, poison in your soup. Well, I'll say it anyway."

The encounter that seals her global reputation as a political interviewer is her interview with Henry Kissinger, the architect of Richard Nixon's foreign policy. In 1972, Oriana requests an interview and is surprised to be given the go-ahead almost immediately. Kissinger has read her piece on General Giáp and is curious to meet her. He receives her on November 4 in his office at the White House for less than an hour, during which they are continually interrupted by phone calls and urgent requests for his signature. The interview ends earlier than expected because Kissinger is called in for a meeting with the president. After a long wait, she receives the message that Kissinger has departed with Nixon. If she would like to continue the interview, she will have to wait a month. Oriana declines: "It wasn't worth it. What would have been the point of confirming a portrait I already had in my hands? A portrait made up of conflicting lines, colors, evasive answers, reticent statements, irritating silences?"

The problem is that she doesn't like him. "What an icy man! During the entire interview, he never altered his blank expression, his ironic, hard look. He never altered the monotonous, sad tone of voice, perfectly even toned. Usually during an interview the dial on the tape recorder goes up and down according to the person's tone of voice. In his case it remained unchanged, and, more than once, I coughed intentionally just to make sure it was working." They discuss Vietnam, obviously. Oriana wants to push him to admit that the American withdrawal was a defeat and that the war had been pointless.

Then she moves on to more personal questions, for example about his reputation as a ladies' man. But the quote that will make the interview famous is his answer to a more innocuous question. She asks him how he explains his popularity. At first he declines to answer. Then he gives in to her line of questioning: "The main point arises from the fact that I've always acted alone," he says. "Americans like that immensely. Americans like the cowboy who leads the wagon train by riding ahead alone on his horse, the cowboy who rides all alone into the town, the village, with his horse and nothing else."

After being published in *L'Europeo*, the article is reprinted in several American newspapers and read all over the United States, where it becomes a scandal. Nixon is not at all pleased by the cowboy metaphor. Kissinger tries to deny that he has said these things, but he is contradicted by Oriana, who has a recording. Years later in his memoirs, Kissinger will confess that this interview was one of the most disastrous decisions of his career. Oriana, too, is irritated by the reach of the scandal. "Don't make me talk about Kissinger!" she will say during an interview at an American college in 1981. "I did that interview in 1972, and ever since, both of us have been questioned endlessly about it. If we'd run off and gotten married, we wouldn't still be asked about it to this day."

After this incident she is crowned as the most feared political interviewer in the world. She can choose her own subjects. She keeps the number down to fewer than twenty per year because each meeting drains her completely. She prepares assiduously, reading every scrap of information that exists about the person. The ingredients are always the same: careful research, impertinent questions, theatrical setup. Like the boy in the famous folktale who cries out that the emperor has no clothes, she is intimidated by no one.

In 1974, when she publishes *Interview with History*, a book containing her most famous profiles, she dedicates it to her mother: "Practically speaking, this is a book about power. A libertarian book about power. My mother, in her innocence, does not understand why there should be a man or a woman up there who decides what should and shouldn't be done. Do you understand? This is the anarchic attitude of the boy in the story. And mine." The book is an extraordinary success, the first of her series of worldwide best sellers.

In her interviews, Oriana articulates her lofty view of the journalist's role. She considers herself a witness, a stand-in for the public, and this is enough to make her feel that anything is allowed. She asks very direct questions, and, if these are deflected, she returns to them. She often asks her interlocutor to repeat an answer in order to be sure she has understood it. If something is unclear, she asks for a clarification. She speaks simply and doesn't allow herself to be drawn into the obscure language of politics and politicians. "My mother used to say, 'Oriana, what you write has to be understood by everyone; don't try to complicate things.' I always followed her advice. Whenever I interview a head of state or a prime minister, I don't allow myself to play the game of politics, of sociology."

She's never detached. She undertakes each meeting with the same passion and radical approach: "In my interviews I don't act only on my opinions but also on my emotions. All of my interviews are dramas. I involve myself even on a physical level." She doesn't believe in objectivity: "When I take the subway in New York and see ads for newspapers that claim 'Facts not Opinions,' I laugh so hard the whole subway car shakes. What does that mean? I'm the one interpreting the facts. I always write in the first person. And what am I? I'm a human being!" She claims the right to be fully present in her interviews, a person with her own ideas and impressions. An American colleague confirms this: "If I'm a painter and I'm painting your portrait, don't I have the right to paint you as I wish?" But there are rules: "I write everything they say, but I don't publish things that slip out in conversation. If they say, 'Don't print this,' I don't. It's a pact, a contract. If not, what are we? Word thieves? I respect the contract. But I don't allow any of my subjects to review my articles before publication."

Her interviews can go on for four to six hours. "In those hours I burn so much energy that I lose more weight than a boxer in the ring." Whenever possible, she likes to meet the subject a second time in order to confirm her first impressions. She also works tirelessly on the logic of the article. She transcribes everything, checking her translations with a dictionary, then puts her text together like a play, cutting and pasting, crafting the rhythm and flow.

She doesn't like it when her colleagues, especially in the United States, praise her interviewing skills. She considers herself a writer. She argues that her interviews are stories, with characters, surprises, conflict, and, especially, suspense: "My interviews are the interviews of a writer, conceived by the imagination of a writer, conducted with the sensibility of a writer." They require space in the newspaper, pages upon pages, a fact that drives her editor, who is under strict orders not to cut them, to despair. Each interview represents a point of view, for or against something. Sometimes she makes a mistake or is derailed. It happens, as she will admit later, when she interviews the Palestinian leader George Habash, the founder of the Popular Front for the Liberation of Palestine. Habash is a supporter of international terrorism, but Oriana likes him, despite her better judgment. He moves her with his stories about working with refugees and setting up a clinic in Jordan (he is also a doctor). When she realizes her error of judgment, much later, she admits it publicly. This is a risk when one practices passionate journalism, as she does. Oriana knows this and is not afraid to admit it: "My naïveté is a quality I value intensely because it is born from a faith in humanity and love for my fellow man. This love and faith swell up in me whenever I see suffering."

For her, an interview is never neutral. It is an encounter, a collision, sometimes a love story. This exchange with a colleague regarding her methods is especially illuminating: "'Do you go into your interviews with the powerful men of the earth with the intention of berating them?' 'Of course not! I go in with the desire to understand them.' 'Without preconceptions?' 'No, I have preconceptions, of course. But because I'm a reasonable human being, I can change my mind.'" She doesn't like to be described as a journalist who is feared. "If they're afraid of me, that's too bad. I need a partner. An interview is like a duet in an opera."

She doesn't use insults as a weapon. When she is about to strike, she warns her interlocutor: "When I have to ask a brutal question, I always say, 'Now I'm going to ask you a brutal question.' I don't write it down each time because it would be boring for the reader.

My questions are brutal because the search for truth is a kind of surgery. And surgery hurts." She is frequently accused of combativeness, which she considers merely courage, as she explains to an American colleague: "Most of my colleagues don't have the courage to ask the right questions. I asked Thiệu, the dictator in Saigon, 'How corrupt are you?'"

Her interviews are not always sparring matches. Sometimes she admires the politicians she meets. She is immediately struck by Prime Minister Golda Meir, whom she interviews in October 1972. From the start she takes a liking to this elderly lady in black who receives her in her home, offering her a cup of coffee as if she were a family friend. Meir reminds her a bit of her mother. "Even if one is not at all in agreement with her, with her politics, her ideology, one cannot help but respect her, admire her, even love her." Oriana loves her old-style socialism, the socialism of her adolescence, and her sincerity in answering questions of a deeply feminine nature. They discover that they have many things in common. Golda, too, smokes dozens of cigarettes each day and lives on coffee. Since the death of her husband more than twenty years earlier, she lives alone and she has worked hard since she was a little girl. Like Oriana, she hates violence. Most of all, Oriana admires what she says about war: "War is an immense stupidity... I'm sure that someday children in school will study the history of the men who made war as you study an absurdity. They'll be shocked, just as today we're shocked by cannibalism." Oriana finds nothing to criticize in her, not even her appearance: "Many maintain that Golda is ugly and rejoice in drawing cruel caricatures of her. I answer: Certainly beauty is an opinion, but to me Golda seems like a beautiful old woman."

Another woman who impresses her immensely is Indira Gandhi, the daughter of India's first prime minister, Jawaharlal Nehru, herself now serving as prime minister. As with Meir,

With Golda Meir during a 1972 interview.

Oriana feels they have much in common. They both grew up in the shadow of heroic fathers in the culture of socialism. They meet in February 1972 in New Delhi, in the governmental palace. Oriana approves of her sober appearance — her slender figure enveloped in a sari — and the simplicity with which she gathers her hair at the nape of her neck. Most of all, she appreciates her lack of formality. Two days after their interview, she realizes she needs more material and returns to her house to request a second meeting. "I rang the bell, and her secretary opened the door. I asked if the prime minister might be willing to sit down with me for another half hour. The secretary said, 'I'll ask,' walked off, and then returned with Gandhi. 'Take a seat,' she said, 'let's have some tea.'" We sat in the parlor overlooking the garden and talked for another hour." Oriana asks challenging questions, just as she had with Meir. For example, she asks whether the rumors that India has initiated hostilities against Bangladesh are true, and what her thoughts are on war, given her upbringing in a family dedicated to the idea of nonviolence. And how she squares her policy of nonalignment with India's recent treaty with the USSR.

When Oriana returns to India in 1975, after Indira Gandhi has taken a turn toward authoritarianism and declared a state of emergency in order to discourage opposition protests, Oriana declares herself disappointed and surprised. But it is clear that in politics she has a preference for women: "First of all, they're not arrogant. They are far more modest, simpler. They don't play a part. They are more balanced and have more common sense. Certainly, they're more human."

Unless the interviewee objects, she always uses a tape recorder. At first these objects are as big as suitcases, but over time they become more manageable. They are a precious ally. The recorder allows her to focus on her interlocutor's behavior and supplies proof of what has been said: "When I took notes in pencil, I couldn't look the person in the face, and I scribbled down things I couldn't read. And I have no memory." She laughingly describes the first time she used the recorder, with Ingrid Bergman in 1956: "I had to rent it. It was huge. When I saw it, my mind went blank. I asked my first question and blushed. Ingrid Bergman answered the question and then, even though she was a movie star, she blushed as well. 'Is that okay?' she asked. 'Well, who knows, I think so,' I answered. With time, I got used to it."

Oriana elaborates on her interview habits. "When I prepare to interview someone, I'm deadly serious. I dress in the least sexy manner imaginable, hair messy, no lipstick. It's not only a question of professional pride. It's also, let's say, a political choice, a form of advanced feminism." She knows that her pleasing appearance works in her favor, but she has rules, which she refuses to compromise. "I'm a woman. That helps. I'll do anything — I'll yell, I'll scream — but I will not sleep with anyone for a scoop." She prefers to use her sixth sense: "I have instinct. I really listen to the people I interview. I imagine their feelings. In a way, I'm kind of a witch." Whenever it is allowed, she smokes, and, if she can offer a cigarette to her interlocutor, she's happy. Sometimes it helps break the ice, as with Makarios, the exiled Cypriot president, who has recently quit. "I asked if I could smoke. With a sigh of relief, he asked, 'Can I have one too? I desperately need a cigarette.'"

Practically every person of importance agrees to sit down with her: Shah Mohammad Reza Pahlavi; Norodom Sihanouk, the exiled leader of Cambodia; Emperor Haile Selassie of Ethiopia; Kurt Waldheim, secretary-general of the United Nations; Mário Soares, leader of the Portuguese Socialist Party; Álvaro Cunhal, leader of the Portuguese Communist Party; Sheikh Zaki Yamani, the Saudi oil minister; Santiago Carrillo, secretary of the Spanish Communist Party exiled from Franco's Spain. She asks difficult questions, no matter the consequences. This is how she conceives her job. "Journalists do not simply recount events. They create events. Or at least provoke them. When I interview a political leader and ask him certain questions, I obtain certain answers; this in turn becomes an event that provokes discussion. These discussions have political consequences."

In 1972, for example, she causes a diplomatic brouhaha between Pakistan and India, two countries that have been on the verge of war since independence. Ali Bhutto, the prime minister of Pakistan, invites her to his country. He has read her interviews with various Asian leaders and does not want to miss out on an opportunity to be included in her gallery of political figures. Oriana stays with him for six days, visiting a number of provinces. She taunts him by referring to comments made by his historic enemy Indira Gandhi during their interview in India: "[I told him she had said] that he is an unbalanced man, that one day he says one thing and the next he says another, that it's impossible to know what he really thinks." She describes Bhutto's irritated response: "I don't think about her at all. I consider her a mediocre woman with a mediocre intelligence." Gandhi, who is scheduled to travel to Pakistan for an official visit, cancels her trip. Only after intense diplomatic negotiations is the meeting between the two heads of state reconfirmed.

She is often pitiless in her descriptions of the powerful, as she had been in her interviews with movie stars. She is dismayed by the elderly emperor of Ethiopia, Haile Selassie: "He was senile, arrogant, and stupid. He had contempt for women. Even when I'm going to meet with the most important men in the world, I wear trousers. But I was told that I couldn't meet His Majesty in trousers. At first I responded, 'Would you please let His Majesty know that I can either come in trousers, or in the nude?'" She calls Jean-Claude "Baby Doc" Duvalier, who has just succeeded his father as the dictator of Haiti, an idiot. "Instead of answering my questions, he read senseless phrases that had been written out for him. I lost patience with him. 'Listen, I don't have time to waste. I'm leaving. This situation is too idiotic. And so are you.'" And she describes Mujibur Rahman, prime minister of Bangladesh, as a madman. She writes that he sprawls on the couch, intent on saying things that make no sense. When she asks him about the massacres of opposition protesters arrested by his men, he erupts. The article she sends to the newspaper is accompanied by these words: "Dear editor. I went to Dacca, where you sent me. I wish you hadn't. That Mujib is not serious. Nor would it be serious to write up an interview with him. So I won't. Just look at my notes. Do what you like with them. Affectionately yours."

Generally speaking, she doesn't like people who hold positions of power, because she doesn't like power. She has her own ideas, which always emerge in her interviews. She believes in social justice combined with democracy, and she believes in liberty. She hates every dictatorship, on the Left or the Right, and also theocracies, no matter what religion they are based upon. She feels the same about the Orthodox dictatorship in Cyprus as she does about the Islamic system in Saudi Arabia. After spending several days with the Saudi minister of petroleum, she asks, "Yamani, has anyone ever told you you're a real reactionary?" At the same time, she has such mental freedom that anything can happen in an interview. For example, she is utterly charmed by Santiago Carrillo, the secretary of the Spanish Communist Party: "Carrillo is an extraordinary man, a heretic but also an intelligent and extremely good man. Listening to him you begin to wonder whether intelligence and goodness aren't the same thing."

She shares her thoughts with her readers, and, when possible, with her interlocutor, creating an extremely personal style that combines seriousness and fancifulness, public and private. She asks the German chancellor Willy Brandt whether he believes in the union of Europe, and also whether he ever cries. She asks the exiled Cambodian leader Sihanouk whether he has ever tried to speak with Kissinger, and also whether he still plays the saxophone. She's impulsive and deeply theatrical. She carefully sets up her position in each article, without ever forgetting her readers. Always, she tries to ask the questions a regular person in the street might want the answer to. She asks Kurt Waldheim, the secretary-general of the UN, about the five permanent member states in the Security Council: "The five of them are having a field day with the veto. Veto here, veto there...Does this veto thing seem right to you?"

If she doesn't like someone, she lets her readers know, and if she is unable to understand the person she is interviewing, she does the same. After a long interview with the shah of Iran, she confesses, "I sat for two hours, trying to get under His Majesty's skin. Then, because I still had a feeling I hadn't gotten him, I asked to see him again." She is struck by his rigid and controlling manner, which imposes itself like a shield, and eventually asks, "Don't you ever laugh, Your Majesty?" Even in this situation, face-to-face with an unsmiling monarch in his gold-filled palace, she takes her usual approach. She alternates highly explicit questions, like, "How many political prisoners are there in Iran today?" with oddball questions like, "Why do you look so sad, Your Majesty?" She manages to get him to formulate ideas he hasn't expressed in other interviews, for example regarding his contempt for women, the mystic visions he claims to experience in his sleep, and even the fact that the price of oil will go up tenfold, an explosive item that the Iranian embassy in Italy does its best to quash.

A few famous people, including Fidel Castro and Pope John Paul II, refuse to be interviewed. Reading over her notes, preserved among her papers, it is clear that their prudence is well-founded.

The folder dedicated to Castro includes provocative questions: "Is it true that you can't stand Americans?" "Why do you send so many of your soldiers to their deaths in foreign wars?" "You, who were once persecuted, are now a persecutor." Her preparatory notes for an interview with John Paul II are even more surprising, full of questions that verge on insolence: "There is something I don't understand. Why do you expect a lack of political engagement by Latin American priests but not by Polish priests?" "What do you think of the Inquisition?" "Why is the Church so obsessed with sex?" "You don't have the angelic air one expects in a pope. Even your feet are a man's feet, and your voice as well. So what led you to renounce your destiny as a man?" "Can one ask a pope if he has ever been in love? Why not? I would ask the same of Jesus Christ…"

When she conducts an interview, she is unable to leave herself out of it. Her meeting with William Colby, the head of the CIA, quickly devolves into an argument. Oriana accuses the United States of meddling in Italian politics. "I'm trying to make you admit that Italy is an independent state, not a banana republic, not a colony of yours." Her former admiration for the United States has long since become openly critical. In a speech to the New York Overseas Press Club in 1975, she launches into a tirade about America's obsession with the Communist threat: "The reality is that, here in America, you're all unbearably ignorant about Europe. When I speak with you about the struggle between the Socialists and the Communists in countries like Portugal, France, Italy, or Germany, I realize you don't have the slightest idea what I'm talking about. At the most, you look at me with a surprised expression and ask, 'Aren't they the same thing?' Forget the man in the street. Europe is far away. But what parts of the paper do your political leaders read? The comics?"

Regarding Italian politics, she is obsessed with the danger of the return of fascism and scandalized by the fact that since 1948, one of the parties in Parliament — the Movimento Sociale Italiano — has had ties with the Fascists. "These Fascists aren't our only disgrace. They are, if anything, the darkest expression of our irresponsibility, our lack of seriousness. I'm often abroad for work, and every time I return I find the country in a worse state. Morally, materially. It's like watching someone rolling down a steep downward slope." In 1973 and 1974, she completes a series of interviews with Italian political figures for *L'Europeo* at the request of her editor.

She inaugurates the series with Sandro Pertini, president of the Chamber of Deputies, who easily wins her over with stories about his experiences during the antifascist Resistance. As a young man, he had spent fifteen years in prison and internment: "One doesn't interview Sandro Pertini. One listens to Sandro Pertini. During the six hours I spent with him, I may have asked four or five questions and made two or three comments. And yet they were six enthralling hours." Then she proceeds with the Communist leader Giorgio Amendola, whom she admires but teases. She opens that interview with the words: "First of all, congratulations, Mr. Amendola. I've read your book, and I was never bored! Forgive me, but you Communists are usually so boring." And the Liberal Giovanni Malagodi, whom she portrays as cold and a snob, who tries to pressure her into drinking whiskey, which tastes to her of medicine. The Christian Democrat Giulio Andreotti, whom she describes as shrewd, never loses his sangfroid, even when she asks the most irreverent questions. "Listen, Andreotti, have you ever considered becoming a priest?" she asks him. "Can you actually talk to the supporters of the Movimento Sociale Italiano?" "Are you always so controlled?" She describes the Christian Democrat Giovanni Leone as a little man who looks lost behind his overly large desk in the presidential office and receives her with an apologetic expression, as if to say, "My dear girl, do you see the mess I'm in?" Finally, she interviews Pietro Nenni, whom she meets with for days, at his house, with a short break for lunch. They sit together until the sun goes down and the housekeeper comes in and scolds them: "Why are you sitting here talking like two blind people?"

Many people criticize her style, finding it too provocative. There are those who accuse her, without evidence, of making things up or embellishing. However, Kissinger admits, after her death, that "she was a great Italian woman. The essence of my answers in that interview was accurate." François, who was at her side during this period of political interviews, defends her: "Those who criticized her were in the wrong. I was present at some of her interviews and can tell you that she was absolutely rigorous about her work. She recorded everything and worked on the text for hours. There is a lot of labor behind each interview, but they were faithful to the truth. No one was as good as she was." He recalls that her interviews were unique, personal, and different from all the others one read in the papers. "When she was with these powerful people, she was never influenced by public opinion. It was about her and the tape recorder, that's it. She had an unparalleled ability to discover people's foibles, their vanities."

Oriana and François feel a profound mutual admiration. He describes her as an unequaled interviewer, and she does not hide the fact that she considers him highly professional and her equal. For years, during their relationship, he becomes almost the paradigm of manhood for her. Half a century later, François admits to feeling irritated by the title of Oriana's book on Alexandros Panagoulis, *A Man*: "I've always thought that that title was Oriana's vendetta against me, a kind of taunt. As if she were saying, *See, this is a man*. I think she did it to provoke me."

16. A HERO

Oriana and Alexandros Panagoulis meet on August 23, 1973. He has just been released from jail in Greece. She has agreed to interview him for *L'Europeo*, between a trip to Italy to see her parents and a trip to Bonn to interview the German premier Willy Brandt. She sends a telegram ahead to alert him of her arrival and boards a plane to Athens before receiving confirmation. She is now known as "La Fallaci." Her name opens all doors. But in reality, until that moment she has not been closely following the Panagoulis case. When he attempts to assassinate Georgios Papadopoulos, the leader of the Greek military coup, with a bomb on August 13, 1968, she is in Vietnam. And when, on November 17 of the same year, Panagoulis is condemned to death, and then to life in prison, she is recovering from the shrapnel wounds she has sustained in Mexico City. There are no notes or clippings relating to the Panagoulis case among her papers. Greece, in those years, appears to have been far from her thoughts.

So why is their meeting so momentous? Is this truly a great love? Or does it represent the crowning glory of years of militant journalism and the crystallization of a type that has always lain at the heart of her worldview, the "hero"? The truth lies somewhere in the middle. Years later, Oriana will not hide that for her this was, above all, a cerebral love.

She meets Panagoulis at a moment of profound crisis. Her relationship with François has ended on a dramatic note, and she feels her journalistic verve beginning to flag. In an interview, she has declared, "I've had enough of war. Professionally speaking, it doesn't interest me anymore. Recently, in India, I wrote a very detached reportage. I'm afraid of repeating myself. I can't keep writing Vietnam over and over. I can't just keep going to wars. I'm unsatisfied. I want to see something new."

She has begun writing a love story inspired by François but has given up, unable to continue. Alexandros Panagoulis, Alekos to his friends and family, is a young, solitary Greek hero battling against the dictatorship. He offers her a new cause, someone to identify with completely and also a great love around whom to build her long-dreamed-of novel. "Alekos was the male version of me," she will say later, when all is said and done.

By the time she arrives at the interview, she is well prepared. She has studied Alekos's story and the extraordinary courage with which he faced his jailers. For six years, even under intense torture, he has revealed nothing. This man embodies everything Oriana believes in: physical and moral courage, the obsession with freedom, the struggle against power. When the taxi drops her off, she finds his house full of family and friends. Plainclothes policemen outside keep track of comings and goings. The crowd makes way for this famous journalist who has come to meet the hero of the Greek Resistance. Oriana is wearing trousers and a flowered shirt, her hair hanging loose over her shoulders. Alekos is ten years younger, but his experiences have made him look much older. Oriana looks like a young girl next to him. Soon, he will call her *alitaki*, Greek for "scamp."

As soon as he sees her, he jumps up and embraces her, exclaiming, in Italian, "You're here!" She doesn't know that he is an admirer, that he has read many of her articles while sitting in jail, and studied Italian. He sent a friend to meet her at the airport with a bouquet of roses, but he missed her.

He is shattered and physically weak, and this touches her deeply from the first moment, as she will describe later in an interview: "Something happened between us when I entered that room and I saw this man advancing toward me, smiling, his hands tense. He was not the handsome young man people saw when I brought him to Italy. By then he had begun nourishing himself again with sun and good food. He was no longer pale. But that day he was ashen, with a greenish tint to his skin and purple shadows under his sunken eyes. I didn't feel a physical attraction, but I recognized in him so many people I had come across in this world, people who had given their lives for an ideal, and because of it had known unspeakable tortures, prison, even death."

Oriana accepts Alekos's embrace and then tries to calm his agitation. She places the recorder on the table and begins to ask questions. He answers, calmly. That is the first thing she is struck by: his beautiful voice. After his death she will say, "I can look at photographs of him. Even photos of his dead body. I can touch and wear his clothes. This shirt, for example, was made out of one of his shirts. I can touch his pipes, his papers, his things. But there are two things I can't do: watch him on film and, worst of all, hear his voice. That wonderfully guttural, deep voice that went straight to your heart like a knife. I'm terrified of hearing it again. Because he is dead, but his voice is alive." The interview goes on for hours. Every so often, Alekos's mother brings coffee. He speaks with a pipe in his mouth; at particularly intense moments in the interview, he grips it tightly with his teeth. His story unfolds before Oriana, and captures her heart.

Alekos comes from a family of heroes. His father was decorated several times in war. His two brothers were also involved in the

Resistance against the dictatorship. The youngest, Stathis, was imprisoned for many years. The eldest, Georgios, disappeared from the ship that was carrying him back to Greece under arrest. It is not known whether he was pushed overboard by his jailers or whether he died during an escape attempt. His body was never found. Every time a body washes up in the port of Piraeus, Alekos's mother, Athena, is called to identify the corpse. Each time she raises the sheet and says, "No, it's not Georgios." Of her sons, who fight without ever bending to power, she says, "Trees die standing up."

After his arrest for the attempted murder of Georgios Papadopoulos, Alekos is tortured for more than two months at the headquarters of ESA, the military police. A motor runs continually outside on the balcony in order to drown out the prisoners' screams. They want him to confess to receiving help from abroad and to give them the names of his comrades. Alekos reveals nothing, opening his mouth only to hurl insults at his torturers. He fights with all his strength against the torture. The torturers have everything on their side, he explains to Oriana, especially the weapon of time: "In time, the victim surrenders. In order to avoid this, the victim must neutralize this weapon by mounting a counteroffensive that impedes the usual playing out of events. Hunger strikes, refusing water, aggressive behavior, in other words opposing violence with violence so that they will hit you harder and cause you to lose consciousness."

Alekos's imprisonment is the drawn-out struggle of a lone man fighting against everyone around him. He is condemned to death and held for three nights, waiting for his execution, which is repeatedly postponed. The world has begun to take an interest in his case. The military junta is unsure how to proceed, whether to kill him and make a hero out of him, or to commute the sentence. In the end, he is transferred to a prison in Boyati where Alekos will stay for five years in inhumane conditions, held in a cell constructed

specifically for him. It is a cement cube in the middle of a courtyard, three meters by five meters, with a slit to allow in a sliver of
light. As tiny as a tomb, as Oriana will say when she visits it after
his death.

On August 19, 1973, he is set free, thanks to a general amnesty.
A few days later, he meets with Oriana, whom he has admired
for a long time. He knows she is the most important journalist
in Italy, a woman who performs her job as if going to war — with
great courage. Their meeting, Oriana remembers later, is almost
like a reunion: "You used to ask, almost with regret, 'Why didn't
we meet earlier? Where were you when I was lighting fuses, when
I was being tortured, during my trial, when I was condemned
to death, and when they buried me in that tomb?' And I would
answer, remorsefully: in Saigon, Hanoi, Phnom Penh, Mexico
City, São Paulo, Rio, Hong Kong, La Paz, Cochabamba, Amman,
Dacca, Calcutta, Colombo, New York."

The interview concludes at three in the morning. Oriana has
only a few hours to rest in a bed in Alekos's family home before
departing for the airport. Her assignments require her presence in
Bonn. She hardly sleeps and instead takes in all the objects in that
room. She is especially struck by a photo of Alekos as a boy, a tiny
figure wearing shorts several sizes too big for him. But already he
has the firm expression of someone who doesn't back down. She
is destabilized by this man in a way that she is still unable to completely understand. Alekos, too, is unable to sleep. She can hear him
pacing around the house all night long. For a moment she has the
impression that he places his hand on the doorknob to her room,
as if unsure whether or not to enter.

Oriana's first reaction to these powerful feelings is to flee. "I thought
to myself, 'Here we go, it's happened, it's happening.' And then I
had another thought or, rather, a fear. I ran away, saying to myself,

ORIANA FALLACI

'Please! P-lease!'" The next day Alekos insists upon accompanying her in the taxi to the airport. He forces her to promise that she
will come back to see him as soon as possible. Just a few days later,
he calls her — as she will soon find out, Alekos loves to talk on the
phone. He yells into the receiver in his approximate Italian, "*Sono io!
Sono me!*"

Among Oriana's papers is a letter that is probably the first he
sent her. It is a short note dated September 4, 1973, twelve days
after the interview. Alekos writes in a joking tone, asking whether
she has stolen two of his pipe cleaners, which he can't find. But he
closes the letter with a short poem dedicated to her: "Laughter of
life / Distant joys / Thoughts of love / Luminous instants." When
she gets word that he has been hospitalized, she rushes back to Athens. She is worried. Alekos's body has suffered from the tortures
and long imprisonment. It is covered with scars. Every so often he
discovers another one and wonders, *When did this happen?*

Once she is convinced he is out of danger, Oriana returns to
Italy. But she comes back almost immediately. She has requested
an interview with Papadopoulos, but the interview is canceled at
the last moment. Each time she lands in Athens, she is subjected
to a lengthy search, meant to discourage her visits. She is worried
for Alekos's safety. He seems set on defying the regime and continues to express his thoughts about the military junta. He knows his
home is being watched, his phone is tapped.

She convinces him to request a passport and come to Italy with
her. She is sure she can protect him with her fame. With her at his
side, no one will dare kill him. She takes him to Tuscany, which is
beautiful in autumn. She tells him that the woods are fragrant and
the grapevines that cover the walls are a fiery red. She promises
tranquil walks in the golden late-afternoon sun. But as soon as he
arrives, he shuts himself indoors with the shutters closed. After all
those years in a minuscule cell, he can't tolerate large spaces.

With Alekos Panagoulis in October 1973 at Fiumicino Airport in Rome.

Oriana's parents take to him immediately. Edoardo had been tortured during the war. Tosca treats him like a son, and he calls her Mamma. For a while, they travel between Casole and a hotel in Rome. Then they move into an apartment in Florence. It is the first time Oriana has lived with a man, and she finds it difficult. Years later, she will write in her notes, "I tried to live with my partner like a married couple. Or rather, I was forced to do so by certain circumstances, noble ones, I might add. I slowly went crazy. I couldn't handle it. And I must say he suffered as well. Because in this respect we are the same: We both thirst for independence. He suffered even though he had the better deal; it was easier for him. I had to take care of the house, cook, etc. He didn't lift a finger. But even more than this, I felt squashed by the obligatory cohabitation. I could feel him there even when he was silent or when he slept. Sharing the phone. Not having secrets!"

They fight over nothing. She can't stand his idleness. She wakes him when he stays in bed all day. "I'm thinking," he counters. "No, you're sleeping," she complains. They hurl insults at each other, yell, and even have physical fights. Years later, when a journalist asks whether they fought, Oriana responds, "All the time. He used to say, 'We were born to fight!' They were Homeric fights, endless grudges. Neither of us knew how to admit defeat."

Alekos is old-fashioned and finds it difficult to adapt to an emancipated woman like Oriana. They are competitive with each other. "I have a bad habit of not opening letters, or opening them weeks, months after receiving them. It drove Alekos crazy. He would get angry. 'Open the letter,' he would insist. 'No,' I would answer. 'It's my letter and I won't open it.' So he'd say, 'I'll open it.' 'Open it! Open it!' 'And I'll read it too.' 'Go ahead!' So he would open it, read it, and ask, 'You want to know what it says?' 'I don't care.' Such was the enormous, delicious antagonism between us."

Quickly, she understands the difference between admiring a

hero and living with a man of flesh and blood. Especially a man like Alekos, traumatized by his experiences. Years later, she will say, "Once, someone asked me, 'Are you happy with Alekos?' I answered, sharply, 'How can one be happy with someone who is unhappy?'" From the beginning, he is moody, unpredictable. Sometimes he says, "I want to see you look elegant tonight. Wear something red." And he drags her on an interminable night out. Other times he is quiet and dark. He talks obsessively about death. At night he has terrible dreams and wakes up covered in sweat. There is a touch of madness in him. He has several personalities. In a poem written in jail in his own blood on a fragment of paper he addresses this multitude of personalities that haunts him: "How many lives I have birthed in my brain / In order to banish my own solitude."

Oriana admires his poetry. She patiently helps him reconstruct the verses written while he was in prison; some of them, when there was no paper, are stored simply in his memory. He puts together a book, *Vi Scrivo da un carcere in Grecia* (I write to you from a prison in Greece). Oriana works on it for weeks, between her own articles. When the book is published, she is as happy as if it were hers. "I guarded the proofs with childish pride, and when the book was published I brought the first copy to Alekos. We were in Rome, it was during the referendum about divorce. It was a victorious day for progressives because the divorce bill passed with a huge majority. Rome was full of celebrations and flags, and the roads were crammed with beeping cars, but Alekos was asleep at the hotel. I placed the book on his pillow, near his head, and went out to write my article for the paper. When I came back he was still sleeping, but the book was in his arms. He held it as if it were a child, not a book."

The poet and movie director Pier Paolo Pasolini has written the introduction. Oriana has known and admired him for years.

From their first meeting, she is intrigued by this unique man with almost feminine sensibilities and a hidden coarseness, who speaks about Jesus and Saint Francis in a way that no priest has, and at night wanders the poor neighborhoods in search of young men to pay for sex. She describes one of his visits to New York: "We were near Lincoln Center looking for a taxi to take you to a place you wouldn't name. You were trembling with impatience. I whispered, 'You'll get your throat cut, Pier Paolo.' And you stared at me with lucid, unhappy eyes — your eyes were always sad, even when you laughed — and answered, sarcastically, 'Yes?'"

When he is murdered, on the night of November 1–2, 1975, Oriana is in Rome. She and Alekos are sitting at a restaurant on Piazza Navona. A young boy selling copies of *L'Unità* draws near and the news begins to spread. Pasolini has been killed. His body has been found near the beach at Ostia, where he has been beaten up and run over with a car. Oriana, who has seen terrible violence in Vietnam, is sickened: "They said it didn't even look like a body, because of the state he was in. He looked like a pile of trash."

Impulsively, she tells the director of *L'Europeo* that she wants to write about the crime. She starts to make inquiries in the underworld of Rome. She follows a lead given to her by an American journalist in Rome who has heard rumors of a witness who saw everything but is afraid to speak. When the article comes out, it's clear from the first line what she thinks: "There is another version of the events surrounding Pasolini's death." She contests the official version of the killing, according to which Pasolini was killed by a seventeen-year-old male prostitute, Giuseppe Pelosi, after an argument over his sexual services. She says that her secret witness saw at least two other men beat up and kill the writer. Pelosi, who according to this witness had been more or less a spectator to the crime, had been left behind to take the rap. He is underage and will not have to spend much time in jail. He ends up coming across more as the victim, a poor kid forced to prostitute himself and accept the advances of a man who could have been his father. The investigation and media focus more on Pasolini's sexual predilections than on discovering what really happened at Ostia. Oriana is disgusted: "They want to kill him a second time, physically and morally, to shame him." She argues that the murder was a conspiracy, that someone wanted to get rid of Pasolini, an intellectual who for a long time has been a thorn in the side of many in the elite.

When the judges in the case ask for her source's name, she refuses, taking refuge in an article of the journalists' statute that permits journalists to protect their sources. She knows that Italian law grants professional confidentiality only to doctors, priests, lawyers, and midwives, but she argues her position on principle. She is tried and found in contempt of court,* and declares to the press: "I performed my duty, and my conscience is clear, my dignity intact. We shouldn't be afraid or allow ourselves to be intimidated when questions of principle are at play." Then she keeps a disdainful silence on the matter. Years later, Pelosi, now free, will admit he was not alone that night.

Alekos, too, is overwhelmed by Pasolini's death. He is obsessed with and fascinated by death. He talks about it all the time, as if suspecting that his own death is near. Oriana advises him to leave politics, but he doesn't listen. He continues to struggle against the dictatorship. Every so often he visits Athens incognito. He travels incessantly in search of funds for the Greek Resistance, which he obtains from Greek émigré circles and European politicians. Often he involves Oriana in his activities, and she finds herself in surreal situations, with suitcases full of cash passed from one person to the next. She describes one of these occasions, during a stop at the

---

*She received a four-month suspended sentence.

Venice Film Festival where Alekos is speaking, to Isabella Rossellini: "When we were at the Ducal Palace, where the opening cer-
emonies were being held, Alekos went onstage and handed me
a suitcase. I was sitting next to your father," the director Roberto
Rossellini. "'Don't let go of that suitcase!' he warned me. 'I want
to see it on your lap while I speak,' he insisted. The suitcase was
uncomfortable. 'Put it on the floor,' your father told me. And I
answered, 'I can't. It contains valuable documents.' 'Give it to me,'
he said, 'I'll hold it.' And just like that he took it and placed it on his
lap. Alekos stopped speaking and stared at me from the stage with
a murderous look in his eye. So I leaned over to take the suitcase
back, saying, 'Please, I don't want to disturb you.' 'It's no bother
at all, I'm happy to hold it.' Alekos kept staring at me, at us, with
daggers in his eyes. It was a real struggle to get it back; your father
couldn't understand why I would not accept this act of courtesy.
'Who was that handsome man dressed in blue who wanted to steal
my money?' Alekos asked as soon as he left the stage. 'That was
Roberto Rossellini. He didn't want to steal your money, he only
wanted to help,' I explained."

She tolerates certain things from Alekos because she believes he
is the incarnation of the hero she has been searching for ever since
she was a girl fighting in the Resistance with her father. "Panagoulis is an extraordinary man. He truly loves freedom, and not just
with words. If he had lived in Italy thirty years ago, he would have
joined the Partito d'Azione." She stays away from her apartment in
New York for over a year because Alekos is unable to obtain a visa
to travel to the United States. She reduces her traveling to be near
him, sacrificing the opportunity to report on events that interest
her intensely—the coup in Chile that ousts Salvador Allende, the
Yom Kippur War in Israel, and the fall of the regime in Portugal.

She even accepts his proposal, in her own way, with a secret
exchange of rings. "He gave me a very beautiful ring, with

diamonds. I gave him a very simple one, because that's what he wanted. Actually, he wanted a ring made out of steel, but such a thing doesn't exist, so I had to buy him a simple silver ring. I got the size wrong. Alekos was amused by that and wore it on his little finger; but even on his little finger it was a bit tight. He had pudgy fingers. He never took it off, never."

She fears for his life. She often has the impression that they are being followed. In August 1974, after the fall of the Greek regime, Alekos decides to return to Athens and run for Parliament. Oriana doesn't go with him. She prefers to return to New York and get back to work. The last year by his side has been exhausting, and she needs a break.

Every so often she visits him in Athens, even though she can't stand the entourage that surrounds him, made up of real friends but also a large number of hangers-on, spongers, flatterers, and women who want to sleep with him. She isn't jealous, but abhors the vulgarity of certain situations: the way Alekos refers to his many amorous adventures as "one shot and off I go," the evenings he drinks too much and she has to help him home and put him to bed, still dressed. At least on her side, their relationship is not based on physical attraction. She has known jealousy — that feeling that "empties your veins at the idea that the man you love is penetrating another body, that jealousy that hobbles you and steals your sleep" — and she knows desire, a feeling that "clouds your vision and takes your breath away when you lay eyes on one you love." She had experienced both in her relationships with Alfredo and François. With Alekos, it's different. The truth of the matter is that she's not particularly attracted to him. A friend she will spend time with many years later remembers telling her about a Greek boyfriend who was obsessed with sex. "Just like Alekos. I kept telling him our relationship was mental, but he wanted to have sex all the time," she would confide.

Alekos is elected to Parliament, where he begins another solitary battle, this time against certain segments of the new Greek government, whom he accuses of being too close to the dictatorship. In particular, he attacks the minister of defense, who leads an army that has not been purged of pro-junta elements. For months, he seeks evidence of his collaboration with the colonels, but the military police archives have mysteriously disappeared. He becomes obsessed. Oriana worries. She suspects that there is a hidden, more personal motive — the desire to find out the truth about what happened to his brother Georgios.

17. UNBORN CHILDREN

"Last night I knew you existed: a drop of life escaped from nothingness." It is without a doubt Oriana's most famous opening. The words are from Oriana's novel, *Letter to a Child Never Born*, published in September 1975. The book is an extraordinary success, even by Oriana's already high standards. It sells almost half a million copies in six months and is translated into more than twenty languages. It is reprinted several times and is still one of her most admired and widely sold books. Its subject — the conflict between being born and not being born — creates an immediate sensation. It scandalizes progressives with its notion that a child is a life from the first division of cells, and scandalizes conservatives with the notion that a woman is the only person who can make decisions about her own pregnancy. Most of all, it takes everyone by surprise, because it approaches the problem backward. It begins with the mother's refusal of maternity, only to transform itself into a moving defense of the relationship between mother and child.

The success of the book stems first of all from Oriana's decision to shape the narrative as the monologue of a mother directed toward to her unborn child. From the first line, the reader is captivated by this solitary voice. A woman lies in the dark with her eyes wide open, convinced, even before going to the doctor, that she is carrying a child. She has no name, no age, no nationality. Oriana does this so that every woman in the world will be able to identify with her protagonist. She lives alone by choice, is passionate about her work, and loves freely, without desiring marriage or expecting the protection of a man. Faced with the reality of her pregnancy, she is conflicted from the get-go. She isn't sure she wants a child, nor is she sure the child wants to be born. "I'm not interested in bringing you into the world only for myself and no one else. I don't need you at all," she says early in the book. And yet, by choosing to speak to this "cluster of cells that has barely begun," she has given it a shape; there is someone in her life to whom she refers as a "child."

The monologue is her way of writing a manifesto for life, because her body — and she can feel it — is working hard. "Who says you're inert matter, little more than a vegetable that can be extirpated with a spoon? If I want to be free of you, they insist, now is the moment to do it. Or rather the moment begins now. In other words, I was to wait for you to become a human being with eyes and fingers and a mouth in order to kill you. Not before. Before, you were too small to be singled out and torn away. They are crazy." But in difficult moments she has doubts: "Tell me, you who know everything: When does life begin? Tell me, I beg you: Has yours really begun? For how long? From the moment when the drop of light they call sperm pierced and split the cell? From the moment you developed a heart and began to pump blood? From the moment you grew a brain, a spinal column, and were on your way to assuming a human form? Or else is the moment still to come? Are you only a motor in the making?"

One emotion follows hard and fast upon the other: amazement, affection, anger, rebellion. Every so often she gets angry, because the doctor insists that she must rest: "What do you think I am: a container, a jar where you put some object for safekeeping?" Finally, she decides to get out of bed. She has a work trip to prepare for, which she doesn't want to cancel. "If you succeed in being born, you'll be born. If you don't succeed, you'll die. I'm not going to kill you, understand: I simply refuse to help you exercise your tyranny to the end." She is optimistic; she has even bought a cradle and baby clothes. The night before her departure, she wishes him, "Good night, child." She worries because she hasn't felt movement in her belly for a while. During the trip, while she's driving, alone, on a highway, she feels pain for the first time. She has to undergo emergency treatment; the fetus, which is already dead, is extracted from her womb. She is unconscious, lost in delirium. Then she utters a last word for her child: "You're dead. Maybe I'm dying too. But it doesn't matter. Because life doesn't die."

These words, which for decades confronted readers as they finished the book, were not the ending Oriana had planned. Alekos had fought for that "maybe," to leave an opening for some hope. In the 1990s, Oriana alters the line, removing all ambiguity: "Now I'm dying too." She explains her decision: "I never doubted that the woman died at the end. There is something behind this change. A beautiful story. That's all. The proofs of the book weren't corrected in Italy. They were corrected in Athens, in the apartment-office where Alekos Panagoulis lived after being elected to Parliament. We argued because Alekos wanted to take part in the revisions. Because he was a poet, and because he loved the meter I often use in my writing, he insisted that the book should be in verse rather than in prose. One day I found the proofs all marked up with lines to indicate verse endings. Here's an example: 'Last night / I knew you existed / a drop of life / escaped from nothingness.' Or he would make suggestions about verbs, adjectives, punctuation. I didn't know what to do, where to hide the proofs. One time, as I was leaving the house, I stuck them in a flower pot. But he found them, even there. But more than anything he hated the ending. The fact that the woman died. 'Murderer! You killed, you're killing, poor woman!' he would yell in his funny Italian without pronouns.

It was useless to explain to him that her death was the logical outcome of the story. But there was no point saying, 'Buzz off, this is my book and I will end it as I please.' When I read the final proof, I suddenly realized he had struck the line, 'Now I'm dying too.' I got truly angry. Furious! I was so mad that I packed my bags and went back to Italy. Without saying goodbye. I took it very, very badly. It was like an act of violence, a mutilation of my creation. But three days later when I was in the studio we kept in Florence at Poggio Imperiale, Alekos showed up with a contrite look and a piece of paper in his hand. 'I came to propose a compromise,' he said. 'To sign an armistice.' Then he held out the piece of paper, and on it was written, 'Maybe I'm dying too.' What could I do?"

This book, so close to Oriana's heart, was a novel but also a precious testimonial of one of the most private chapters of her existence: the children she never had. "It was always extremely painful to me to lose these children before they were born. Because you die twice when you die without children." Based on the accounts of family members and on her own stories, it seems likely that she became pregnant at least twice and each time lost the baby. "It was destiny's choice," she will say later. "I never had an abortion. I always lost them. Maybe I decided too late to have a child. Or maybe I didn't take good enough care of myself. Actually, I never took care of myself at all. I never had the time, to be honest. It's not healthy to fly so much or to feel so many emotions and fears, or to work as much as I do, when you're pregnant. You lose the child. The problem of abortion never arose for me. Or the issue of the pill. My problem was finding a pill in order to *have* a child. The only pill that helps you do that is calm, and I never had that." Oriana does not say much more about this aspect of her life, refusing to elaborate on a subject that she considers extremely private. Only a few isolated facts can be reconstructed.

The first child is lost in Paris in 1958, during her relationship with Alfredo. It is a terrible trauma that takes place in the context of an unhappy love affair, an episode she will barely make reference to in the future. It is her secret wound. At the time, she is unable to share it with anyone. It is a time of absolute solitude in which she feels rejected, along with her minuscule unnamed fetus, by a man who doesn't want her.

The second miscarriage takes place in 1965. The father is probably American; all that is known is that he is a person of note. He is married and fears a scandal. Perhaps he is one of the NASA astronauts. Oriana decides to say nothing and to face the pregnancy alone, though she does tell her family. They all support her decision, even her parents, who are always on her side. One of her sisters sends a package containing a pair of tiny white shoes: "It was so beautiful that she sent them just like that, without anything else. When I was little, we were poor, and shoes were important. They were expensive. My mother would always buy them a size too big, so they would last longer. Throughout my entire childhood, my shoes were too big. One time on my birthday, my mother decided to give me a pair in my exact size. They were white, and lightweight. But my grandfather reinforced them with nails and they became as heavy as the others."

Against the tide, she decides to raise the child on her own, and she is proud of her decision. The sudden miscarriage occurs in the fifth month of her pregnancy. It is a heavy blow. Perhaps in part because of what had happened in Paris years earlier, this child has become deeply important to her, a surprise after years of thinking she couldn't conceive. In a way, it is also a form of reparation. As in the novel, it is the frenetic pace of her working life that causes the miscarriage. In a letter, she describes her life at the time: "I wish I could write more, but I'm drowning in work, in worry, and in travel. I'll write more when things are calmer, maybe from California or Texas or Florida or Mexico, the next legs of my travels that await me, and which I await. The days are longer there than they are in Europe. And I hope to see you at Christmas when I come to Casole to rest my 48 kilos, soon 47, 46, 44, 43, then nothing."

She is unwell after the miscarriage, physically and psychologically. She writes to a friend who has offered to pay her to take some time off: "I don't want to spend a month doing nothing. Exhaustion and worrying about work are the only things that keep me from thinking too much and going crazy. What happened at Christmas was a big shock. I haven't gotten over it and I wonder if I ever will. As I told you, I had so much anxious, desperate desire for that child, and to lose it that way..." It is July, six months later, but Oriana hasn't fully recovered. In this letter she mentions a detail which, transfigured, will become the heart of her novel: "The world seems like such a hostile place and I just can't understand it. Sometimes I get a feeling, like when you take a tram and get off at the wrong stop. You look around and don't recognize anything. You don't know what to do, and the tram is already gone. It has left you there with your mistake and your embarrassed solitude... Maybe I shouldn't have taken the tram in the first place. Maybe I've gotten off at the wrong stop. Maybe I shouldn't have been born. Maybe my child made the right choice to avoid all that suffering. Maybe oblivion is the best solution."

The loss of this second child brings to the surface the contradictions that have always accompanied her desire to be a mother. Oriana suffers because she doesn't have children, but at the same time she isn't sure she is prepared to take care of a child. She tells a friend about the difficult decision in 1969 to leave her little dog, whom she loves, with her mother because she can't travel with it all over the world: "There were tears at the airport. We kissed, we cried, we made promises. But as soon as the airplane took off I felt so free, so light. And in the weeks after that I was so free and light, and I quickly realized that the last thing I was made for was living with someone: a man, a child, even a dog. I realized, to my shame, that my desire to be a mother is highly abstract."

To her a child is a symbol, an affirmation of her will. It is life, the supreme form of resistance against a scandalous reality that she cannot accept: death. This is why her maternal desire is rekindled in Saigon. "When I was in Vietnam and I saw all those corpses in Dak To, my desire to become pregnant redoubled," she says in an interview. "I know, and you can write this, what it means to be pregnant. But not a long-term pregnancy. I always loose them early in my pregnancy. But it is a sensation a man can't understand. You're so conscious of this other life growing inside of you. You feel so important." While living in Vietnam, she considers adopting a child. She visits an orphanage, where she experiences conflicting feelings. On the one hand, she thinks that a child will give her a sense of peace: "I won't need to be shot at to feel alive." On the other, the idea terrifies her. She walks through room after room full of orphans. She begins to feel light-headed. She feels herself being watched by too many eyes, reflecting all the suffering of the world. Finally, she tells her guide, "Let's go, please."

During her relationship with François, more than once she wonders whether she is pregnant. Each time she feels great joy, followed by great disappointment. In a poem, she writes, "I thought I had extended you / in the form of a child. / I walked on the beach alone / with my illusion, thinking up names." Years later, she transforms these sensations — an overwhelming fullness, followed by the pain of emptiness — into a scene in *A Man*. She and Alekos argue in front of a closed door. He wants to go out and confront his enemies, she tries to stop him; a kick accidentally strikes her in the belly. "A powerful pain. The key is in your hand. My voice breaks the silence to utter the word you ignore: the baby." There is no way to know if this scene is real. At the time of her relationship with Alekos, Oriana is over forty years old. She still feels regret; with the years it will become only stronger. "I would have liked to have a child. I did what I could to make it possible, but each time I tried I lost the baby."

She writes *Letter to a Child Never Born* quickly, in 1966, after losing her second child. Then she leaves it in a drawer for almost ten years, overwhelmed by its vividness and rawness. When, in 1974, the director of *L'Europeo* asks her to prepare an essay on abortion, she takes her time and, instead, writes a short story. She locks herself in for four months and comes out of isolation with a finished novel. She has gone back and revised the original version, removed overly personal details to create a more universal tale: "There are only a few hints of the bloodcurdling scream I uttered at the time: the beginning, the ending, and the episode of the moon dissolving in my fingers. In that long-ago scream, I was the protagonist, but in today's more rational version I no longer am. At the most, she is a woman who resembles me."

The first version of the novel, which is written in diary form and hews more closely to real-life events, has survived among her papers. The dates correspond perfectly with Oriana's time line. Oriana discovers she is pregnant in the summer of 1965, in New York. In late September her doctor prescribes bed rest, but she is unable to comply: "I explained to him that I can't allow myself the luxury of not doing anything. Nor can I tell people that I'm pregnant." She says little about the father. One gets the sense that he is someone she sees from time to time and with whom passion has abated. She has probably become pregnant in a paradoxical situation in which she finds herself unable to say no to a former lover without wounding him. "It's not civil to say no to a man who has been important to you," she writes. When she realizes she is pregnant, she does not tell him. He is convinced, like everyone else, that she can't have children. She nurses her pregnancy in secret, like a miracle. A sentence lies at the heart of this first version, a secret wellspring from which will emerge the novel years later: "If you died, I too would die. I would die even if I survived, because I would go back to being what I was. A dried-out tree, without a future. A vain wait for nothing at all."

The novel is published in 1975 as Italy debates the issue of abortion, which will be legalized three years later. Oriana's position is clear: She is always on the side of life, almost desperately so. "Imagine that when I was an embryo, just a few millimeters long, someone asked me, 'Listen, Oriana, if you're born, you will be hungry and die at the age of six in an oven in Mauthausen. Do you still want to be born?' I would have answered, 'Yes. At least I will have lived those six years. I will have seen the sun, the trees, the sky, and will have breathed in the fragrance of life.'" But she believes that only women can decide. So she believes strongly in the legalization of abortion. "I'm willing to go to jail to defend a woman's right to an abortion when necessary."

In reality, she's not terribly interested in arguments over abortion. They will help sales of her book, she knows that, but not her understanding of the issue. In a letter, she describes the polemic unleashed by the publication of her book: "Women are indignant, men are angry, the pro-abortion camp curses me because it has concluded that I'm opposed to abortion, the anti-abortion camp insults me because it has concluded I'm for abortion. And no one, or almost no one, understands what the book is really about. No one is right, or rather everyone is." She says over and over that the subject of her book is not abortion, but doubt. And her own suffering: "A friend, Giorgio Amendola, helped me understand this. Some time ago he lost a thirty-seven-year-old daughter, and it was as if he had lost a child just before or after birth. He said it just like that: This is a book about suffering. For a moment I couldn't breathe. I didn't know I had written a book about suffering. Then I remembered the circumstance in which I began writing the book, years earlier, in tears."

18. THE ARABIAN DESERT

For a short period, in March 1976, Oriana has the illusion that Alekos is no longer obsessed with his research into the Greek military police archives. He even agrees to write a book about his time in prison, as she has long been pushing him to do. He returns to their apartment in Florence and starts to work. Every morning he lines up paper, pens, his pipe, and a lighter on the desk and applies himself to his task. He starts with the moment he places the bomb and the image of himself trying to unravel the fuse, which has become tangled and needs to be clipped. This detail is what dooms the assassination attempt and results in his arrest. When he begins writing about his arrest and the first, extremely violent days of torture, he stops, unable to go on. Oriana tries everything. She carefully prepares an outline of the book. But he gives up and goes back to Greece. Before leaving, he says to her, "You write it."

In the last months of Alekos's life, they see little of each other. He lives in Athens, she's in New York. Apart from him, she can preserve her idealized image, the product of her memories or her fantasies. In the ensuing years she will romanticize this arrangement, explaining, in interviews, that living apart had been the choice of two people equally obsessed with freedom. "When Alekos went back to Greece, we lived at separate addresses. And everything was better, because it was much freer." The truth is that their relationship has deteriorated, even if they are still very close. They never let more than a few days pass without speaking on the phone. His death interrupts this process of letting go, binding them together forever.

Alekos is killed in a car crash on the night between Friday, April 30 and Saturday, May 1, 1976. The following Monday, he was planning to present the papers he had finally located in the files of the military police. His death is officially ruled an accident, but Oriana is convinced that he was assassinated by two killers chasing him in separate cars. She personally finances forensic tests but is unable to obtain clarification. The accident happens at night, and there are no witnesses. The only thing that is known is that Alekos's car crashed into a wall near a downward-leading driveway. The car had been a Christmas gift from Oriana. It was a bright, cheerful green. Alekos had named it Spring.

Alekos's death is followed by Tosca's in January 1977. It is a terrible time in Oriana's life. Whereas Alekos's death is unexpected — the dangers of the dictatorship have receded into the past — her mother's death is slow, preceded by a protracted decline. "A death that arrives drop by drop, like a leaky faucet: drip…drip…drip… It drips away, without ever overflowing. But you know that it's coming and you don't want it to come, even though once it does, it will be a relief. Watching this person who loves you, whom you love, suffer like Christ crucified, with an oxygen tube in her nose to help her breathe…Her vocal chords can't utter a sound but those eyes watch you, attempting to say what her mouth cannot. So you try different things. Is it this? Or this? Or this? And her head moves slowly, saying, no, no, no."

After Alekos's death, Tosca, weakened by a tumor, takes to her bed. When Oriana becomes aware of the seriousness of her mother's condition, she decides to stay in Casole to spend time with her. "I wandered around the house like a tourist, up and down the thirty rooms, filled with a silence that reminded me of death, space, time. I observed myself with a certain irony, like a Romantic character in a novel, someone imagined by the likes of Emily Brontë, and I thought, 'This is what my old age will be like. A very solitary old age.'"

In the end, she reacts as she always has—by writing. She gets to work on the novel that Alekos abandoned before leaving for Greece. Even though the house has dozens of rooms and big, sunfilled windows, she chooses to work in a narrow hallway between her bedroom and a bathroom. There is just one tiny window there, with a view of a field. "One morning I stopped writing for a moment to follow a train of thought. Suddenly I saw the white wall before me, in my eyes. I looked around and wondered, 'Why have I encased myself in this tiny hallway, with no air or light?' Only then did I understand that my subconscious had led me to create a jail cell for myself. That little hallway, the smallest corner of the house, was the closest thing to Alekos's cell in Boyati: tiny, suffocating, solitary, punitive."

She feels the need to write a novel about Alekos, as if to build a monument for him out of words. The tomb his family erects for him in Athens seems to her like a vulgar theme park, full of saints and colored lights. She protests, vainly, that Alekos would not have wanted this and offers to build it herself, to have marble brought from Carrara. His mother and brother respond that they would prefer that she send them the money and let them decide.

The relationship between Oriana and his family quickly deteriorates in the days after the funeral. The family requests that she return the money Alekos had collected abroad and kept in Italy, in Oriana's bank account. She answers that Alekos had intended to donate it to the Spanish and Chilean Resistance, one million lire [approximately $700] to each. He was planning to do so on May 5, in Rome, and had already purchased a plane ticket. She stands fast, respecting his wishes. She gives the family the receipt for the two bank transfers and the remaining funds. The idea that the family thinks she might be keeping money that does not belong to her offends her deeply. She writes a very strong letter, underlining that she doesn't need Alekos's money and that she is a person who gives money away, not one who takes it. From that moment forward, she has no more relations with the Panagoulis family.

Once she begins to write the novel, her work absorbs her completely. She gets up from her desk only to sleep and to visit her mother's room, where Tosca patiently awaits death. In her final days, when the situation appears desperate, Oriana never leaves the room, not even to sleep. Many years later, in a letter to a friend, she will describe the final hours spent at her mother's bedside: "Even though I had gone to live in the country in order to be close to her, and even though I had 'accepted' the idea that she was dying, I suffered terribly. The only comfort was that I was able to find a priest for her the night before…Around midnight, she mumbled the word 'priest' with an imploring look. I ran out without even putting on a coat. It was winter, and it was snowing. In the dark, I reached the village church and called on a certain Don Gori, who didn't want to come. 'Tomorrow, tomorrow. It's too late, and too cold.' Pushing and screaming, threatening to kill him if he didn't follow, I forced him to come to the house with his purple stole and the rest. When she saw him arrive, her imploring eyes were illuminated by a senseless joy. Sublime and senseless. She had always hated him because each time he celebrated Mass in our chapel, he demanded twenty thousand lire. And because, during the service, he would kick York, her Yorkshire terrier, who liked to sit at the base of the altar. Then, absolved from the sins that she had not committed, by a man like that, she fell asleep with a smile on her face."

Oriana recognizes that "a mother's death is not comparable to the death of a man you love. It is the foreshadowing of your own death. Because it is the death of the person who conceived you and carried you in her belly." Before Tosca's death, Oriana becomes even more cruelly aware of the outrage of death. Even though she has grown up in war and has returned to it as a war correspondent, and even though she has seen and described death in her articles and books, she has never accepted it. Death is a problem that has always obsessed her. It is in this terrible year that Oriana finally stares it in the face, and is transformed by it. Her face develops wrinkles and shadows that will never disappear, as if she has suddenly aged.

"It was traumatizing. Something happened inside of me. If you asked me, 'What is the word you think about the most, day and night?' I would say 'death.' Always," she will tell an American journalist years later. "There is an American TV series, *The Bionic Woman*, the story of a woman pilot who crashes in her plane. Her body is broken. There is nothing left, nothing but her brain, which they salvage. They recreate her, piece by piece, in the operating room, with pieces of metal and plastic, electronic eyes, a pump instead of a heart. The only original piece is her brain. Well, I won't give the imbeciles an excuse to say that I have a pump for a heart. But one thing is certain: There is little left of the woman I was before crashing down from the sky to the ground."

Oriana sums up her state of mind: "Two people in my life were more important to me than my own life: my man and my mother. They died in quick succession, over the course of eight months. Now that this double tragedy has taken place, I don't know what to do with my freedom. I'm like the Arabian Desert."

That year, 1977, changes her life. She resigns from *L'Europeo*, a decision precipitated in part by the firing of the editor in chief, Tommaso Giglio, to whom she is close. She has grown tired of being a reporter and wants to dedicate herself to writing books. "I stared myself in the face and realized I was over forty and thought, What am I doing? Why am I still giving all of myself to this profession that I love but that I also accepted out of need and compromise?"

After being in the public eye for so long, she becomes extremely private, obsessed with the need for silence. She disconnects the phone and refuses interviews about topical issues, as well as invitations to speak in public. For three years, she stays in her refuge at Casole, working on the book about Alekos. The book is born of the loss of her mother and of her partner. "These were the two people I loved the most. I loved them so much that it was almost painful to divide my love between them. What I mean is that the time I spent with one felt like time stolen from the other... One of the staircases in my country house, between the ground floor and the second floor, connected my mother's apartment and the area where I lived with Alekos. When I was there with both of them, I was always running up and down those stairs. Up and down." As she will with every book after that, she retires completely from the world and works in complete silence. No one is allowed to talk about the book she is working on. To those who ask to meet with her, her friends and family are instructed to say, "She's working."

"I wrote it three times. No, four. Five if you count the proof revisions. At a certain point, the typographers started to hate me, and the editors too. 'She hasn't given permission to go to print! She keeps starting over! She's crazy! Crazy!' They thought I had lost it. And in a way they were right. I couldn't pull myself away from those proofs, I couldn't leave them alone. I always found something to correct, to change, to cut or to add." *A Man* requires an enormous effort from her. "In order to tell his story I had to suffer too," she will say later. "It was as if I carried inside of myself the soul of this dead man. Listening to his voice. I didn't live for two years; I spoke only to a few very intimate friends. I cut myself off from the world."

The book opens with a description of Alekos's funeral, a great crowd scene. Then it goes on to tell the story of the assassination attempt and his arrest. She vividly describes his time in prison and the experience of torture, and then moves on to their love story, which illuminates the second half of the book, before finishing with the dramatic scene of Alekos's death. Everything is described in great detail, as if she had lived it. Dissatisfied with the prison chapter, she takes an extremely rare break from her isolation to visit Alekos's cell in Boyati. "I asked my guides if I could be locked in the cell alone. 'I want to stay here, alone, as long as I can.' They shut the door and walked away. I sat down on what was left of the camp bed. Even though it was summer, it was dark. Light filtered in between the bars of the tiny gate facing the atrium. The pale light from the atrium seeped through the grate and left a patch on the ceiling. I tried to imagine what it must have been like to live in that cell in winter. I had brought a measuring stick with me. I carefully measured every wall. Thirty centimeters here, forty centimeters there, 1.8 meters over there. And that's it. I drew a map of the cell. *Finito.* I sat down to think. I couldn't think! A feeling of oppression, even senseless fear, was growing inside of me. What if they forgot about me and left me in there? I thought an interminable amount of time had passed — in fact, as I learned later, I had been there only twenty minutes. I grabbed the bars and began to yell, '*Basta!* I get it! *Basta!*' Alekos had lived in there for years."

The book is published in July 1979 and is an immediate success, in Italy and abroad. According to her usual formula, it is a novel based on real events. It is unclassifiable, both an elegy for a lost love and a *roman vérité.* "It's not possible to define *A Man,*" she herself will acknowledge, "because it is a book full of other books." It is particularly important to her that it be read as a fable about the solitary struggle of a man against power: "The book follows the classic structure of a fable, which is always the same, in Greek myths as in the popular legends of every era. Initiation, period of great trials, homecoming, final challenge, death and apotheosis." Even though she maintains that every event in the book is true, she insists that it is a novel. She argues that only a novel allows her to take on the wider, more universal significance of the events she describes.

The result is a six-hundred-page book that is dramatic, violent, and excessive. Through this novel Oriana describes a brief but very intense season of her life. She has made peace with her obsession with courage and tells the story of a very difficult love with a man who is too different from herself. "I did violence to myself because I wanted to be good to him, to Alekos. I was not happy with how I had behaved with him. I didn't always try to understand him, to meet him halfway. When he died, everything transformed itself into a terrible feeling of guilt."

The book's dedication reads, in Greek and Italian, "*Ghia sena. Per te*" (For you). It is the title of a poem he had written for her: "Forgotten thoughts of love / revive / and restore me to life." With this book, Oriana links her name to Alekos's for eternity: "Journalists ask me whether I will fall in love again. And I say, Are you joking? I can't even imagine such a thing. I think people see me like one of those Indian widows who burn themselves with the bodies of their dead husbands."

Now that the book is finished, she can talk about—and sometimes reinvent—*her* Alekos. In interviews, she describes an extraordinary love story: "At a certain point in my life I experienced a miracle: I met Alexandros Panagoulis and fell in love with him and was loved by him. I say it was a miracle because it wasn't an ordinary love—it was a great love." She can love him even more now that he is gone. Now that she has created a legend around him, she can turn him into the love of her life.

19. THE RETURN

The publication of *A Man* forces Oriana to leave Casole to promote the book in Italy and abroad. After three years of total isolation, she returns to the world, starts traveling again, begins reading the newspapers and watching television. Once in a while — when the subject interests her — she even does interviews, for the *Washington Post*, the *New York Times*, and the most important Italian newspaper, *Corriere della Sera*.

She obtains an interview with Ayatollah Khomeini, who agrees to meet her in Qom, a city considered sacred by Shiites, in September 1979, when the country is still in the middle of the revolution that will overthrow the shah. Khomeini, who has been in Iran for less than a year after a long exile, is the spiritual leader of the revolt. From his refuge in Qom, he is plotting to take control of the country and impose his vision of an Islamic state managed by the clergy. Two months later, the Islamic Republic will be proclaimed, with Khomeini as its Supreme Leader. It is not easy for a Western journalist, much less a woman, to obtain an audience with him. As in the past, her fame smoothes the way. Oriana is a star in Iran: "In 1973, I interviewed the shah and wrote that he was a son of a bitch. And so Khomeini granted me an interview thinking I would praise him. In truth, even I thought I would like him more than I had the shah, but it was enough to meet him to know

During her famous interview with Ayatollah Khomeini in September 1979, in which she removed her chador in protest.

that I wouldn't like him at all, that he was as tyrannical as the shah, and that one tyrant had replaced another. I wrote about him in the same terms."

She agrees to wear a chador for the meeting, as has been requested. Khomeini, annoyed by her questions about the conditions of women in Iran, makes a sarcastic quip: "If you do not like Islamic dress you are not obliged to follow it. The chador is only for young and respectable women." Oriana reacts by removing the chador with an angry gesture. There is a commotion. Khomeini, who refuses to meet with a woman without a chador, leaves the room. Oriana refuses to leave, saying that she has been given only half an interview. She sits there for hours until Khomeini's son swears on the Koran that she will be received again the next day. The next day, she says, "Khomeini arrived and I looked him in the eye and said, 'Let's start where we left off yesterday. You were saying that I was indecent...' And Khomeini did something very interesting. He never looks you in the face; he always looks down at the floor. But at that moment he looked me in the eye with an amused smile. It was funny, because he couldn't laugh." Her friends recall Oriana's hilarious imitation of the elderly imam, particularly that half smile.

The interview is published around the world and proves that Oriana has not lost her touch. She seeks out conflict, asks polemical questions, like why Khomeini is persecuting the rebels who had driven out the shah, and why he wants to push his country back into the Middle Ages. He is unperturbed, never loses his temper, and avoids conflict. When she asks a particularly shameless question, he sighs and whispers that this foreign journalist is tiring him. Oriana is frustrated by the interview but cannot deny Khomeini's charisma: "It may be banal, but the simple truth about Khomeini is that he is a fanatic. To me, a fanatic cannot be intelligent, but I must admit that he is the exception that confirms the rule. I thought I would be meeting an idiot, but instead I encountered an extremely acute man."

A month later, on November 4, a crowd of revolutionaries overruns the American embassy in Tehran and takes hostage everyone inside. This causes a dramatic diplomatic crisis. Fifty-two people are held hostage for more than a year, while a power struggle rages within the ranks of the Iranian Revolution, between moderates and radicals. Then there is the standoff between Iran and the United States regarding the fate of the shah, who is in a hospital in New York awaiting surgery.

Several months later, Oriana will return to Iran as an envoy of the *New York Times*. She obtains a visa in March 1980 and requests entry to the embassy to interview the hostages and the revolutionaries. The request is denied. Her act of defiance toward Khomeini is still fresh in people's minds. In front of the embassy, a hostile crowd gathers and begins to push and pull at her. She is forced to retreat and rushes off to the airport.

Almost immediately after meeting Khomeini, Oriana interviews Colonel Muammar Gaddafi, who had seized control of Libya ten years earlier in a coup. The dictator has made a bet that, unlike Khomeini, he will obtain a positive interview with Oriana. "He adores a challenge," says the government functionary who takes her to the dictator. "Everyone likes him, men and women, but especially women. Many of the women who interview him end up falling in love with him."

Oriana meets with him twice, the first time in his office and the second time in a tent in the desert. She has read his *Green Book*, concluding, "The book had only showed me that the Colonel was an idiot, and I knew that already." As usual she arrives for the meeting armed with a list of polemical questions, about his financing of the Red Brigades, his alliance with Fiat, and his friendship with

With Muammar Gaddafi in December 1979.

With Deng Xiaoping in August 1980.

Idi Amin, the dictator of Uganda. But Gaddafi eludes her by confusing everything in his answers: Vietnam and Italian colonialism, the Palestinian question and neutron bombs. "Good God. It was like being caught up in a riptide, not knowing where it was taking you," Oriana writes of the interview, which turns out like something from the theater of the absurd. She doesn't even try to follow Gaddafi's stream of consciousness and instead depicts him as a comic character. Years later she will say, "That interview was truly horrible. Gaddafi is clinically infirm, mentally ill, a crazed idiot. If I had Alekos's courage, I would have killed him at our meeting. I should have had the courage to die killing Gaddafi, but I didn't."

After her long isolation in Casole, Oriana decides to visit China. Thanks to the Italian president, Sandro Pertini, she joins an official party traveling to China in August 1980. She is full of curiosity. She wants to see everything and requests permission to look inside Mao's tomb, a request that is predictably denied. She is, however, granted a meeting with Premier Deng Xiaoping. The resulting interview also becomes famous. The writer Tiziano Terzani, in China at the time, writes to her, "At every lunch and dinner or cocktail party, everyone is talking about you, and I've become your defense lawyer; you should hear me. That interview is fantastic; it's the first time a Chinese leader has come across as a human being, not just a parrot. He is the first Chinese Communist to appear natural, who explains the challenges of being emperor of this Middle Kingdom."

As usual, she manages to ask the leader exactly the questions most normal people are interested in. She opens the interview by offering greetings for his birthday, which is the next day. "My birthday? Is it my birthday tomorrow?!" "Yes, I read it in your biography." "Humph! If you say so...I don't know. I never know when my birthday is, and, even if it is, it's hardly something to be congratulated about. It means I'm turning sixty-six. And sixty-six means decay." "My father is sixty-six, Mr. Deng, and if I tell my father that this means decay, I think he'll clock me."

She finds him simpatico, funny, charmingly hard of hearing. She eggs him on with impertinent questions: regarding the portrait of Stalin in Tiananmen Square, which she says he should remove; about the Gang of Four, who are blamed for every possible crime while Mao is held in high regard; and about the number of people who died during the Cultural Revolution. But she doesn't hide the fact that this man, who can laugh at himself, pleases her. And she knows he likes her as well. "Honestly, it may have helped not only that I was a woman but that I am a petite woman. Deng is also small; he is shorter than I am."

Finally, in the spring of 1981, she travels to Poland. She is curious to meet Lech Wałęsa, the dockworker who leads the Solidarność trade union and is creating trouble for the Soviet Union. The interview is not an easy one. Wałęsa doesn't trust this famous journalist who has torn apart men far more powerful than he is. He repeats that he is an ignorant man who has never read a book. "Why are you looking at me like that?" he complains, irritated by Oriana's inquisitive demeanor. "I'm looking at you because you resemble Stalin," she answers calmly. "How will the interview be written?" he insists, nervously. "Question and answer, question and answer, or like a narrative with your comments throughout? Because I don't like the idea of the comments at all. It's not honest, the reader should be making the comments, deciding if I'm an idiot or not." When she pushes him too much, he complains, "What's wrong is your authoritarian style: you're so dictatorial. Seeing as how I am too, we've got a problem. We need to find a modus vivendi, we need to figure out a way to proceed. Let's make a deal: From here on out I'll be nice to you, and you'll be nice to me. If not we'll beat each other's heads in, okay?"

Oriana interviews him over the course of two long meetings, about three hours each, and writes a portrait that is picturesque but, overall, quite positive. Years later, she will say to an Italian newspaper, "I didn't like Wałęsa. I understood that I was dealing with a vain, presumptuous man, a bigot imposed by the Catholic Church the way a film producer imposes a third-rate, talentless actor. I even intuited a certain air of protofascism about him; he seemed like the kind of man who, once in power, will name his horse or his driver to a senate post. But after a long internal struggle, should I say so or shouldn't I, I decided that by saying I didn't like him, I would be helping the Communists, or even Moscow. The problem is that journalism, because of its immediacy, doesn't really let us think things through."

In this period of her return to the world, the Middle East interests her the most. In June 1982, Israel invades Lebanon, driving out the Palestinian forces. Oriana decides to go and see for herself. After a long hiatus, she returns to a war zone. A colleague remembers seeing her on a bench at the airport in Pisa, waiting for her flight to Beirut. "What are you going to do in Lebanon? Are you doing a reportage?" he asks. She pulls herself up in her big jacket and shrugs. "I'm going to look," she answers. Then she closes her eyes and pretends to fall asleep, in order to avoid more questions. She hasn't been sent by a newspaper. It is her decision to go. Another Italian journalist recalls her arrival at the Hôtel Alexandre in Beirut: "A bomb had just gone off. There was shattered glass everywhere. I cut my fingers picking shards out of my singed hair. Suddenly, amid the chaos and injured, confused people, Oriana appears. 'What the hell is going on?' she asks, then complains because they've given her a room filled with broken glass. Then she declares that she wants to interview the leader of the Lebanese forces, Bachir Gemayel."

Ten years earlier, she had interviewed Palestinian fighters and written an important portrait of Golda Meir. This time, too, she wants to accomplish something that will have a lasting impact. When she realizes that she won't be able to obtain an interview with Gemayel, she turns her focus toward General Ariel Sharon, the commander of the Israeli Army. Her Italian colleague recalls, "Sharon's car arrived at the Alexandre Hôtel. Suddenly a woman appears in front of the car. I hear a bodyguard yell out, 'Crazy woman, she's crazy!' Then that familiar voice: 'I am Oriana Fallaci, you must give me an interview!' One of Sharon's companions must have read one of her books, because he whispers into Sharon's ear and the general lowers his window. He leans out and says, 'No problem, Mrs. Fallaci. Come to my office in Tel Aviv Monday morning at ten o'clock!' All the international correspondents look on in shock and Oriana glares back with a satisfied look, like the cat who ate the canary."

The interview with Sharon lasts all day. At regular intervals the general's wife brings in food, which is devoured by Sharon. Oriana prefers to stick to coffee and cigarettes. She does not tread lightly. She reminds Sharon that many people describe him as "a killer, a brute, a bulldozer, a rube, power-hungry." She attempts to demonstrate that the purge of Palestinians from Southern Lebanon was a Pyrrhic victory, or worse, since it inspired international condemnation. She points out that Jews, too, once planted bombs: "The fact is that you are using that word 'terrorist' as an insult, and rightly so. But what were you when you were fighting the Arabs and the English to found Israel?" At the end of the interview, Sharon shakes her hand and says, "I knew you had come to add another scalp to your necklace. You are hard, very hard. But I enjoyed every moment of this tempestuous conversation because you are a courageous, loyal, capable woman. No one has ever come to me as well prepared as you have. No one goes into a war zone, under the bombs, just to get an interview."

20. INSHALLAH

After the Israeli operation has come to an end in September 1982, a multinational peace force is sent in to protect the cease-fire in Lebanon and usher in a return to normalcy. Italy takes part in the mission. Oriana decides to go to Beirut to visit the Italian contingent. She is surprised by these soldiers, most of them draftees fulfilling their military service, who behave with great professionalism. In October 1983, she is devastated when two trucks full of explosives, driven by suicide bombers, destroy the barracks of the American and French forces, killing more than three hundred soldiers in their sleep. She returns immediately to Beirut and interviews Italian soldiers living under the threat of another attack.

She takes a liking to a sergeant by the name of Paolo Nespoli, who is almost half her age. He was born in 1957, and in Beirut he is in charge of the Italian journalists who come to report on the conflict. He is ordered to escort this famous Italian journalist around, making sure that nothing happens to her. Paolo Nespoli is an admirer. *Un Uomo* is one of his mother's favorite books. When he was a boy, his girlfriend in middle school gave him *If the Sun Dies* as a present, because he had a passion for space travel. During those long days in Beirut, between an interview and a visit to the Palestinian camps, Oriana and Paolo get to know each other. They talk about war, history, family, ideals, the future. Oriana is surprised that she has so much in common with a young man who could be her son.

She returns to Beirut several times, including in February 1984, when the situation in the city has become very dangerous. General Franco Angioni, the commander of the Italian contingent, remembers, "At that time the situation in Lebanon had deteriorated completely and everyone was shooting at everyone else. It was no longer possible to travel there with ordinary modes of transport. She demanded that the minister of defense make it possible for her to go." Oriana takes a military flight to Cyprus, then transfers to a frigate, and, when the coast comes into view, climbs aboard a helicopter that approaches the coast after dark, landing at a spot indicated by torches. She jumps out while the helicopter is still in motion, just before the pilot reverses course and flies off. "It took courage; not many would have done it," Angioni commented.

She had planned to stay at a hotel downtown but is stuck in East Beirut, on the Italian base. She sleeps on a cot next to the soldiers. One night the order to evacuate Beirut arrives from Rome and the retreat begins. The soldiers are loaded onto trucks and taken to the port, where ships are waiting. The last to be evacuated are the soldiers who man the command post. Paolo finds a helmet and a bulletproof vest for Oriana. Both are too big, unsurprising given Oriana's small and slender frame. He puts her in a jeep and grants her a final wish: to see, for the last time, the hospital built by the Italians, which has been ceded to the local population. When they arrive, bands of armed men are already sacking the structure and destroying whatever they are unable to take with them, as religious men burn the food stores, which they consider impure. Oriana, standing in the jeep, watches the destruction and swears. On their way out, she sees a dozen children. Instead of sticking out their hands to ask for chocolate, as they usually do, they stand at attention and salute the passing jeep. The soldiers respond to their salute as if it were an honor guard. Oriana cannot hold back her tears. As the ship leaves the port of Beirut, she stands on the bridge watching the city recede into the distance.

During the four-day journey home, she has long conversations with Paolo. They finally switch from the formal *lei* to the informal *tu* as they discuss the present and the future. Oriana asks him what he'd like to do when he grows up. He confesses that he has always dreamed of becoming an astronaut, but at the age of twenty-seven, with no knowledge of English or a degree, he knows it is too late. Oriana gets angry. She tells him that if he truly believes in his dream, he must really give it a try. When they arrive at their destination, she embraces him and promises to help.

In the following months, they see each other often. They spend some weekends together. Oriana is amazed that she can still feel something for a man. After Alekos's death, she had closed herself off in complete emotional isolation: "I had sworn that I would never touch another man. Then I met you," she writes in a letter. In the summer of 1984, when they are finally able to spend some time together, she finds herself saying things she thought she would never say again and writing poetry, which she collects in a notebook, as if speaking with the man she loves.

One of these poems describes Paolo going on a skydiving mission. Oriana stands in a field, worried at first when he is only a tiny speck in the sky falling toward the earth. She is relieved when the great sail of the parachute opens: "The little dot opened up, released a sail / wide and blue, descending slowly / coasting, spinning, trembling / carrying you toward me, and I returned to life. / Finally I heard my name, as you called me / joyfully, happily. / And a great bird, / all green, hanging from ropes / fell beside me, safe and sound, and smiled."

Paolo has strong feelings for Oriana. He isn't deterred by the years that separate them. This woman who had intimidated him at first, as she does everyone, infuses him with an enormous vitality. Her enthusiasm and her hunger for life make her seem younger than many women his age. He writes to her in a letter, "I think that this period in Italy will be useful to you, and that in solving the problems you face you will draw on your usual grit. Nothing can stop you. I think that this is the secret of your eternal youth and your stupefying lucidity."

Oriana's poems reveal a love full of great tenderness and, at the same time, infused with complete honesty. Oriana knows from the start that it is doomed to end quickly. "Will you discard it in a drawer / like an old shoe or a passport / that no longer serves a purpose? / Or will you make up a delicate excuse / to painlessly remove the blade?" From the outside, everything about them seems wrong: "The two of us, together / we are a heresy / an improbable hypothesis / an interesting phenomenon / like black holes and quantum theory. / Nothing between us makes sense, / neither age nor height nor weight. / Neither profession nor address." And yet she celebrates this relationship like a miracle: "Then, why / are the two of us / so happy and content? / Why, when we're apart / do we seek each other out and wait / impatiently to be together? / Is it because we laugh when we're together / and suffer the same torments, / because, together, we sleep / as calmly as two stones / buffed by the current, / side by side?" In her apartment she keeps a map of La Brianza and an enlarged photo of Paolo's eyes. When people ask what they are, she doesn't answer. "How can I explain to people / that I keep the map of Brianza / because you were born there, / and that your eyes are there because / they know how to look and see / beyond my tired face?" She doesn't talk about him with anyone. To her friends, Paolo is just a protégé. She tries to ignore the perplexed looks when people see them together at a restaurant or on the street, surprised by this tall young man with this tiny mature woman. "People look at us / but can't believe it. / They suspect / but, confused, conclude: no."

In April 1985, Paolo leaves the army and moves into Oriana's apartment in New York. For four years, the two of them work determinedly, side by side, on their own projects. Paolo works on his aerospace engineering degree at New York University, and Oriana is writing a new book, which will keep her busy for almost ten years. *Inshallah* is her most complex novel, an eight-hundred-page book that is a world, a kind of *Iliad* that challenges the reader with sixty-six main characters and thirty-six secondary figures, and a radical writing approach. Each soldier speaks his own language, everything from American slang for the Marines to various Italian dialects. The arc of the story covers three months beginning with the attack on the UN peacekeepers' bases, and hinges on the possible existence of a third truck destined for the Italian troops. The book is an attempt to come to terms with the "eternal massacre called war," as she says in the dedication, and she dedicates it to the men, women, old people, and children killed in Beirut.

Oriana, who has seen so much violence in her life, is deeply affected by the massacres perpetrated by the differing factions in Lebanon. "I was overwhelmed when I went to West Beirut. To see that savage destruction... savage... to smell that horrible stench of death and see the dismembered bodies of the dead," she will write in a letter. A character in her book utters this sad truth: "War accomplishes nothing, he used to say, it resolves nothing. As soon as it ends, you realize that the reasons for which it was fought have not disappeared or that new reasons have taken the place of the old: new pretexts for which another one will break out."

The book opens with an image: bands of stray dogs taking over the deserted streets. It is a symbol of the militias fighting for control of the city. She doesn't spare the reader any violence or crudeness. But there are also love stories, which flower continually in the most unlikely settings, illustrating how life refuses to stop even amid daily destruction. It is a novel about war in the fullest sense. Everyone in Beirut is armed, and you can die over nothing. Each event is sparked by another, minuscule, apparently unrelated event, in a chaotic chain reaction that escalates over time. The force of chaos is constantly at work. In order to express this, Oriana uses Boltzmann's entropy formula. At the end of the nineteenth century, the Austrian physicist had devised the equation as a way to explain entropy, or chaos, in mathematical terms, before committing suicide. Oriana is fascinated by it. In the novel, the protagonist, Sargent Angelo, a math student, is tormented by the equation, which he calls the formula of Death. He asks himself if its opposite, a formula of Life, exists.

Inshallah is in many ways a prophetic book. It shows Lebanon as a laboratory for terrorism, a toxic mix of politics and religion that will soon become explosive. Here, Islam becomes a political weapon and the Middle Eastern conflict is transformed into something new. Almost twenty years before September 11, Oriana suggests that radical Islam will expand beyond the Middle Eastern arena and confront the West in a much wider war. An Italian friend remembers her being preoccupied by the problem of the Arab world and the West: "She didn't predict the disaster in new York but already in conversations in the eighties she said, I'm telling you, here in America we underestimate the hatred that exists. Who knows how it will manifest itself…"

Having followed international conflicts for decades, she can intuit the nature of future conflicts, the new tensions that will divide the world. One of the characters in the novel says, unambiguously, "Forget the Communists and the capitalists! The next war wouldn't take place between the rich and the poor: it would break out between the Guelphs and the Ghibellines! That is, between those who eat pig meat and those who don't, those who drink wine and those who don't, those who mumble Pater Noster and those who whimper Allah rassullillah."

She involves Paolo in her research. He digs up maps, photographs, descriptions, details. In the evenings, at dinner or surrounded by the material she accumulates to create the background of her novel, they talk for hours about the characters and situations she describes. Oriana reads the pages she has written that day, seeking advice or a small gesture of approval, or simply an attentive ear. She is oppressed by the myriad stories that crowd her mind. It's almost as if everything she has learned in her life as a war reporter is clamoring inside of her to be told. She can't say no to anyone. In order to keep the characters in order, she hangs a large chalkboard in her study on which she writes every name, connecting them with arrows and comments, adding a mark when one of them dies. There is a lot of death in *Inshallah*. One of the few friends allowed to visit during that time recalls, "Sometimes I would come in the evening. She would arrive like a fury and say, 'I killed him today, I killed him!' She meant one of her characters. And after a bit she couldn't take it anymore... 'I killed him, I made him suffer...' She was happy because she had killed off one of her characters."

As always when she's working on a novel, she devotes all her time to writing. She takes a break just before Christmas 1987 to assist her father, who has been diagnosed with a tumor. She returns to Italy and stays with him for two months. She is shaken by the sight of her childhood hero reduced to a birdlike shadow of himself. "I feel like his mother. He's so tiny now, you know," she tells friend. "When I pick him up and carry him to the bathroom, it's no effort at all."

Edoardo dies in her arms. "I was desperate. I knew it was almost over. He was suffering terribly. Suddenly, I had an illumination.

I said to him, 'What a wonderful man you are, Papà, what courage you have! Bravo! Bravo!' He opened his eyes and smiled. And then he died." During the brief ceremony at the cemetery, amid flags with the emblem of Giustizia e Libertà, the National Association of Partisans, and the metalworkers' union, Oriana gives the funeral oration she has written while sitting at his bedside. Then she returns to New York and gets back to work on the novel.

Her relationship with Paolo lasts five years. It is a long period living with someone, exceptional for Oriana. Because of the age difference, she often feels herself to be in a position of weakness. And because she hates to show weakness, she reacts furiously to things that she considers betrayals, from friendships with fellow students his own age to arguments in which she feels he hasn't taken her side. Every tiny incident unleashes long acrimonious discussions, after which she refuses to speak to Paolo for days and floods him with letters full of reproaches. For the first time in her life, she feels the weight of her age: "I've always felt much younger than I was and am. And that's how I have behaved. Suddenly, now, the years weigh on me. I feel, you have made me feel, you make me feel, old."

Despite these clashes, they live together until 1990, the year in which *Inshallah* is published in Italy. As often happens with Oriana, their separation is caused by a disappointment. In 1989, the Italian space program announces a public examination to select the first Italian astronaut. Paolo decides to take part and, despite being very busy with the final phase of her novel, Oriana does everything she can to help him, putting pressure on all her connections. Paolo complains. He finds her activism excessive and perhaps even counterproductive. They fight furiously. Oriana accuses him of being naïve and argues that when he is selected he'll have to admit she was right. Paolo obtains a good score but isn't selected. It is a difficult defeat for both of them, but especially for Oriana.

After getting his degree, Paolo finds a job in an aerospace research lab in Italy, then in Germany, with the European Space Agency. When he leaves for Germany in 1991, Oriana tells him that she does not want to see or hear from him again. She keeps her promise, as she always does whenever she eliminates someone from her life.

The book is finished. Another chapter of her life has come to an end. A few years later, in her final novel, one of the main characters, a mature woman in love with a much younger man who decides to break things off cleanly, says, "He said ours had been the most beautiful love of his life. The purest, the most honest, the best. But in truth he wanted it to end today and in this manner. No love lasts forever. Every love dries up, fades." She will never speak with him again, even when, ten years later, he manages to fulfill his dream and becomes an astronaut.

21. ILDEBRANDA'S TRUNK

During the winter of 1991, while she is working on the English and French translations of *Inshallah*, she notices something strange in one of her breasts, like a pebble. She knows she should see a doctor, but she delays so as not to interrupt her work. It is only a year later, once *Inshallah* has come out in the United States, that she finally goes to the doctor. The results are incontestable: a tumor in the breast. She has to be operated on immediately.

After the surgery, she asks to see the tumor. "The doctors said, 'Come on, no one does that, it's a terrible sight.' But I insisted: 'It's mine, and I want to see it.' It was a small, white, elongated object. How I hated it. I talked to it: 'You goddamned bastard, don't even think about coming back. Did you leave offspring inside of me? I'll kill you! You won't defeat me!' The doctors couldn't believe their ears. They kept saying, 'Oh, dear.'"

Her parents had both died of tumors, as had her sister Neera when she was still young, in 1984. Oriana is sure that her turn has come and that the tumor will return. Her health has always been delicate, and she is something of a hypochondriac. A friend remembers, with a smile, the day she received a medical encyclopedia as a gift: "She read it and discovered that she suffered from every single illness. The fatal ones, of course." She has already undergone an operation on her vocal chords, compromised by her smoking, and for years she has been at war with her teeth, weakened by smoking and a series of infections that require constant care. Her datebooks are full of dentists' names; she switches dentists at a frenetic pace. A friend says of her, "Oriana was a courageous woman, but she was afraid of one thing: the dentist." Now she feels that life is beginning to close in on her. She has always had a difficult relationship with time. Even as a child she felt that there wasn't enough of it to do everything she wanted to do. Now she has the impression that it's slipping through her fingers.

She returns to New York and decides to begin the family saga she has been contemplating for a long time. "I'm ready to write the book that I've been wanting to write for at least twenty—maybe thirty—years, and which, until now I haven't written because I didn't feel ready. It's a book about my life, my childhood, my youth. I'm working on it now, the early stages. It's what I'm dedicating all my thoughts to, my energies; it is my life's purpose now. Or, I should say: it's what keeps me alive. If it weren't for this book, I wouldn't get treatment. I would let myself die like my sister Neera. I would give myself over to the cancer with resignation."

She has been thinking about this project ever since she was a little girl fascinated by her ancestor Ildebranda's wooden chest. In 1972, after the death of her uncle Bruno, this vague notion begins to take more conscious shape. His death is a blow, marking the passing of her first teacher, the man who guided her toward her dream of becoming a journalist: "They say that before closing his eyes he murmured, 'Where is Oriana?' 'In Saigon, again.' 'Good, that's where she should be.'" When she receives the telegram announcing his death, she realizes that all the witnesses to the family history will die one after another, and that if she wants to record their stories she must start soon. She keeps his diaries and begins to research the past. All this material will help her reconstruct the family tree, with its four branches: the Fallacis and the Ferrieris on her father's side, the Launaros and the Cantinis on her mother's. All four are Tuscan, with two outside grafts, one from Spain and one from Emilia-Romagna. "A terrible combination, as you can see from the temperamental results."

The novel, which will be published posthumously under the title *Un cappello pieno di ciliege*, amounts to a lengthy farewell: "A woman who feels she is close to death returns, through her memories, to her past, her childhood, even her arrival in this world. Almost as if she were trying to explain the mystery of life, why she was born and from whom, she digs around her memories searching for a past about which she knows almost nothing. She has never asked, but has retained overheard fragments, perhaps even against her will, recounted by relatives who are now dead. There's no one left to ask in order to satisfy her existential curiosity, so she attaches herself to those few fragments like a drowning man to a piece of wood after a shipwreck. She elaborates on them, builds upon them with her imagination, creating fantastical stories."

She has to do it on her own. There are no relatives left to ply for stories. "There was just a single ninety-four-year-old aunt who, when I begged her please-Auntie-please tell me, barely moved her pupils and murmured, 'Are you the postman?'" She is determined to follow each branch of the family tree as far as she can, an almost impossible attempt to recreate a lost past. She wants to tell the stories of her ancestors in detail, to investigate and reinvent them, in order to understand herself, as if a part of her lies there, in these lives that preceded her. To answer, "now that the future has been shortened," a question about herself: "Why was I born, why did I live, and what or who molded the mosaic of people who, on a long-ago summer afternoon, became me." To her, the idea of finding the answer to the mystery of life through the idea of God is an expedient she "has never understood and will never accept." She can only look toward the past, to the memory of her ancestors in the years before she was born. As she writes in a letter, it is "a search that reveals that in all my lives, life has been chaos and torment. My family is filled with farmers, sailors, riffraff, and impoverished folk, but also aristocrats, to whom I owe my arrogance."

Painstaking as always, she seeks to reconstruct every detail of the periods in which her ancestors lived. She accumulates boxes of notes and materials on the most disparate topics: the salaries of stone carvers in 1880, the trials of the Waldenses in Piedmont, the history of Livorno, steamboats, the telegraph, nineteenth-century stamps, air balloons, Polish exiles, Singer sewing machines. She contacts the Museum of the Risorgimento in Turin, the Gabinetto Vieusseux in Florence, Lloyd's of London, *National Geographic*, the Italian Naval History Office in Rome, parish and public records. No stone is left unturned. Her papers contain mountains of notes about rural Tuscan life, plants that attract lightning and those that repel it, animals whose behavior changes before storms, popular beliefs. There is a two-page list of proverbs relating to weather. The novel is an enormous open construction site. Oriana carries the manuscript with her in a bag that never leaves her side.

In 1994, she writes a letter to a British historian with whom she has been in contact in the course of her research: "At this moment I am completely immersed in the first part of the book, which begins at the end of the 1700s and ends, with some lacunae, in 1944. Imagine, I've reached the point when the French Revolution is about to erupt. In America, George Washington is angling to become president; Marie Antoinette's head is still attached to her shoulders; Robespierre's too; and Napoleon is a young man. I'm surrounded by wigs and three-cornered hats. The Resistance is still far off into the future. At the beginning, in my frenzied search for information and facts, I mixed everything together: 1700s, 1800s, 1900s. But at a certain point I realized it was mad, or rather stupid. I stopped looking at anything after 1900 and decided to concentrate, in a more logical fashion, on the period I'm currently working on." She asks him about the Resistance, which she hopes to get to within a year. In fact, six years later, in 2001, she will not yet have finished the section on the 1900s. "I'm a slow, wordy, uncontainable writer. And this is the most difficult book I have ever written, because it is based on historic events and precise research. There is no room for vagueness or errors."

Now that both her parents are gone, she returns less frequently to Italy. To travel to Casole from New York, she must take a transatlantic flight and then hire a car to drive her from the Rome or Milan airport to the Tuscan hills. Relations with her sister Paola are often tense, marked by long silences and periods when they refuse to see each other. Her adoptive sister, Elisabetta, now an adult, has cut off all contact with the family. "One has to resign oneself to one's own destiny. Mine is to live, in monstrous solitude, this final chapter of an existence that only the superficial and the ill-informed can describe as charmed," she writes to her nephew Edoardo, Paola's eldest, whom she sees regularly.

She is glad that he visits her every time he is in New York for work, and she is enchanted by his wife, a beautiful girl from Puglia who wants to raise a large family, filled with children. As a wedding gift, Oriana sends him a tape on which she has recorded herself reciting the Song of Songs; she sends gifts marking the birth of each child, usually made with her own hands. Strange antique-looking embroidery, purses sewn out of vintage fabric. She has always had a passion for embroidery, lace, tassels, exotic textiles. It is the old-fashioned side of her nature, which exists alongside her extraordinarily modern side, often ahead of her time.

Her arguments with Paola usually stem from disagreements about the maintenance of Casole, which requires constant repairs.

Since the death of their parents, Paola has been in charge of the property. Oriana seldom visits, but she is closely involved with every change and every repair. No one dares make a move without consulting her. "We won't proceed without your approval," is the formula Paola uses in her letters, which are often long lists of projects and expenses, repairs to the well, pipes damaged by frost, mold on the walls, rotting doors and gates, termites in the wooden beams. Oriana knows that the maintenance is endless, but she wants the place to stay the same. She wants to be able to show up, without warning, open the gate, and have the dogs run to meet her, barking, and the cats raise their tails, intrigued.

In a family where everyone has been poor for generations, she has been the person who earned the most, from the time she was a young woman. This has affected, and sometimes profoundly deformed, her relationships. Since the 1950s, various relatives have asked her for money, even old unmarried aunts, and she, generous by nature, has always obliged. She arranges for a part of her income to be paid directly to her parents. She sends extravagant gifts to her sisters. When the mood hits, she can give an apartment, a fur coat, a car. She hates to think about money and doesn't know how to manage what she has. She doesn't even keep track of the royalties from her books. "I hate money," she says. "Nothing disgusts me more than those lurid scraps of paper. When I have money, it burns my hand; I have to give it away and so I spend it on the silliest, most useless things. And then I need more. That's why I work." When asked about her lifestyle by an American journalist in the 1960s, she answers, impatiently, "I live like a millionaire. Why not? The hell with it."

She spends most of her time in her New York home, working on her family saga. It matters to her because she knows it will be her last book. She fears that she will die before finishing it, extinguished by her illness. "I'm afraid that one day they'll break the door down and find me dried up or mummified, like that woman in Varese; it took them seven years to notice she was dead," she writes to her nephew Edoardo. She spends far more time with her ancestors, as they come to life in her book, than with friends. Her house is filled with notes and material. She has brought all the family photos to New York. "It's bizarre: I'm a modern woman, of that there is no doubt. I've always done everything before others did. But I live in the past." The book brings together everything that has preceded and justified her existence, almost a compensation for a life of great professional success with an equal portion of private unhappiness. In a letter written shortly before her death, she says of her life, "Unhappy, yes. Lacking in love, in tenderness, in affection. And, in short, in family. My book is a desperate quest for family."

When she finishes a section, she reads it out loud to herself, in order to listen to its internal music. She does this with all her books. She is obsessed with the notion of musicality; she wants her style to be fluid. "Hemingway used to say that a well-written page is like a snowy field without potholes, stones, or barriers; you can ski or skate on it smoothly without losing your balance or stumbling." Each sentence must be in harmony with the next, as in a musical score: "The written word isn't silent! It's a voice. When I write, I'm not silent. I murmur the words to myself, I dictate and recite them and create a sound track that echoes the tone of the story and the dialogues."

In 1993, when the first audiobooks come out in Italy, she interrupts her work on the book in order to record *Letter to a Child Never Born*. Several famous actresses ask for permission to perform it onstage, but it comes to nothing. Nor, despite many proposals from Hollywood, are any film adaptations made. Oriana turns down all requests, even from the most prestigious directors. Her lawyers block three movie projects based on her life. "Let them do it when I'm dead," she says. She is convinced that no one can perform her words without betraying them.

She does all the work on the audiobook herself — records the text, chooses the music, edits the montage — over the course of a long summer, buried in a sound studio from morning to night with a technician. "My voice is on the low side; it's a throaty voice, and in the morning I was always hoarse. I would arrive at the studio hoarse. 'It won't work! We can't proceed! You have to warm up your voice!' the technician would insist. So I would read for an hour or two without recording. Then, when the time came to record I was already tired. The fatigue would put me in a bad mood and…I cursed a lot!" The process is exhausting, but it makes her happy. This book that is so dear to her, built out of her own internal monologue, has acquired an almost physical concreteness thanks to her voice.

At the beginning and at the end, she plays a recording of her favorite piece of music, "Greensleeves." "We all have a melody that touches our hearts and our minds more than any other. For me, it's 'Greensleeves.' I know nothing, nothing is known, about 'Greensleeves.' Neither who wrote it, nor when, nor where. Some think it's an Irish lullaby. To me it sounds like a medieval troubadour song. A love song composed at the court of King Arthur. Its sweetness and melancholy touch me so deeply that I often say, 'When I die, don't bother with a funeral. Dump me under an olive tree, that's fine with me. But if, while you're dumping me there, you play "Greensleeves," I would be very grateful.'"

She doesn't mind aging, and she's not obsessed with her physical appearance. "My wrinkles are my medals. I've earned them," she likes to say. "Aging is beautiful. As we get older, we acquire a freedom we lack when we're young. A complete freedom." But she knows she has little time to complete her novel. After she finishes recording the audiobook, she returns to New York and submerges herself again in the project.

As usual, when she writes, nothing else exists: "I start early in the morning and continue until six or seven without interruptions, without eating or resting. I smoke more than usual, which usually means about fifty cigarettes a day. I sleep poorly. I don't see anyone. I don't answer the phone. I don't go out. I ignore Sundays, holidays, Christmas, New Years."

Her mind returns constantly to her parents, the only people she feels have never betrayed her. "It seems that we all need full, complete relationships with someone. I had this in the family composed by my mother and father, who didn't constrain or enslave me like a husband. They let me come and go, escape." Her relationship with her father has been conflicted because of their difficult personalities. But the connection with her mother has been visceral and cloudless. "My father was a war hero, but in peaceful times he was just a man. But my mother was an extraordinary human being."

Tosca was gentle by nature, and in a family where people were endlessly fighting, she was the peacemaker. She had been a beautiful woman, taller than her husband; she had stopped wearing heels when she married him, a detail Oriana loves to repeat, with a smile. Her whole life, Oriana will venerate her mother. In 1973, when she becomes famous, she says in an interview by an American newspaper, "I find it intolerable that a woman like my mother — a great mind unable to fulfill her potential — spent her life as a housewife. She dreamed of studying astronomy and traveling." At every stage of her career, the idea of this brilliant woman held back by her condition as a woman returns, insistently. Tosca is the reverse image she confronts at every step: "Don't tell me, 'Oriana, you're so good at what you do,' she interjects in an interview. I do my job, and I do it well. We should always work well, every day. My mother is a fantastic cook, but *Time* doesn't put her on the cover because she has prepared a fantastic roast."

Throughout her career, she always finds a way to place a call, even from the most difficult locations, to hear Tosca yelling into the phone with her limpid voice: "Ciao! Where are you?" And she has always written long letters full of anecdotes, which her mother reads out loud to the others. Tosca writes less often, and her letters have the habit of chasing Oriana across the planet: "Here I am, pointlessly writing to you for the fourth time. I write to you in Saigon, and you're in India. I write to you in India and you're in Saigon."

Like all mothers, she begs her daughter to look after herself: "I hope you're well and that you're not in danger, considering you do nothing to avoid it." Oriana's correspondence with Tosca reveals her fragile side, a side that others don't see. Oriana admits that she's exhausted, her nerves on edge. She describes her periods of depression, when she can barely get out of bed. Her insomnia, migraines, fevers, terrible toothaches. Tosca's exhortations to smoke less and eat more go unheeded. Oriana forges ahead, cursing her situation but unwilling to change her way of life.

At times, even her relationship with her mother has weighed on her. Especially in the 1960s, when her work is at its zenith and she is becoming a global star. "Don't worry. It makes me unhappy, you know, to see you sad when I leave," she writes. "It would be so much easier for me if you could understand that this is my life and I can't live any other way, or stay in the same place. I would go crazy." Casole is the constant reference point on her world map; Oriana stays there whenever she goes to Italy, despite the complicated logistics. "If I manage to return to Vietnam, I'll stop in Europe on my way back," she writes. "If I go to China, I have to stop in Warsaw, so I'll be in Europe. If I don't go to either place, in two months I'll be back in Europe. So, as you can see...And of course I can't completely abandon America, or else everything I've built here will collapse."

Like her other books, the family saga is a dialogue with someone who is no longer present. In *Penelope at War*, she writes of her romantic dream with Alfredo. In *Letter to a Child Never Born*, she speaks of the children she has lost. In *A Man*, she speaks of Alekos, a man killed by those in power. *Inshallah* is about Paolo, who leaves her in order to live his own life. Edoardo and Tosca — rarely named but central to the project — lie at the heart of this book. "I was exhuming, in equal measure, the sounds and images of my parents, who for years had lain beneath a fragrant flower bed. Not in their old age, when they had become almost my children, so that when I lifted my father to place him in a chair he seemed light and small and defenseless, and when I saw his sweet, bald head resting on my neck, I felt like I was holding an octogenarian child. As young people. Back when they picked me up and held me in their arms. Strong, beautiful, brash."

She writes about their ancestors, through two centuries of adventures, using her signature formula: a novel that reinvents the past, retelling actual events. The Fallacis, ancestors of her grandfather Antonio, are sharecroppers from Chianti, hard workers, devoted Catholics. She writes at length about Carlo Fallaci and his wife Caterina Zani, whom she admires immensely. Caterina is an indomitable redheaded beauty who rides horses and swears as a way to show her contempt for the Church, which burned her great-grandmother — Ildebranda of the wooden chest — at the stake.

On the other side of the paternal line, there are the Ferrieris. She admires Anastasia, an adventurous beauty who, as an adolescent, becomes the lover of a nobleman from Turin, with whom she will have a daughter, Grandmother Giacoma. In the family, this mysterious forebear is referred to as "L'innominato," or "the unnamed."

There are rumors that he was a great man, even the king himself. Giacoma reveals his name on her deathbed but makes Oriana solemnly swear that she will never reveal it. Oriana keeps her promise. Even in the book, he is referred to only as "L'innominato." She likes to say, with a smile, that she has a photograph of this man at home and that sometimes she pulls it out and talks to him.

The maternal line, too, is full of twists and turns. Here lie the fortunes of the Cantini, poor laborers constantly at war with the powers that be, and the Launaros, sailors and adventurers. Oriana is particularly struck by Francesco Launaro, a quarrelsome sailor, and his wife Montserrat Grimaldi, the illegitimate daughter of a Spanish nobleman who ends her days in an asylum, moved to madness by the death of her four children in a shipwreck. "I sensed that unhappy, unlucky and unhappy couple inside of me like a weight, an unwanted guest. Each time something goes wrong I think, just like Montserrat, just like Francesco. Their story frightens me." She is convinced that they are the source of the family's predisposition to cancer, which has affected so many of her relatives. According to this theory, it is Montserrat, the Catalan ancestor, who carries the illness, or *mal dolent*, as they call it in her language, in her genes.

Oriana's plan is to proceed from the eighteenth century to the Second World War and conclude with her childhood, in 1944, under the bombs: "The final scene will be a great fire, with the family home enveloped in flames." But the novel ends in 1889, the year of the marriage between Oriana's grandparents, Antonio Fallaci and Giacoma.

22. THE GREAT SILENCE

In the 1990s, Oriana rarely leaves New York. She's working on the novel, and when she is writing she doesn't like distractions. She is in her sixties and, convinced that the tumor will return soon, can't abide the idea of wasting time. She loves to be alone. For her it is the only condition that allows her to work. "I have a degree from the Sorbonne in solitude," she once told a journalist. "I love solitude. I'm never bored when I'm alone. It's when I'm with people that I often feel bored."

She spends most of her time in her four-story town house on East Sixty-first Street. She's proud of this home, which she bought with the royalties from her books. Using an old Tuscan phrase, she likes to say, "It cost me as much as the Serchio cost the Lucchesi," in other words, an arm and a leg. The house is filled with books, for which Oriana has an absolute, almost physical love. She is especially fond of antique books and collects early editions of Shakespeare's plays, as well as Latin and Greek literature and the works of philosophers like Voltaire. In every city she visits regularly, she frequents certain antiquarian bookstores, whose owners know her well. She spends hours riffling through the stacks, excited by every new discovery. "I can't get used to a room without books. When I'm in a room without books I feel as if the room were bare. There are no rooms without books in my house, neither in Florence nor in New York. There are books in the kitchen, in the hallways, in the living room — it goes without saying — and in the bedroom, where there are shelves all the way up to the ceiling. When I fall asleep and when I wake up I see them, just as I did when I was a little girl. I love them as objects too. I like to look at them, touch them, leaf through them. And I can never throw them away."

Over the years she has filled the house with furniture brought over from Italy and objects collected on her travels. They accumulate in a joyful mess in rooms full to bursting. The walls are hung with Asian prints and paintings of every kind: "I'm mad for paintings. I'll spend a fortune, sometimes, on a painting. I have everything from Russian icons to Haitian primitive paintings," she writes in a letter. And she loves antique furnishings, Fabergé eggs, colored-glass lamps, military maps. There is a phone on every floor, though few people have her direct number. People who seek her out must go through her secretary at the Rizzoli offices in New York, who is under instructions to say, "Oriana is away, in China." She sticks colored Post-its all over the place, on the pages of her manuscripts, on knickknacks, and on the walls. Often, she attaches one to the doorbell; it says "Go Away."

Her difficult nature worsens. Sometimes she slips into paranoia. She gets into constant arguments. With the other diners at her local restaurant, who talk too loudly at the next table. With her neighbors, who leave trash on the sidewalk. With chauffeurs who listen to the radio as they wait for their rides. Sometimes she goes out into the street to yell at them. She regularly quarrels with her Italian editor and also, often, with her foreign editors. The secretaries who deal with her at Rizzoli in New York change frequently, fired after she makes wild accusations. And the Italian editors who work with her on her books are dismissed one after the other; some of them continue working with her via email, under false names.

When the editor in chief of the *Corriere della Sera* asks her for an article, she snaps at him: "You're all the same, you all want the same thing, I know you." She doesn't want to write for newspapers anymore; she considers herself a writer of books and nothing else. The great family saga is her last project, and in her eyes it deserves her full engagement, even at the cost of denying herself rest. Once, she said, "Writing steals from life. When I write, I go to bed with the book. We sleep together, and I dream about it. And in the dream I can see the letters on the typewriter, the chapter I'm working on, the dialogue or the passage that didn't turn out as I wanted. I'm not crazy or a masochist, so after every book I swear: 'This is the last one. I won't write any more.' Then I fall into a slumber that lasts three, four, five years. Deaf to my editors and readers who keep asking, When will you write another book? I sit still, like a turtle hibernating in winter under the snow. But one day the snow begins to melt and winter comes to an end. It always happens. Then I wake up and, forgetting my oath, I let myself be swept away by the madness, and I write another book."

She still writes on an Olivetti typewriter, despite the advent of the computer. She loves the physical sensation of typing: "Porters have calluses on the palms of their hands and I have them on the tips of my fingers. And I like them. Nice and hard. If I cut myself there, I don't feel it." She needs to hear the sound of her fingers pounding on the keys, which are worn with use. She rests her cigarette on the edge of the typewriter, leaving burn marks. She has never used a different model, though with time it has become more and more difficult to find ribbons and get repairs. A friend remembers, "One night she calls me, devastated. 'An idiot, a cretin came to the house... He wasn't able to fix the typewriter. What will I do now? I'm done for. I'll never get used to a different typewriter.' Luckily I owned the same typewriter. 'You're a genius. You've fixed everything. God bless you...' The next morning, very early, I bring her the typewriter, and then come home. Half an hour later, she's on the phone again. Her voice is somber: 'Your typewriter's keys aren't indented like mine. I almost cried. You have to understand, I'm not used to it. I won't be able to write anymore...' That time I was tough with her. 'Get used to it!'"

When she goes out, she hides her face behind dark glasses and big hats. She wants to be left alone and regrets having once been in the spotlight. "A writer should never reveal himself to his readers. He should hide, not let himself be seen close up. The problem is that I realized this too late, once people started recognizing me in the street. They would stop me, and this made me very anxious. It was my punishment for allowing my photo to be published on the cover of my books. If I could go back, I wouldn't allow it." She has a conflicted relationship with success. She appreciates the fact that it allows her to reach so many people, but she also feels imprisoned by it: "I never sought out success. It was success that sought me out."

For years, she has refused to read her mail; she receives too much. "You have no idea how many hundreds of letters I receive," she tells an American journalist in 1979. "I can't even open them, and I don't read them. A friend said, 'Okay, I'll read them for you.' But soon she gave up, saying, 'I can't keep up, there are too many.'" Over the years she receives letters from all over the world: readers who love her books, committees seeking her support for their causes, institutions and universities inviting her to speak.

Her papers include a letter from an American university inviting her to give a lecture. She responds by apologizing because two and a half years have passed since the invitation. Nor does she immediately answer Howard Gotlieb when he proposes a scholarship in her name at Boston University. But this time the reason is different: "I thought he was pulling my leg so I didn't answer his letter. Then he wrote me again, asking whether I'd received his first letter. I called him and asked if he really meant what I thought he meant, that he wanted to create an Oriana Fallaci Collection. He said yes, yes. I was embarrassed." The same thing happens with a letter from Columbia College in Chicago, informing her that the college would like to give her an honorary degree. At the time, she is writing *A Man*; months pass before she reads the letter. "I was cooking dinner. I like to cook, it relaxes me. This letter came from Columbia and I opened it, distractedly. I looked out the window and called out to my father who was pruning his roses in the garden. I told him, 'Listen, Dad. They want to give me a degree in the States, with a cap and gown and everything.' My father looked up and said, 'Good for them,' and kept on trimming the roses."

She's always surprised by the affection shown to her by her readers. All kinds of people write to her from every part of the world. Children in elementary school, adolescents who want to get in touch with the astronauts, young people worried about being drafted to Vietnam, a woman who sends the name of a clinic where they might be able to help her carry a child to term. "It's a strange phenomenon for a writer like me, who writes books that are neither easy nor entertaining, to be popular around the world. My books are never light and they're never easy. Never amusing. I'm mortally serious and I always talk about mortally serious, even tragic subjects."

Every so often she opens a letter, and if she is struck by something, she even takes the time to answer. A Danish couple that names it newborn daughter after her receives a note addressed to the child: "I hope you have a good life, Oriana. A full, honest, useful, courageous life. And if possible a happy one. Never, never be frightened by the obstacles and pain it will present you with." A group of Italian university students receive a long reply. Oriana explains the reasons behind this exception: "The chance of having opened it. The fact that I had 45 minutes of free time, the hope to do something useful, and the fact that you made me smile. I smiled when I read that you wouldn't have been able to scrounge the money for a phone call, and that your savings amount to barely enough to buy a pizza." She has a soft spot for young people. When her foreign publishers insist on organizing promotional book tours, she accepts only if they include events for students: "I like going to universities when I'm on tour; I like talking to young people. They matter."

She does, however, carefully read the reviews of all her books, even though she has a difficult relationship with critics. She believes that they're lazy and often don't get beyond the first pages of a book, and that they're envious, because many of them would like to be writers themselves. For her, the true critic is the public, who has always bought her books and shown its appreciation. "A writer without readers is a like a voice speaking into the void, into silence, like a spring where no one goes to quench his thirst. As lonely as the last fish in the sea. Whenever I see someone holding one of my books, I want to go up to him and do what my uncle Bruno used to do when he was the editor in chief of one of the most important Italian weeklies. In order to gauge how well a certain issue was doing, he would linger by the newsstand for a few minutes. As soon as someone bought a copy, he would tip his hat, bow, and say, 'Thank you sir, thank you madam.'"

She is one of the most popular Italian writers of the twentieth century. Stories pour out of her with the potency of fruit and flowers in nature. One of her admirers, the American author Janet Flanner, writes, "You belong to the category of natural creators, with the same kind of creativity a fruit-bearing tree has." Every element of her life passes through the filter of her imagination and becomes a novel. "What I know is that I see literature everywhere. When I eat and when I do an interview. It's a bit like pantheism."

She writes not for intellectuals, a category she often speaks of with contempt, but for the general public. When, in 1969, a critic asks her whom she is addressing with her books and articles, she responds, "Romeo, a farmworker on my property and a man of refined intellect, infinite curiosity, and complete ignorance." When she thinks of her audience, she thinks of a seamstress, a housekeeper, a builder, a housepainter. "I detest difficult words, complicated and impenetrable. I learned to detest them from my mother, who was a highly intelligent but not highly educated woman, because she hadn't gone to school. My mother used to always say, Write simply, please! I want to understand as well!"

Her books descend directly from the writings of Curzio Malaparte, whom she knew as a young girl thanks to her uncle Bruno. "Malaparte would take me for walks in the Tuscan countryside and, like an oracle who studies the patterns of birds in flight, he would predict a glorious future for me. 'You're like me, Oriana!' he would say, using the formal *lei*. 'One day you will have tremendous success. But not in Italy, abroad. In Italy they will hate you as they hate me.' 'Why, Malaparte?' 'Because in Italy, in order to be accepted, you have to be dead and buried beneath the cypress trees.'" Like him, she writes in an aggressive style that is never neutral, and like him, she describes violence and death in the crudest terms. "When I write, I too try to do violence to the reader, to oblige him to read me. I do this by surprising him, scandalizing him, irritating him, seducing him. It's a tiring process, but, in the end, so entertaining." Yet the Italian writers she admires most are Italo Calvino and Natalia Ginzburg, whose writing could not be more different from her own.

Her style is extremely natural, like a conversation. "I write as if I were composing a letter to my mother or the man I love," she explains. But if one looks at the preparatory materials, one sees that the extremely smooth language is actually the result of an enormous amount of hard work. She writes and rewrites, throwing out hundreds of pages and even entire versions of a book, until she is satisfied with the result. "I'm a perfectionist. Obsessed with precision. I'm always afraid of making a mistake; I'm never satisfied with what I write." She considers and measures every word, every line, obsessed by the rhythm of the text: "It is possible to write prose that is as musical as poetry, with a rhythm that respects meter, the way poetry does. There is no clear line between poetry and prose; free verse and prose are almost interchangeable." She considers every translation to be a betrayal because the rhythm of her Italian is lost in the process. She torments her foreign editors.

When a book is translated into a language she speaks — English, French, Spanish — the editing process becomes a protracted drama, in which she fights for something impossible: a text that exactly reproduces the original. She insists that everything be preserved, even the punctuation and the line breaks. It doesn't worry her if this creates awkwardness in the language her words are being translated into.

Many years later, the American editor Jonathan Burnham describes a trip he made to Italy in order to convince her to approve the translation of one of her novels. It had been finalized, but she was still contesting it. "Oriana insisted that I travel to Italy and go over the translation with her, page by page. I went to Florence. I would arrive at her apartment at nine and we would begin right away, without even a hello, and continue until six o'clock in the evening. There was no food, nothing to drink, just coffee and water. I remember that on the first day we worked on the first line for about twenty minutes. I was shocked. Only then did I realize that she wanted her own English, 'Fallaci English,' and it would be difficult to change her mind."

As her fame increases, her relations with editors, and especially her Italian publisher, Rizzoli, become more difficult. When she is working on a book, she's terrified of leaks. Often, she sends her manuscripts under a false title and pseudonym, in order to divert attention. To an editor to whom she has just sent a manuscript, she writes, "No one must see this text, other than the typesetter and the editor. That 'no one' includes close relatives. The fact that a text arrives at a publishing house does not authorize strangers to read it, no matter who they are. And that includes the pope." She personally oversees each detail, from the typeface to the cover. She does not accept any changes. Again to the same editor, she writes, "Don't ever, I mean ever, change the chapter breaks. They are my obsession, and I check them ferociously, even in translations. They are where they should be. Not one more, not one less. They are as sacred as the Holy Father."

Every tiny disagreement irritates her, inspiring one of her legendary rages. A few friends are still welcome in her home, but they must be willing to accept her brusque manner. One of them remembers her at dinner, screaming as she cuts the leaves of lettuce in his salad, which he finds too large: "You're such a spoiled asshole, how can your wife stand you?" On the other hand, the political scientist Giovanni Sartori, who had met her in his youth and saw her in those final years, remembers long and delicious dinners: "She was an excellent cook, and when she was calm, the conversation in her home was extraordinary." Oriana loves to cook for her friends; she's especially famous for her fry-ups, which are extremely light. She likes to say that even a shoe is good if it is fried.

Sartori is the one who convinces her to see a doctor at Memorial Sloan Kettering Cancer Center in New York. After she stops going to the oncologist who operated on her in Italy in 1992, Oriana refuses to see a doctor, even though it's obvious from various symptoms that the cancer has metastasized. Monica Fornier, an Italian oncologist at Sloan Kettering, remembers her well: "She did radiotherapy and chemotherapy, but in reality she hardly ever came in, because she didn't feel like it, because she found it tiresome, because she didn't want to go out. Often, we would go to her. She would only accept certain treatments, only the least toxic ones. There were a lot of things she wouldn't do because of the side effects." She remembers that the thing that bothered Oriana the most was that the illness had spread to her eyes, which made it difficult to work. "She refused the idea of being constantly medicated and under treatment. She would say that when a person is in treatment, she is chained to the hospital, to doctors' visits, to tests. Existence is reduced to a 'so-called life.'"

Oriana does not conceal the fact that she has cancer. In 1992, at the time of the first diagnosis, she mentions it in an interview with the *Washington Post*. A year later she mentions it on Italian television. She can't stand the silence that often surrounds the illness in Italy. "I don't understand this shame, this aversion that surrounds the word 'cancer.' It's not an infection or a contagious disease. People should do as they do here in America. We have to say the word. Serenely, openly, without feeling intimidated. I have cancer. We should say it, just as if it were hepatitis, pneumonia, a broken leg. That's what I did. I say it, and by saying it I feel as if I were exorcising it." Like everything in her life, the illness becomes a battle: "My relationship with cancer is a war; it is a face-off between two enemies who are trying to destroy each other, as in a war. He wants to kill me and I want to kill him. I say 'him' because I'm incapable of speaking of the disease as if it were an abstract entity. To me, he is alive, an animal from another planet, an alien who has invaded my body in order to destroy it."

While she speaks about her tumor in that television interview, she lights one cigarette after another. Now that the cancer is full-blown, she has no reason to stop smoking, she says. And she is convinced that if the disease spreads to her lungs, it will not be

A close-up of Oriana taken during the final years of her life.

because of her smoking but because of the black cloud she inhaled in Kuwait, along with the U.S. Army, as the retreating Iraqi armies set the oil fields alight.

In 1991, when international forces, led by the Americans, invade the Persian Gulf, she returns one last time to the front. She wants to see war in a time of mass communication. The American command regulates every movement by accredited journalists, and her experience is very different from that in previous wars: "For someone like me, who has been a war reporter most of her life, it's disheartening, mortifying, and unpleasant. They don't want people to see the dead bodies. In Vietnam, we saw too much. We saw too many corpses and we revealed too much, in words and images."

The illness is one of the reasons for the solitude she experiences in her last years. "I worry about making appointments because I don't know if I'll be well enough; I can never predict how I'll feel," she writes in a letter. She lives alone in New York. She doesn't even want a cleaning lady, though many friends try to convince her to get one. Not even someone highly trusted, or who doesn't speak English or Italian, in order to protect the secrecy of her work. She hates to be seen in this state, weakened by the disease. One day an Italian journalist manages to convince her to receive him. He brings a young colleague with him. She remembers her surprise at seeing Oriana so diminished by the disease: "The lock turned twice and a tiny woman emerged, wearing a knee-length skirt, a blue sweater, and flesh-colored hose. I was struck by her tiny feet, in felt slippers. It reminded me of the Tuscan countryside, where you see little old women in the medieval towns, sitting on their doorsteps. She pointed at me and said, 'If you tell anyone that you were here, I'll have your head cut off.'"

23. THE RAGE AND THE PRIDE

On the morning of September 11, 2001, Oriana is at home in New York. As on every other day, she's working on her book. Suddenly, something alarms her. A strange silence, as if time had stopped. She turns on the TV. The sound is off, but the images speak for themselves. One of the Twin Towers is burning after being hit by an airplane. While the reporter interviews a witness, a second airplane flies into the other tower.

The whole country is in shock. Terrorism has hit the United States, and in the most spectacular way possible. Two planes have destroyed two skyscrapers, symbols of the New York skyline, a third has crashed into a wing of the Pentagon, and a fourth, which had been headed for the Capitol, crashes in a field after the passengers overcome the hijackers. Al Qaeda has hit the United States in an unprecedented attack, and Oriana is there, just a few miles from the attack in New York. She calls up a policeman who is a friend of hers because she wants to see what's happening: "She asked me to take her downtown, she wanted to enter the perimeter of the World Trade Center, which was closed to traffic, to be close. I tried to get her a permit; I said she was a writer and a war correspondent, but it wasn't possible."

Since she can't go to the site itself, she watches footage of the burning towers incessantly on TV. She is spellbound by the images of people throwing themselves from the skyscrapers in order to escape the flames, falling for hundreds of feet. "God almighty, I thought I'd seen everything in war. I thought I was vaccinated, and for the most part I am. Nothing surprises me. Not even when I get angry, not even when I feel contempt. But in war I always saw people killed by other people. I've never seen people kill themselves, throw themselves without a parachute from windows on the eightieth, ninetieth, one hundredth floor."

Many people call to see if she's all right. Those who don't manage to speak to her send telegrams. She answers everyone, in order to reassure them, but doesn't want visitors. She is too upset to speak. She writes to a French friend, "Even despite the horrors I've seen in war, I'm distraught. And furious. The city is a graveyard. Instead of the infernal noise of the city, there is a glacial silence. Like a cemetery. Everything is still. The bridges, the tunnels, the offices. Only the hospitals are open. And the funeral parlors." She feels the wounds upon this frenetic, vertical city, her home of half a century, celebrated in her 1962 book *Penelope at War*, as if they were her own. In that novel, with a kind of foresight, she almost prefigures the attack. The protagonist goes up to the top of the Empire State Building at night with the man she loves and points at something on the ground. "You see that terrace below us? Once, it was hit by a plane." "O no! And it didn't break?" "No, the airplane broke."

She paces around the house for days, unable to do anything else. She knows she should get back to work on her book. She's ill, doesn't have much time left, and knows that she'll never finish it if she lets this interruption distract her. Finally, unable to calm down, she does something unlike her: She calls Ferruccio de Bortoli, the editor in chief of the *Corriere della Sera*. After listening to her rant on the phone, he makes a proposal: "Why don't we do an interview? What do you say?" Oriana accepts the offer, as long as he is the interviewer.

Ferruccio de Bortoli takes one of the first flights to New York after the United States reopens its airspace. He arrives at Fallaci's home on September 15. He doesn't even have to do the interview because Oriana has already done it, writing both the questions and the answers while she waited for him to arrive. When he suggests publishing it as an editorial, Oriana accepts but asks a lot of questions. How much space will she have? Will it be on the front page? What photos will he use? She chooses a portrait with the Twin Towers behind her. She comes up with the title as well: "The Rage and the Pride."

The article is published on September 29 as a four-page insert in the *Corriere della Sera*, and in Italy its effect on public opinion is like a second explosion. The tone is passionate, as always, but solemn, almost like a sermon. The subject is the attack on New York, but even more, she accuses Europe of cowardice in the face of radical Islam. Oriana praises the American public's capacity to come together in adversity, as well as its patriotism, a sentiment she doesn't see in the people of Italy. The article ends with these words: "I have said what I had to say. My rage and my pride ordered me to do so. My clean conscience and my age permitted me to obey that order, that duty. But now the duty is fulfilled. Thus, stop. Enough. Stop."

She plans to return to her novel, but in reality this is only the beginning. The waves caused by this article set in motion a mechanism that will overtake the final years of her life. The newspaper edition sells out in a few hours. Over the following days, many opinion writers write responses in the *Corriere della Sera* and other Italian newspapers, creating a fierce debate. Soon the polemic spreads abroad.

Three months later, Oriana republishes the text in a book. The volume, which has the same title as the article, includes sections cut by the newspaper for space. The book is an immediate success and sells seven hundred thousand copies in Italy in its first two weeks. Ultimately the number will reach almost a million. The book is translated into sixteen languages. Each time, Oriana revises the translation, sometimes adding things. She involves herself personally in every aspect.

Some accuse her of inciting racial and religious hatred, which only encourages her to intervene again. Many years earlier she had written to a foreign colleague, "To me, being a journalist means being disobedient. And being disobedient means being in opposition. In order to be in opposition, you have to tell the truth. And the truth is always the opposite of what people say." The threats she receives from radical Islamist sites encourage her to continue saying what she thinks, without being intimidated. Years earlier, an interviewer had asked what qualities she had brought to her profession. "First of all, I hope I brought courage, because courage is one of my few virtues, and this is something no one can deny. I'm obsessed with courage, physical and moral."

Dragged into this polemic, she writes two more books, both published in 2004: *Oriana Fallaci intervista sé stessa: L'Apocalisse* (Oriana Fallaci interviews herself: The Apocalypse) and *The Force of Reason*, focused on the history of Islamic pressures on Europe. With *The Rage and the Pride*, they form a trilogy. She writes for the people of Europe, in order to shake them and spur them to defend their identity and values, like a medieval sermonizer. She prefers a different comparison. She compares her editorial with a speech given by the exiled Italian historian Gaetano Salvemini in New York in 1933, warning the United States of the danger represented by Hitler and Mussolini. The speech, organized by a meeting of the antifascist party Giustizia e Libertà, took place on May 7 at the Irving Plaza Hotel. A framed poster of the event hangs on the wall of Oriana's living room.

The polemic occupies her full time; her desk is covered in new books. She studies the history of relations between Islam and Europe with the same intensity with which, a few months earlier, she had studied eighteenth-century Tuscan land records and the price of stagecoach travel in nineteenth-century America. She watches interviews with Islamic leaders on television and reads documents, everything from European Union resolutions to the proceedings of conferences on Islam. She follows the polemics and discussions going on in Italy regarding local Islamic communities. Obsessed by a single subject, increasingly weakened by disease, she concentrates her last remaining energy on this intellectual labor, which has become pure polemical fire. In a letter she writes, "I'm a disaster, from my eyes to my feet. Nothing works anymore. Except the brain. In fact, I feel like it has improved with age, like wine."

In these three books she returns to old topics. Her criticisms of Islam weren't born on September 11. In 1960, she had denounced the way women were treated in Islam. Her war reporting often revealed the explosive result of mixing politics, religious fanaticism, and ignorance. She had been particularly horrified in 1971, when she witnessed Islamic soldiers committing a massacre in Bangladesh: Some prisoners had been executed in a stadium, struck down with bayonets while twenty-thousand people yelled, "Allah akbar." They kicked the corpses as they filed by, one by one. "Oh, yes: I hear very well what you are thinking... All over Europe the Catholics, those Catholics whose contribution to the History of Thought I acknowledge and respect, used to amuse themselves with watching the heretics burn alive. But a lot of time has passed by."

The trilogy allows her to recall episodes from her career that she has never written about before. In Qom, where she had gone to interview Khomeini, she was forced to sign a temporary marriage contract with her driver because a mullah had discovered her alone with him in a room. She describes Ali Bhutto, the Pakistani head of state, crying when he revealed, in confidence, at the end of an interview that he had been forced to marry his first wife, a twenty-three-year-old woman, when he was just fifteen. And the macabre trick played on her by a group of Palestinian fighters during an air attack. They had taken refuge in a bunker but refused to let her join them because she was a woman. Instead, they told her to hide alone in a shed that turned out to be an explosives depot.

Her complaints about immigrants who work as street vendors in the historic districts of Florence are more personal. Oriana considers her native city to be the epicenter of European civilization and is scandalized to see it turned into a bazaar. "I remember that already in 1978 they occupied the historic district. 'When did they arrive?!?' I asked the tobacconist in Piazza Repubblica. He shrugged and sighed and said, 'Boh! One day I opened the shop and there they were.'" Oriana campaigns to discourage activities that endanger the beauty of the city. She tries to block a social forum meant to attract several thousand protesters. She campaigns for the removal of a tent set up by a group of Somali immigrants near the Duomo. To a Florentine friend, she describes her disgust at the state of the city: "Vicolo dell'Inferno, Vicolo del Purgatorio, and Vicolo della Bombarda have become public, open-air toilets, and no one says anything."

She wages battles, as she has since she was a girl, convinced that, as she writes in the trilogy, "there is no getting away from war because it belongs to human nature." She doesn't slow down, even though she is now very weakened by the disease. Paradoxically, she is capable of great surges of energy, as if she were holding herself together through force of will. Once she has finalized the American edition of *The Rage and the Pride*, after a marathon of revisions and corrections, she writes in a letter, "The editor who came from

New York, who is young and robust, collapsed from exhaustion on the last night."

She writes articles, open letters, statements. In Italy, her positions are published mainly in Right-leaning newspapers, which hold her up as an icon. She opines on various topical issues, for example, denouncing the euthanasia of Terri Schiavo, who died in 2005 after her feeding tube was removed at her husband's request, after a lengthy struggle with her family. She also takes a stand on medically assisted fertility treatments, which Italy votes on in a referendum in June 2005. She passionately supports contradictory positions, underscoring her attachment to life, always and in every situation, whether it is a woman in a vegetative state after an accident or an embryo at the moment of conception. It seems like another lifetime when she was accused of being a Communist in the United States. Back then she had affirmed in an interview, "I am what is called a person of the Left. I don't know what these words mean today — right, left, all shit — but I care a lot about freedom." In reality she defends her own ideas and most of all her freedom to express them. She has always believed that impeding speech is a Fascist act. "Fascism isn't an ideology, it's a behavior," she says.

Once the trilogy and the translations are finished, she goes back to the family saga, which is behind schedule: "Even though I never leave this desk, I'm proceeding as slowly as a sailboat against the wind. Often I'm afraid that I'll be finished before the book is. I'm too slow, too exacting." She writes all day, even though the lesions to her eyes caused by the metastases make it difficult to see the typewriter keys. She knows she doesn't have much time, and this makes her frenetic. A friend remembers that she no longer leaves the house: "She would call once in a while and I would say, 'Let's see each other,' and she would answer, 'No, no, I can't, I'm writing, I'm writing, don't distract me.'"

Because she wants to be left alone to work, and because of her infamous rages, she no longer receives visitors. "I don't answer the phone, and if someone approaches me, I bite," she writes to a journalist who asks for her phone number. She has become the caricature many people believe her to be: aggressive, intractable. And yet she finds this image grotesque and is deeply hurt by it. Years earlier she had said in an interview, "One evening I was watching TV with my father. Maurizio Costanzo was interviewing the adventurer Ambrogio Fogar. 'Mr. Fogar,' he asked, 'whom would you like to travel around the world with on your boat?' 'One person: Oriana Fallaci,' Fogar said. 'Why is that?' responded Costanzo. 'Because she has courage,' Fogar declared. 'But Fallaci is mean! Watch out, she's mean!' Costanzo retorted. My father was furious. I was dismayed."

She doesn't deny her flaws: "I'm too argumentative and aggressive and I don't forgive people. I don't know how to forgive. Never! I don't know how to forget. Never! It's a terrible trait. And sometimes, I like to take revenge on people. And I do. It's terrible, but at least I'm straightforward about it, like a dog, I bark before I bite." And also: "I only smile when I feel like smiling, I only talk when I feel like talking, and when I talk, I say what I mean." She is the first to admit that she doesn't like herself much. But she respects herself: "Because, with all my faults, I'm a truly decent person. That's what counts. I never shoot first, never. I always hold out my hand first. But if someone bites that hand, I kill, that's true. I'm not ashamed of anything. Nothing. I've never sold myself, morally or physically."

She has spoken of herself in articles and books and interviews for years, and asserts, "I know few people as strong as I am." Raised like a soldier, she chooses to reveal only this side of herself, refusing to show her fragility, the side that yearns for tenderness. Those closest to her speak of her complexity. "She is both the simplest and the most complex person I have ever known, the most open and the most mysterious," writes her sister Paola, the person who has come closest to capturing the manner in which Oriana reveals herself by hiding herself. This sister of hers, famous around the world, is like an open book, she says, using an apt metaphor, but written in Chinese. Oriana is voluble and seemingly extroverted, but in reality she hides herself behind her words. She reveals only what she wants to reveal, always retelling the same stories, building a wall to protect herself from prying eyes. "The more I talk, the less I say. I've locked myself away," she admits to an American interviewer.

Italian journalists repeat the stereotype of the irascible, difficult woman to the point of caricature. This is not surprising. As a colleague observes after her death, "Even the honors and tributes given to her are different from those given to the 'great men' of our profession, in life and after death. They celebrate the exceptional nature of her talent, her personality, her character, her unpredictability. But no one, not even the most broad-minded of her admirers, is willing to recognize her authoritativeness. She knew this, and was hurt by it. Oriana was the most revealing example of male chauvinism in the world of Italian journalism. This international star whom the *Washington Post* had under exclusive contract was treated, in Italy, like a madwoman, an eccentric, and, in the final years, as someone who had sold herself to the Right."

Oriana is well aware that not everyone is happy that the most famous Italian journalist is a woman: "Years ago I received a prize, but I couldn't pick it up because I was covering the war in Bangladesh. So I sent a male colleague in my place, and when he stood up, a woman's voice screeched, 'I told you that Fallaci was a man!' When I heard about this, it didn't make me laugh. To the contrary, I was offended."

In the last year of her life, nothing exists outside of her book. She barely leaves the house. She writes, rereads, adjusts, and at night calls a friend or two, sometimes waking them because of the time difference with Italy. One of the few people who has her private number is Archbishop Rino Fisichella, the rector of the Pontifical Lateran University. Their friendship is as improvised as it is profound. She reaches out to him in June 2005, after reading an article in which Fisichella defends her. "I was moved by your action," she writes to him, without preamble. As always when a person touches her, she is open to an immediate friendship: "I'm here, half blind, skin and bones, but still here." Everything should separate them, especially their ideas about faith, but instead they begin an assiduous and affectionate correspondence.

Oriana doesn't hide the darkness she feels, especially as the illness advances: "I have periods of gelid depression, it's true. Especially at night when, instead of sleeping, I stay up reflecting on what I should have done and didn't do, what I deserved to have and didn't obtain." She talks about her unfinished novel: "That book sleeps in the wooden chest in the blue room on the fourth floor. Damn September 11, damn Islam, damn me." She invites him to visit. "The house is pretty, charming, and slightly démodé as one would expect from someone who swims against the current, like me. And it offers absolute privacy, bombproof. No one knows where I live. Not even the mailman, who always gets confused when he delivers the mail. My neighbors don't know who I am. I don't speak to anyone, and no one speaks to me."

She admires Fisichella's generosity, his optimism, his culture. The more she corresponds with him, the more certain areas of the Vatican seem like "an oasis of civility in the midst of barbarity." She learns, to her surprise, that this tiny theocracy preserves certain manners from another time, which she finds touching. She describes herself as a Christian atheist, because she appreciates the cultural patrimony of Christianity. "I grew up in a landscape full of churches, convents, Christs, Madonnas, saints. The first music I heard when I came into this world was the ringing of bells."

The church bells that accompanied her birth, ringing out from the towers of Santa Maria del Fiore and the Duomo, are a detail that returns again and again in interviews. She admits, too, that she is fascinated by Christ's message: "Christianity is an irresistible provocation. A clamorous challenge that man sets for himself." But her position on faith hasn't changed, and the idea of changing it now feels like an act of cowardice: "Living is difficult, dying is unpleasant, and the idea of God helping us face these two things offers an infinite sense of relief. I understand it well. I envy those who believe. Sometimes I'm envious of their belief."

Through Fisichella, she meets Pope Benedict XVI, for whom she has great esteem. "I adore Ratzinger, not just because he is intelligent and cultivated, but because he has balls. He is the only person in the Vatican who took a clear position against the pedophile priests in America. And the only one to defend the West. I like everything about him. Even his face and his funny voice, the voice of a benevolent grandmother who, if provoked, is prepared to spank you." She has been reading his books and speeches, and wishes she could meet him. She's not up to doing an interview — she's too tired — but dreams of a private meeting. She writes to a colleague, "Apart from the fact that an interview with Ratzinger would require ten degrees in philosophy and eleven in theology, as well as lengthy research, I have always selfishly imagined a simple tête-à-tête. In order to express my gratitude and my sympathy. To tell him that he makes me feel less alone."

The meeting with Benedict XVI takes place on August 27, 2005, at Castel Gandolfo, the pope's summer residence. It is draped in secrecy and prepared with care. Oriana hardly travels anymore, for reasons of safety but also, mainly, of ill health. She writes to Fisichella, "I will have to fly in a few days earlier. Traveling exhausts me. For the last eight months I've only left home to go to the hospital, which is just five blocks away. When I come home, I buckle and sway like a limp blade of grass. After eight hours on a plane I'll need to rest for at least 48 hours. That's the minimum. I'm not a wimp. I'm a tough nut who can take exhaustion and physical pain with some stoicism. At the hospital they call me 'the fakir.'"

The news seeps out three days after the meeting and ends up in all the Italian newspapers. The writer who has become the standard-bearer for the war against Islam meets with the head of the religion of love; the great atheist and her spiritual guide... The headlines express surprise on the one hand and polemicism on the other. But the subject of their conversation is not leaked.

Her final months are dedicated to preparations for death. She finishes as much as she can of her novel and leaves precise instructions for the publication of her posthumous books. She insists that the title of her book, *Un cappello pieno di ciliege* be spelled like that, without an *i* at the end of *ciliege*, because that is how her mother wrote it, in the Tuscan manner, on her jars of homemade marmalade. She settles questions of money and inheritance, leaving most of her possessions to her nephew Edoardo. She donates her antique books to the Pontifical Lateran University. She leaves instructions for her funeral, which, according to her wishes, is to be private and secular. She wishes to be buried next to her parents in the Cimitero Evangelico degli Allori, a cemetery filled with foreigners who have loved Florence, on a hill just outside the city.

She carefully prepares every detail. She wants to be dressed in a certain outfit, with a Napoleonic-period pin that she used to wear when she interviewed heads of state. "I wear it in order to intimidate them," she likes to say, with a malicious smile. Most of all, she wants to die in Florence in a room from which she can see Brunelleschi's dome and the Giotto bell tower. She dreams of the church bells of her native city ringing for her. She loves the sound they make, filling the air with joyous chiming. In a letter to Fisichella, she writes, "I love the paschal sound of bells. If I were a king I would order the bells to be rung every day as if it were a feast day."

I have never understood death. I have never understood those who say that it's normal and logical, that everything ends and so will I. I have always thought that death is unjust and illogical, and that since we are born, we shouldn't die.

The plane lands in Florence early on the morning of September 4, 2006. As the plane approaches the gate, her traveling companions move around her. Oriana is too weak to get up without help. She turns her head slowly and looks out the window. She blinks. Recently, her vision has been blurry, and she feels as though she were surrounded by a permanent mist.

She sees an ambulance approaching on the tarmac. It reminds her of the jeeps, years earlier, in Saigon, amid the soldiers and sandbags. She is afraid of flying, as she always has been. And she is afraid of death. But she has never backed away from danger. She hears the cabin door open and prepares to leave the plane. She's going into battle for the last time.

She dies during the night of September 14–15, in the Santa Chiara clinic. She can see the entire city from her window. The bells of the Duomo ring as her coffin is carried out of the building.

ACKNOWLEDGMENTS

"I have never authorized, nor will I ever authorize, a biography. I've told you a million times. My lawyers have always blocked anyone who wanted to write my biography, the story of my life and that of my family. You know my reasons. One is that I would never entrust anyone with the story of my life. Another is that biographers are traitors, just as translators, whether in good or bad faith, always err. Another is that I am obsessed with privacy." With these words, Oriana responded to an American academic who wanted to write her biography in the 1990s. And she would have disapproved of this book.

In truth, at first she fought me, even though she was no longer of this world. She visited me at night. And even though I am not someone who normally remembers her dreams, I had terrible nightmares for years. I had a recurring nightmare in which Oriana insulted me, screaming that I didn't understand anything, and then showed me her diary. But when I drew close to read it, the words faded, as if immersed in water. In the daytime, things weren't much better. The material in her notes was full of lacunae. Many people refused to meet with me, because around Oriana there was a web of disputes, envy, grudges. The memories of those who did meet with me were often confused or contradictory. The life of this woman who had so often spoken about herself revealed itself to be a series of empty spaces. I started to understand that Oriana had spoken often and only about certain experiences, hiding herself behind a wall of words.

I took inspiration from her famous tenaciousness. I put my head down and proceeded for years, one step at a time, filling in the empty spaces, cross-checking information, comparing letters with witness accounts. I needed to understand the weave of this long life, which had been exposed to bright lights but also kept in secret, and I knew I had to find it in her private life, the hidden part. I intuited a few themes: the humble origins, her relationship with her mother, the struggle between her internal fragility and external aggressiveness, the obsession with roots, the continual mirroring between life and work. Finally, one night, I had a beautiful dream in which she was no longer angry. Maybe she was too weak, too old. I lifted her in my arms, and she weighed nothing. I whispered in her ear, "Oriana, if you promise not to yell at me anymore, I'll take care of you." In that moment the writing began, and proceeded surprisingly quickly.

Since I had never met her, I searched for her in her work. I read everything she wrote, articles and books, over and over. She is so deeply present in her writing that it was like speaking with her. Thanks to many documents supplied by her heirs, I was able to consult her appointment books, look at her photographs, and read her poems, correspondence, and notes. I interviewed many people, obtaining a fragment from each person which, directly or indirectly, contributed to the whole. Many people preferred that their names not be used, and I respected their wishes, naming as few as possible so that the story of this woman who knew so many people would remain focused on her and only her.

I chose not to interview any Italian journalists. The issue of Oriana's relationship with the journalistic establishment in Italy is so vast and complex that it merits its own book. Every biographer reinvents her subject and works with the materials at her disposal.

Errors are possible, and if I have made them, I apologize in advance to those who will discover them and to my readers. I've tried to be as rigorous and discreet as possible, listening, leaning in. Perhaps someone will do better someday. Some sources unknown to me will come forward. Oriana's story does not end here.

I thank Edoardo Perazzi, Oriana's nephew and heir, and his wife, Alessandra Ricci, who believed in me from the start; Roberto Santachiara, my agent, who has always encouraged and supported me; Paolo Zaninoni, editorial director at Rizzoli, who christened this project; Giorgio Boatti, writer and friend, who fed me delicious meals when I arrived at his house late, famished after hours of writing, and, more important, checked various passages in the biography with a historian's eye. A particular thanks goes to Gabriela Jacomella and Sara Galinetto, two extraordinary collaborators who helped with the research in the United States and Italy, respectively, and who became my friends. I also want to mention Daniela Di Pace, Oriana's friend and assistant, who, from our first meeting, seated on the couch in her house, listened with great generosity of spirit. I understood why Oriana, who argued with everyone, never fought with her.

In addition, I want to thank all the people who helped me and who shared memories and information about Oriana: Rino Fisichella; François Pelou; Chantal Clappier; Isabella Rossellini; Jane Dreyfus; Monica Fornier; Paolo Klun; Mirella Florita; Alessandro Cannavò; Jonathan Burnham; Katherine Benvin Quinn; Shirley MacLaine; Vita Paladino; Francesca Tramma; Eleonora Vallone; Fabiola Rocha; Giorgio Boccolari; Barbara Zaczek; Ben Bradlee; Bruno Coppi; Christiane Amanpour; Daniel Pipes; Dolly Borgia; Dominic Di Frisco; Francesca Forcella; Howard Modlin; Janet Levy; Jim Lovell; Jurate Kazickas; Maria Campbell; Maristella Lorch; Marta Lotti; Martin Peretz; Mauro Lucentini; Megan Kashour; Nan Talese; Norman Alexandroff; Patricia Violante;

Robert Spencer; Sandro and Anna Fioriti; Scott Manning; Tony D'Angelo; Tunky Varadarajan; Alberto Vitale; Adina, Naomi, and Michelle Kohan; Sirio Maccioni; Alberto Vacchi; Arrigo Brandini; Tommaso Marroncini; Paola Kennealy; Renata Brasca; Piero Gelli; Paola Locchi; Giovanna Govoni Salvadore; Andrea Salvadore; Francesca Della Monica; Maria Luisa Marcolin; and Simonella Condemi.

Among the many institutions that allowed me to access their archives, I would like to thank in particular RCS MediaGroup, Oriana's publishers for decades, and the Fondazione Corriere della Sera, which has preserved Oriana Fallaci's professional papers. In addition, I would like to thank the Howard Gotlieb Archival Research Center at Boston University, the Cesare Zavattini archive at the Panizzi di Reggio Emilia library, the historic archives of the Università degli Studi in Florence, the Istituto Statale di Istruzione Superiore Niccolò Machiavelli in Florence, the Istituto Storico della Resistenza in Toscana, the Ordine dei Giornalisti della Toscana, the Archivio Contemporaneo "A. Bonsanti" at the Gabinetto G. P. Vieusseux in Florence, the Biblioteca Nazionale Centrale in Florence, the Archivio del Novecento at the Università La Sapienza in Rome, the office of vital statistics in Florence, the Fondazione Carlo Cassola at the Soprintendenza Archivistica della Toscana, the Fondazione Sandro Pertini in Florence, and the Fondazione Pietro Nenni in Rome.

Finally, I'd like to thank the oak tree at the Società Canottieri Ticino di Pavia, my sports club on the river, where I wrote the book over the course of three long Italian summers. That tree generously offered me its shade, breeze, and the delicious sound of its leaves, always in motion. One day when I insisted on plugging ahead even though a storm was brewing, it even dropped a branch on my head, as if sending me a message. I hid the branch, out of fear that the gardener might decide to prune the tree, as men do, impeding the tree's natural growth according to its own internal wisdom, which infallibly finds the lines of maximum beauty. I am obsessed with trees, just as Oriana was. I was moved to discover this common trait. There are not many others. Unlike Oriana, who saw politics everywhere and loved to say, laughing, "I have never written a cookbook but if I did I would turn it into a book about politics," I am completely apolitical. My only experience in politics was as a young girl when I took part in a human chain with the people of my neighborhood in order to block the removal of some trees. Sadly, it did no good. I hope that somewhere, someone will plant a tree, or defend one, in memory of Oriana.

BOOKS BY ORIANA FALLACI

I sette peccati di Hollywood. Milan: Longanesi, 1958.
The Useless Sex. New York: Horizon, 1964.
If the Sun Dies. New York: Atheneum, 1966.
Penelope at War. London: Michael Joseph, 1967.
Limelighters. London: Michael Joseph, 1967.
The Egotists: Sixteen Surprising Interviews. Chicago: Regnery, 1968.
Quel giorno sulla Luna. Milan: Rizzoli, 1970.
Nothing, and So Be It. Garden City, NY: Doubleday, 1972.
Letter to a Child Never Born. New York: Simon & Schuster, 1976.
Interview with History. Boston: Houghton Mifflin, 1977.
A Man. New York: Simon & Schuster, 1980.
Inshallah. Garden City, NY: Doubleday, 1992.
The Rage and the Pride. New York: Rizzoli, 2002.
Oriana Fallaci intervista sé stessa: L'Apocalisse. Milan: Rizzoli, 2004.
The Force of Reason. New York: Rizzoli, 2006.
Un cappello pieno di ciliege: Una saga. Milan: Rizzoli, 2008.
Saigon e così sia. Milan: Rizzoli, Milan: Rizzoli, 2010.
Intervista con il mito. Milan: Rizzoli, 2010.
Interviews with History and Conversations with Power.
    New York: Random House, 2011.
Il mio cuore è più stanco della mia voce. Milan: Rizzoli, 2013.

BOOKS ABOUT ORIANA FALLACI

Aricò, Santo L. *Oriana Fallaci: The Woman and the Myth.*
Carbondale: Southern Illinois University Press, 1998.
———, ed. *Contemporary Women Writers in Italy: A Modern
Renaissance.* Amherst: University of Massachusetts Press, 1990.

Cannavò, Alessandro, Alessandro Nicosia, and Edoardo Perazzi,
eds. *Oriana Fallaci: Intervista con la storia: Immagini e parole
di una vita.* Milan: Rizzoli, 2007.

Cecchi, Umberto. *Oriana Fallaci: Cercami dov'è il dolore.*
Florence: Mauro Pagliai, 2013.

Di Pace, Daniela, and Riccardo Mazzoni. *Con Oriana.* Florence:
Le Lettere, 2009.

Gatt-Rutter, John. *Oriana Fallaci: The Rhetoric of Freedom.*
Washington, DC: Berg Publishers, 1996.

Maglie, Maria Giovanna. *Oriana: Incontri e passioni di una grande
Italiana.* Milan: Mondadori, 2006.

Mazzoni, Riccardo. *Grazie Oriana.* Florence: Società Toscana
di Edizioni, 2006.

Nencini, Riccardo. *Oriana Fallaci: Morirò in piedi.* Florence:
Edizioni Polistampa, 2007.

Santini, Aldo. *Lavorando con l'Oriana Fallaci.* Livorno: Debatte
Editore, 2008.

PHOTO CREDITS

INDEX OF NAMES